Conversations with Gabriel García Márquez

Literary Conversations Series

Peggy Whitman Prenshaw
General Editor

D1527802

Photo credit: © Photofest

Conversations with Gabriel García Márquez

Edited by
Gene H. Bell-Villada

University Press of Mississippi
Jackson

www.upress.state.ms.us

The University Press of Mississippi is a member of the Association of American
University Presses.

First edition 2006

∞

Library of Congress Cataloging-in-Publication Data

García Márquez, Gabriel, 1928–
   Conversations with Gabriel García Márquez / edited by Gene H. Bell-Villada.
     p. cm.
   Includes index.
   ISBN 1-57806-783-9 (cloth : alk. paper) — ISBN 1-57806-784-7 (pbk. : alk.
paper)
    1. García Márquez, Gabriel, 1928– —Interviews. 2. Authors, Colombian—
20th century—Interviews. I. Bell-Villada, Gene H., 1941– II. Title.
PQ8180.17.A73Z467   2005
863'.64—dc22   2005005457

British Library Cataloging-in-Publication Data available

Books by Gabriel García Márquez

La hojarasca. Bogotá: Ediciones S. L. B., 1955. (In *Leaf Storm and Other Stories.* New York: Harper & Row, 1972)

El coronel no tiene quien le escriba. Medellín: Aguirre Editor, 1961. (In *No One Writes to the Colonel and Other Stories.* New York: Harper & Row, 1968)

Los funerales de la Mamá Grande. Xalapa, Mexico: Universidad Veracruzana, 1962. (Included in *No One Writes to the Colonel* as *Big Mama's Funeral.* New York: Harper & Row, 1968)

La mala hora. Mexico City: Ediciones Era, 1966. (*In Evil Hour.* New York: Harper & Row, 1979)

Cien años de soledad. Buenos Aires: Editorial Sudamericana, 1967. (*One Hundred Years of Solitude.* New York: Harper & Row, 1970)

Relato de un náufrago. . . . Barcelona: Tusquets Editor, 1970. (*The Story of a Shipwrecked Sailor.* New York: Alfred A. Knopf, 1986)

La increíble y triste historia de la cándida Eréndira y de su abuela desalmada. Buenos Aires: Editorial Sudamericana, 1973. (The title piece, plus "Death Constant beyond Love" and "The Sea of Lost Time," are gathered in *Innocent Eréndira and Other Stories.* New York: Harper & Row, 1978. The rest appear in *Leaf Storm and Other Stories,* New York: Harper & Row, 1972)

El otoño del patriarca. Buenos Aires: Editorial Sudamericana, 1975. (*The Autumn of the Patriarch.* New York: Harper & Row, 1976)

Ojos de perro azul. Buenos Aires: Editorial Sudamericana, 1975. (Youthful stories, gathered in *Innocent Eréndira and Other Stories.* New York: Harper & Row, 1978.)

Cuando era feliz e indocumentado. Bogotá: Editorial Oveja Negra, 1979. (Newspaper articles.)

Crónica de una muerte anunciada. Buenos Aires: Editorial Sudamericana, 1981. (*Chronicle of a Death Foretold.* New York: Alfred A. Knopf, 1983)

El olor de la guayaba: Conversaciones con Plinio Apuleio Mendoza. Barcelona: Bruguera, 1982. (*The Fragrance of Guava.* London: Verso, 1983)

Collected Stories. (Gathers the three previous English-language collections into one.) New York: Harper & Row, 1984.

El amor en los tiempos del cólera. Bogot: Editorial Oveja Negra, 1985. (*Love in the Time of Cholera.* New York: Alfred A. Knopf, 1988)

La aventura de Miguel Littín, clandestine en Chile. Buenos Aires: Editorial Sudamericana, 1986. (*Clandestine in Chile: The Adventures of Miguel Littín.* New York: Henry Holt, 1987)

El general en su laberinto. Buenos Aires: Editorial Sudamericana, 1989. (*The General in His Labyrinth.* New York: Alfred A. Knopf, 1990)

Doce cuentos peregrinos. Buenos Aires: Editorial Sudamericana, 1992. (*Strange Pilgrims.* New York: Alfred A. Knopf, 1993)

Diatriba de amor contra un hombre sentado. Barcelona: Grijalbo Mondadori, 1994. (One-act monologue, untranslated.)

Del amor y otros demonios. Buenos Aires: Editorial Sudamericana, 1994. (*Of Love and Other Demons.* New York: Alfred A. Knopf, 1995)

Noticia de un secuestro. Buenos Aires: Editorial Sudamericana, 1996. (*News of a Kidnapping.* New York: Alfred A. Knopf, 1997)

Vivir para contarla. Barcelona: Cartoné Mondadori, 2002. (*Living to Tell the Tale.* New York: Alfred A. Knopf, 2003)

Memoria de mis putas tristes. Buenos Aires: Editorial Sudamericana, 2004.

Contents

Introduction

The twenty-something woman seated across from me on the train was engrossed in her copy of the *Irish Times*. It was the late 1980s perhaps. Occupancy that mid-afternoon on Boston's chief underground rail artery, the Red Line, was low. From my angle I could glimpse that the multicolumn item being casually savored by the Irish reader had as its title "An Interview with Márquez," or words to that effect. A photograph of the Colombian Nobel laureate's familiar, mustachioed visage accompanied the Irish reporter's text.

An authoritative, ongoing, four-volume *Bibliographic Guide to Gabriel García Márquez*, published by Greenwood Press, registers a total of 197 interviews with the author. The conversation in the *Irish Times* is not among those listed. I mention this not as any kind of criticism of the invaluable job being done by Margaret Estella Fau and Nelly Sfeir de González, the assiduous editors of the series, but as an instance of the logistical difficulties involved in seeking out every personal audience that García Márquez may have granted to diligent world news gatherers and avid paparazzi.

We can thus only speculate as to how many conversations with the novelist may have appeared in Japanese, Russian, Greek, or Arabic venues that, even to the most polyglot of Western readers and researchers, are all but inaccessible. Moreover, at a relatively early stage in García Márquez's career, there must have been interviews that ran in local journals and newspapers—dailies in mid-sized Colombian towns or obscure little magazines in Mexico—and that still sit unacknowledged in private collections somewhere. Add to that the untranscribed talks with the novelist, on several continents, over radio and TV, and the total could conceivably reach four, five, six hundred. The number is anybody's guess and in the end probably undeterminable.

Whatever the exact figure, the fact is that interviews with García Márquez have functioned as a yearned-for scoop and a recurring feature both in the literary press and the mass media. This is only to be expected for an author whose prose works, while highly complex and sophisticated, command a vast, global readership even as the man himself enjoys a prestige and visibility normally associated with soccer players and movie stars.

In gathering interviews for a book such as this, the compiler-editor must perforce be selective. Facing a plethora of items that could fill a multivolume set, the researcher ends up picking those encounters that are particularly distinctive, thorough, or fresh—or that are simply of direct relevance to a specific work and/or moment in García Márquez's artistic growth. Certain conversations, moreover, enjoy the status of key texts in their own right, a fact that in itself calls for their inclusion in these pages.

Given so many press appearances, the author inevitably ends up going more than once over familiar territory: his formative relationship with his grandfather; his parents' troubled courtship; his fractured childhood; his studies away from home; his beginnings as a journalist and novelist; his various phases in Paris, New York, and Mexico City; his struggles with the making of *One Hundred Years of Solitude*; and the problems that arise with having worldwide fame. There are also the cultural and political topics: his Caribbean roots, his own left-wing position, his views of the Cuban Revolution and of Fidel Castro, the bottomless pit of violence in his native Colombia, and U.S. imperialism.

Among the unavoidable literary subjects in García Márquez's interviews are the influences from U.S. authors (notably Faulkner), the images that have smitten him with inspiration for key scenes in his fiction, his own daily routines as scribbler, his indifference to critics, and whatever new volume he has just had published or might be working on. No writer's set of personal topics is without limit, and a certain amount of repetition in subject matter is only to be expected. Given that the editorial policy for the University Press of Mississippi's *Conversations* series is to reprint each interview uncut, in its entirety, some thematic overlap in the course of these encounters is inevitable. Still, the unique flair, good humor, and sheer charm of García Márquez generally help make even his most familiar anecdotes fresh and enjoyable.

This particular Conversations gathering comes with an unusual feature: it contains several interviews that were conducted by Latin Americans and/or Colombians, sometimes on Latin American soil, and always in Spanish, sans interpreters. In each of these instances the culture and nationality of the interviewer makes an enormous difference for the dynamics of the exchange. The encounters in Castilian offer a glimpse of the author at his most informal, forthright, and personable.

With a reporter from the *New York Times*, García Márquez is very much the international man of letters—sober, decorous, and urbane, cosmopolitan and correct. With Latin Americans, by contrast, the author can assume a more jovial manner and be more himself, more direct and down-to-earth. Or he can give vent to his personal anguish about the weekly horrors besieging his native land. The Spanish-language interviews, accordingly, have their share of offhand references to local people and places, culture and folklore. Some of the passing allusions may well be intelligible solely to Colombian readers of this volume.

Moreover, given that most of the author's Latin American interviewers tend to be left-wing, and given also the large numbers of Hispanic readers who lean left, García Márquez in these encounters shows much less restraint in airing his own secular, radical views. Sympathetic interlocutors, who speak and pose questions for a largely sympathetic readership, inevitably bring out the novelist's socialist sympathies.

These views come through quite clearly in the interview with Uruguayan journalist Ernesto González Bermejo. A small classic that is often cited by critics, the conversation takes place just three years after the phenomenal success of García Márquez's celebrated masterpiece, and it communicates some of the excitement being generated by the book and by the "Boom" of the Latin American novel. Toward the end of their dialogue—and a true dialogue it is—García Márquez expresses to González Bermejo his optimistic hopes for Cuba's experiment in socialism. The bulk of their long chat, however, focuses on the Colombian's own growth as a writer: the inner relationship between the news reporter and the narrator and his hitting upon the mythic treatment in fiction. At the time García Márquez is caught up in the long, slow process of crafting *The Autumn of the Patriarch*. Fans of that book will catch his references to a couple of key episodes—the presence of Columbus's three caravels, and the countless small children who are sucked into the dictator's lottery scheme. Discrepancies between this "sneak preview" in 1970 and the final product in 1975 will surely be noted. The interview concludes with a captivating first glimpse of a work that anticipates *Chronicle of a Death Foretold*—and that bears but the most general resemblance to the book-to-be.

When Rita Guibert interviewed the author, she was one of Latin America's better-known journalists, her reports having appeared in such wide-circulation venues as *Life en Español*. Guibert's encounter with the novelist thus carries some weight. Besides passing in review with her the standard topics enumerated above, García Márquez touches on the roles played in his work by his women characters, and he comes out squarely against the traditional ethic of *machismo*. On the matter of socialism, in what almost amounts to a public statement, he speaks as frankly as ever. One particularly striking insight is the author's advance summary of a short fiction that he imagines and hopes to write; admirers of García Márquez will immediately recognize it as the plot of the short story, "Light Is Like Water," which would not appear in print until nearly two decades hence, in the volume *Strange Pilgrims*. It is fascinating to see a writer carry a work within himself for so long and then retain its features just as they had been announced at an early date.

William Kennedy is something of a disciple of García Márquez, having learned from the Colombian master how to mingle reality with magic in his own fiction. His essay-cum-interview, which first appeared in the *Atlantic Monthly*, enjoys a special literary reputation. The piece marshals a great deal of biographical data, much of it presumably gleaned from fellow novelist Mario Vargas Llosa's six-hundred-page study, *García Márquez: Historia de un deicidio* (back then a hot-off-the-press item and the leading book on the subject). Kennedy—himself formerly a reporter for an English-language daily in Puerto Rico—particularly traces the novelist's growth as a newsman and stresses the fantastical side of that process, García Márquez having something to say about the place of magic in everyday life. García Márquez confronts the inevitable matter of Faulkner, and talks about his relationship to books in general, more specifically his love of Graham Greene. He also voices his high opinion of American literature, though he shows scant awareness of the U.S. writers who postdate the "lost generation."

When chatting with the staff writers of *El Manifiesto*—a now-defunct Colombian leftist journal—García Márquez opens up remarkably and reveals his most nostalgic and personal side. And he's unusually frank about his spotty education, his days of poverty, his youthful days residing in brothels, and his having been accidentally cured of boils by putting *No One Writes to the Colonel* to paper. Naturally the conversation brims with Hispanic references: the *Romancero* (Spain's medieval ballad tradition), the *vallenato* (a native music genre from Valledupar, consisting of narrative songs with accompanying accordion, percussion, and bass), Rafael Escalona (the most celebrated writer and singer of *vallenatos*), Caribbean crooners such as Daniel Santos, and the Colombian literary classic *El carnero* (literally

"The Ram"—a fanciful mock-chronicle from the colonial era). He reflects on
the decisive impact that Kafka had on his development and admits to how
much he needed to work at *not* being like Faulkner when he drafted *Leaf
Storm*. Finally, he notes the colloquial, Caribbean flavor of *The Autumn of the
Patriarch*—a trait much valued and savored by Hispanic readers of that book.

The *Playboy* interview with Claudia Dreifus provides the most thorough
and extensive biographical information, thereby overlapping with several
other of these encounters. The author dwells on the oddities of his upbringing (a subject to be covered so eloquently in his memoirs twenty years
hence), and fondly remembers the prostitutes who once shared their daily
lives with him. The chat is also quite political. García Márquez, for one, com-
plains of the use of the English word "America" in denoting the United States
exclusively, a touchy issue that is familiar to most any culturally conscious
Latin American. At the time the U.S. proxy wars in Nicaragua and El Salvador
are heating up, and the novelist analyzes in detail the policies of Presidents
Carter and Reagan toward Spanish-speaking America. He also offers a fascinating glimpse of Fidel Castro as reader of fiction and as a connoisseur of . . .
seafood. The Colombian expresses his frank distaste for solemnity and points
out some of the sources for the magical episodes in his most famous novel,
including a fascinating look at the origins of the chocolate-drinking, levitating priest in *One Hundred Years of Solitude.*

Simply gaining access to the company of García Márquez is a major challenge, and Gene H. Bell-Villada's interview starts out with an account of just
such an adventure. Once the novelist has finally made himself available, however, he speaks fluently and freely. The author talks about the historical bases
for the banana-strike chapters in *One Hundred Years* (a topic little noted by
scholars and critics) and the motives and method that went into the making
of *The Autumn of the Patriarch*. García Márquez admits to his plebeian side
and his feeling for street life, and also suggests the various ways in which both
the figure and music of Bela Bartók have served him as a model for writing.

During the mid-1980s García Márquez was in his prime. The Nobel Prize
had recently been bestowed upon him—to broad, popular acclaim and cele-
bration throughout the Latin American continent. Moreover, he was further
fulfilling himself as an artist with the writing and, later, the astounding critical and commercial success of *Love in the Time of Cholera*. The number of
major interviews increased during this period, and their content takes on a
weightier, more serious cast.

Marlise Simons's series of interviews for the *New York Times Book Review* captures the author precisely at this juncture. In the first such exchange with her, from 1985, the novelist discusses the special challenges involved in writing of old age and the aging process. Accordingly, he raises the universally scanted issue of sexual relations between the loving elderly—a matter that his book seeks to correct. On a similar note, he talks of the shifting methods of composition adopted by a literary artist as he grows older. For the subject of aging, García Márquez claims to have pursued little research other than study Simone de Beauvoir's *The Coming of Age*, though in other interviews (such as the one with Bell-Villada) he owns up to doing massive amounts of reading in preparation for each novel.

In the first (1987) of two interviews that he granted to Mexican journalist Susana Cato, García Márquez reflects on his having just turned sixty. Continuing with the theme of romantic love brought to the fore by the author in his latest thick opus, he admits to his frank fascination with soap operas and with the medium of TV. Accordingly, the novelist comments on his personal involvement with and broad commitments to the visual media. The issue of his having become accidentally wealthy comes up for discussion. He also mentions Fidel Castro's perspicacious mind, at the same time that he as Nobel laureate plays down the importance of his own friendly ties with prominent political figures.

With *Love in the Time of Cholera* now solidly behind him, Marlise Simons returned to the master. The result was two more interviews published in 1988, both of them put together (as she noted to me in a private communication) from a series of earlier talks. In the February 1988 item, the novelist speaks further about aging and life experience, about his interest in plagues, and about the touching, striking genesis of his wondrous tale of eros and illnesses. Other subjects discussed are his struggle to encourage a Latin American cinema and the novel about Simón Bolívar that sits next on his drawing board.

Simons's sequel interview from April 1988 provides some captivating details about the central role played in García Márquez's youth by the mighty Magdalena River. The ever-meticulous novelist goes into his decision not to give a mother to his female protagonist Fermina and admits to a frank dislike for the book's male lead Florentino. García Márquez's comments on translators, and his reports on the recurrence of exactly the same translating doubts and queries, are a revealing insight, as are the accounts of the many letters he receives from fans who've found in his books echoes of their own lives and home towns.

The author's compatriot and fellow journalist María Elvira Samper is just the right sort of person for him to chat with about his Bolívar novel, *The General in His Labyrinth*. The Bolívar mythology is a cultural force to be reckoned with. Citizens of most South American countries have had the idealized lore hammered into their tender minds since grade school, and the ritual veneration of "the Liberator" is further reinforced by public statues, politicians' rhetoric, place names, and even the national currency (as in Venezuela, where the basic monetary unit is the *bolívar*). In this interview, García Márquez airs his dissatisfaction with the monumentalized image of *el libertador*, and elucidates his conscious aim of humanizing the leader, the icon. He goes into the complexities of doing historical research and of consulting with professional historians (all of whom strenuously objected to his scene in which he portrays Bolívar lying naked in a hammock, tapping his foot to some music). García Márquez's intuitive approach and creative imagination are especially foregrounded in this exchange. And we read about the centrality of Caribbean geography to his larger *oeuvre*, with the Magdalena River again holding the spotlight.

Andrew Paxman's encounter with the novelist in Mexico City (for *Variety* magazine) provides an all-too-brief glimpse of García Márquez the man of cinema. We read of his attitudes toward movie-making and, once again, of his hopes for a vital and authentic Latin American film industry.

The next-to-last interview in this volume, and the second one by Susana Cato (1996), is arguably the freshest, most original, most gripping conversation of them all. Following on the heels of the publication of *News of a Kidnapping*, it offers us a long, close look at García Márquez the investigative journalist—his methods, his peculiar difficulties (notably, that of being a Nobel laureate). We learn about the nuts-and-bolts sleuth work that went into the investigation and about the author's having to depend on intermediaries for bringing such labors to fruition, simply in order to avoid calling public attention to the project. He admits to a certain fascination with the notorious drug lord Pablo Escobar, along with a wrenching sensitivity to the unspeakable ordeal of being a kidnapping victim. More dramatically, in this encounter we see García Márquez the *Colombian*, a man personally pained by the horrors taking place in his country, both in official circles and among ordinary people (even and including the drug rings' gunslingers). The concluding paragraph is among the author's most eloquent and impassioned reflections on the endless wounds and sorrows being endured by Colombia and Latin America.

In the 1980s the sheer quantity of interviews with García Márquez peaked, after which the numbers fall precipitously. By contrast with the spate of encounters that had surged in the wake of the Nobel Prize and then *Love in the Time of Cholera*, few such conversations were prompted by the author's luminous little novel from 1994, *Of Love and Other Demons*, and those that existed tended to be brief. At the same time a more positive development arose elsewhere. Among the worthier decisions of President Bill Clinton (whose favorite work of fiction is *One Hundred Years of Solitude*) is his definitively having taken the Colombian Nobel laureate off the U.S. Immigration blacklist.

The concluding interview, by David Streitfeld, arises directly out of that enlightened executive decision and stems from one of the author's few public U.S. appearances where he could be personally approached. In this his first encounter of an academic kind, García Márquez met with a group of students at Georgetown University (perhaps not accidentally Clinton's alma mater). Reporters were not allowed at the colloquy, but Mr. Streitfeld had the good fortune to buttonhole the illustrious visitor during a spare moment and hear him expatiate on President Clinton and on his own relationship to his troubled land. In addition, the interview features some memorable musings on the Colombian fabulator by some other well-known Latin American novelists who happened to be present at the Georgetown events.

In one of those sad surprises that can come with old age, García Márquez in 1999 was diagnosed with lymphatic cancer. As is to be expected, virtually no interviews of note are to be found in this period of treatment and convalescence. However, a bizarre sort of confession did take shape when, over the internet, a "Farewell" statement began circulating under the author's byline, and in more than one language. The lengthy, nostalgic outpouring was to reach millions of sympathetic readers before finally being exposed as a hoax. The novelist himself disavowed it as "*cursi*" (roughly, "corny," "affected," "pretentious") in a public declaration.

Readers of these gathered conversations will get to know Latin America's most famous author about as well as it's possible to know anyone via this medium. There is biographical material aplenty. His political opinions surface time and again. He discusses specific details of his most important works. His independent, intuitive methods and his ironic take on the world come through with wondrous clarity. And in the interviews with fellow Hispanics we see his own Latin and Caribbean side—his warmth, spontaneity, and amiability. Despite his shy streak, García Márquez is at heart a sociable man who simply loves to chat in his native tongue. I got my own glimpse of this aspect of him in my interview with the master in 1982, and I recognize it in the other conversations.

I wish to thank Tomás Eloy Martínez for helping me track down two of the Latin American interviewers or their associates. Without his support, reprinting these conversations might not have been possible. Rebecca Ohm and Christine Menard of Sawyer Library at Williams College were touchingly patient in guiding me through the intricacies of searching for interviews over the newly digitalized information system. The Cultural Attaché's office at the Colombian Embassy in Washington D.C., along with Stella Sánchez and her friends, did whatever they could to locate the whereabouts of *El Manifiesto* magazine. The Writers' Center in Albany, and author William Kennedy himself, led me to the appropriate venues for obtaining permission to reprint his fine piece. Gratitude is due to Seetha Srinivasan, who spent years trying to convince me to take on this project, and I am a prime beneficiary in having yielded at last to her persuasions. Last but not least, to my wife Audrey, for what she is, does, and provides.

GHB-V

Chronology

1927   Gabriel José García Márquez is born on 7 March to Gabriel Eligio
        García and Luisa Santiaga Márquez in Aracataca, Colombia. His
        father, a sometime pharmacist, works as the town's telegraph oper-
        ator. The boy is the eldest of what will be eleven children. He will
        spend his first eight years with his grandparents, Colonel Nicolás
        Márquez and Tranquilina Iguarán. The grandfather, a former hero
        in the country's civil conflicts and a prominent local figure in
        Liberal Party politics, will be a decisive influence on the writer.

1936   GGM moves in with his parents in the town of Sincé, near the river
        port of Sucre.

1937   The Colonel, GGM's grandfather, dies. The boy attends schools in
        Cartagena and Barranquilla.

1940   GGM receives a scholarship to attend the Liceo Nacional de Zipaquirá,
        a prestigious secondary school some thirty miles from Bogotá. He
        reads widely in the European classics. Over this decade and the next,
        la Violencia will spread across the Colombian countryside.

1946   GGM graduates from the Liceo de Zipaquirá.

1947   In order to please his parents, GGM starts attending law school at
        the Universidad Nacional in Bogotá, where he is an indifferent
        student. He publishes his first story, "The Third Resignation," in
        El Espectador, Bogotá's number two daily.

1948   The terrible April 9 riots in Bogotá disrupt GGM's life. The
        Universidad Nacional closes indefinitely, and his rooming house
        burns down. He transfers to the Universidad de Cartagena, where
        he scarcely attends classes, but also rediscovers his Caribbean roots.
        He begins publishing daily columns in that city's daily, *El Universal*.

1949   GGM continues to publish short stories in *El Espectador*. He
        becomes friendly with the writers of the "Barranquilla Group," and
        through them gets to know the major Modernist authors.

1950	After moving to Barranquilla, GGM starts writing a daily column for *El Heraldo*, and begins work on *Leaf Storm*.
1953	GGM travels around the areas of the Magdalena River and the Guajira peninsula, working as a book salesman. In Bogotá, Gen. Gustavo Rojas Pinilla stages a military coup.
1954	GGM moves to Bogotá and begins work as a staff writer for *El Espectador*.
1955	GGM's report on the harrowing experience of a shipwrecked sailor reveals irregularities in the Colombian Navy. The newspaper sends him as a correspondent to Europe. During a lull in the news, he briefly attends film school in Rome. *Leaf Storm* is published.
1956	GGM's short story "One Day after Saturday" wins a Colombian prize. GGM moves to Paris, only to find out that *El Espectador* has been shut down by the Rojas Pinilla dictatorship. He decides to stay, working on drafts for *In Evil Hour* and *No One Writes to the Colonel*. Living in poverty, he ekes out an existence by returning empty bottles and writing occasional freelance pieces.
1957	GGM travels with Plinio Apuleio Mendoza through then-communist Eastern Europe, and will later write about the experience. In Colombia, the Rojas Pinilla dictatorship is overthrown and the Liberal and Conservative Parties agree to alternate in power, in a system called the National Front.
1958	GGM moves to Caracas, where he will hold a series of editorial posts with local glossies. The Venezuelan dictatorship of Gen. Marcos Pérez Jiménez is overthrown by a politically moderate military junta. *No One Writes to the Colonel* is published in *Mito*, a Bogotá magazine.
1959	Fidel Castro overthrows the Batista dictatorship in Cuba. GGM is invited by the revolutionary government to cover the events unfolding there. GGM and Plinio Mendoza set up a branch of Prensa Latina, the Cuban press agency, in Bogotá. GGM marries Mercedes Barcha. Later that year his first son Rodrigo is born.
1960	GGM works briefly for Prensa Latina in Cuba.
1961	GGM works as a staffer for the New York office of Prensa Latina. He later resigns in solidarity with his boss Jorge Massetti, who has been elbowed out by old-guard Stalinists. GGM and his family

travel by Greyhound bus through the U.S. South, and then to
Mexico City. *In Evil Hour*, in manuscript, wins the Esso Prize.

1962   GGM works for fluff magazines. The couple's second son, Gonzalo,
         is born. The author enters a writer's block. *Big Mama's Funeral*, a
         book of stories, is published. *No One Writes to the Colonel* is pub-
         lished in Medellín. An unauthorized edition of *In Evil Hour*
         appears in Madrid. GGM is put on the U.S. immigration blacklist.

1963   GGM works for J. Walter Thompson, then writes scripts for
         Mexican cinema.

1965   GGM starts writing *One Hundred Years of Solitude*.

1966   An authorized version of *In Evil Hour* is published in Mexico City.

1967   *One Hundred Years of Solitude* is published in Buenos Aires, and
         becomes a surprise, massive best-seller in the Hispanic world.

1968   GGM moves with his family to Barcelona.

1969   *One Hundred Years of Solitude* wins the Chianchiano Prize in Italy
         and the Prize for the Best Foreign Book in France.

1970   *Diary of a Shipwrecked Sailor*, based on GGM's news report for
         El Espectador, is published in Barcelona.

1971   GGM receives an honorary doctorate from Columbia University.
         The imprisonment and forced confession of poet Heberto Padilla
         in Cuba provokes two letters of protest from world-renowned
         intellectuals. GGM signs the first letter, but refuses to sign the
         second one.

1972   GGM is awarded the Rómulo Gallegos Prize in Venezuela and the
         Neustadt Prize in the United States. He publicly donates the
         Venezuelan prize money to a local socialist party.

1973   *Innocent Eréndira*, stories, is published.

1975   *The Autumn of the Patriarch* is published. GGM and his family move
         back to Mexico City.

1981   *Chronicle of a Death Foretold* is published. GGM requests political
         asylum in Mexico.

1982   GGM is awarded the Nobel Prize for Literature.

1985   *Love in the Time of Cholera* is published.

1988   Under the generic title *Amores difíciles* (Difficult Loves), a cycle of
         six films based on scripts written by GGM, are produced by
         Spanish National Television.

1989   *The General in His Labyrinth* is published.
1992   *Strange Pilgrims*, stories, is published. Bill Clinton is elected
        President of the United States. Clinton, whose avowedly favorite
        novel is *One Hundred Years of Solitude*, will eventually lift the U.S.
        travel ban on GGM.
1994   *Of Love and Other Demons* is published. *Diatribe of Love against a
        Seated Man*, a play, is published. (No English version exists as yet.)
1996   *News of a Kidnapping*, reportage, is published.
1999   GGM contracts lymphatic cancer. Successive, advanced treatments
        at U.S. hospitals will help put the author's illness in remission.
2002   *Living to Tell the Tale*, the first installment of a three-volume
        memoir, is published.
2004   *Memoria de mis putas tristes* (Memories of My Sad Whores), a
        novel, is published.

Conversations with Gabriel García Márquez

And Now, Two Hundred Years of Solitude

Ernesto González Bermejo / 1971

From *Triunfo* (Madrid) vol. 25 no. 441 (November 1971), pp. 12–18. Reprinted in Alfonso Rentería Mantilla, ed. *García Márquez habla de García Márquez* (Bogotá: Rentería Editores, 1979), pp. 49–64. Translated by Gene H. Bell-Villada.

BARCELONA. One of the greatest writers, or the greatest writer in Spanish. The Amadís of Latin America. The Cervantes of Colombia. Author of *One Hundred Years of Solitude*, one of the most important or *the* most important of contemporary novels. . . . García Márquez shakes off his awards and, in sports clothes, with a wry smile under his hard moustache, comes by for me at my hotel. "Ready? Let's go for a bite to eat out there." And out on the street: "You can interview me all you want and I can interview you about Cuba all you want. Agreed?" And he takes me to the Amaya Restaurant where we have cold soup, sirloin, and green purée, and we talk about everything and about *One Hundred Years of Solitude*, of course, and I say to him, "Not bad, that little novel of yours." And he laughs a toothy laugh, and leads me out of the restaurant and puts me inside his Seat [Spanish Fiat] 1430, and says: "Take note: consumer society. Imagine: if this is my car, what must my publisher's car be like." And we drive around Barcelona, reaching the quiet neighborhood of Sarriá. A spacious living room, sober and clear, and we sink into a couple of armchairs so big you could live in them.

GGM: You know, two weeks after the triumph of the Revolution I was in Cuba. I was in Operation Truth. Then I went to Bogotá, to the Prensa Latina office. In mid-1960 I returned to Havana. I worked for six months and I'll tell you what I got to know of Cuba. I got to know the fifth floor of the Retiro Médico, where Prensa Latina had its offices; I got to know the elevator in the Retiro Médico building; a partial view of la Rampa, and the Indochina shop, which was on the corner; I got to know another elevator that took me on another street to a twentieth floor, where I lived with Haroldo Wall. Ah!

And I got to know the Maracas restaurant, a block and a half from there, where we'd eat. We worked every minute, day and night. I'd tell Massetti [the director of Prensa Latina]: "If anything's going to sink this Revolution, it's the waste of electricity." Hey, what're you doing?

EGB: Setting up the recorder.
GGM: Drop it, it takes away spontaneity.

EGB: No, you'll see how we'll forget about it and talk as if there's nothing there. And we can forget, but the tape, fortunately, can't. And now a bit of formality: Mister García Márquez, what's your opinion of *One Hundred Years of Solitude*?
GGM: Mostly, it was a big surprise. Look, of my previous books, if I may use the only gauge for measuring success—sales figures—a thousand were sold. And *Leaf Storm* had been available since 1955. From that point of reference I'd calculated that *One Hundred Years of Solitude* would sell five thousand copies.

EGB: Did you have confidence in the book?
GGM: I had confidence in the book. I was sure it would be a great critical success.

EGB: But not a best-seller.
GGM: But not a best-seller. Still, the first five thousand copies sold out in almost two weeks only in the entrances to the Metro stations in Buenos Aires. Sudamericana Publishers had done a printing of eight thousand copies, calculating that they'd sell out between June and December of '67. Then they found themselves without any books.

EGB: The readers were the chief protagonists of the book.
GGM: That's what most interests me. In Latin America, here in Spain, everywhere, the book has been sold by readers. It's sold by word-of-mouth publicity, by *radio bemba* as they say in Cuba.

EGB: How many printings so far?
GGM: In Spanish, eighteen or twenty. It's surpassed the half-million copies mark, without counting the two Cuban printings, eighty thousand copies the first time, fifteen thousand the second. In other languages I've signed

seventeen contracts. The ones you see on this bookshelf are in French, Italian, English, Danish, and German. In Russian it's supposed to have come out, and, according to a notice I just received, it was just published in the Soviet magazine *Foreign Literature*.

EGB: How are the translations?
GGM: I like the English one a lot; the language is tighter, gains strength. The Italian one came out really good; we worked quite a bit with the translator, clarifying things. The French version is good, too, but I can't feel the book in French. And the French edition, despite its award for Best Foreign Book in 1969 and good reviews, hasn't sold that much. I think it's reached five thousand copies. I always felt the book wouldn't take off in France, because it's not a Cartesian book. You know how it is: in France, between the rationalism of Descartes and the crazy, overflowing imagination of Rabelais, it was Descartes who won. In the United States it's selling well, especially around universities. Even though it costs eight dollars. The translator tells me that when the paperback edition comes out, it'll sell much better.

EGB: And what do you feel in the face of that polyglot delirium?
GGM: A great joy in having achieved such communication with people.

EGB: What do you think there is about this crazy book that could achieve such a degree of communication?
GGM: That's what I wonder. Because apparently there are two levels, but maybe there are three or four, who knows how many? The British have seen this very well and have made an edition with two different covers, and they sell it accordingly here or there: one for readers who're interested in the literary side, another one for those interested simply in an adventure story. And I believe that between those two extremes there are other levels I haven't the slightest idea about and don't want to know about either. That is, I don't want to become conscious of the recipe to *One Hundred Years of Solitude*.

EGB: Are you afraid it'll influence you?
GGM: A couple of years ago I stopped reading the reviews of *One Hundred Years of Solitude*. My wife keeps them and I'll read them when I finish this other book I'm writing. There comes a time when you realize that the critics are discovering and, in some way, asking for something that I don't know up

to what point, unconsciously, you can't start giving them. I think that to find the recipe as to why *One Hundred Years of Solitude* sells so much is quite dangerous. Now it's a curious phenomenon, isn't it, taxi drivers in Barcelona read *One Hundred Years of Solitude*.

EGB: And, in Cuba, telephone operators, the girl who sets up the cows for milking, the hydraulic engineer, a cattle inseminator in Oriente province, cane cutters in Camagüey . . .
GGM: Yes, it's odd. To me, one of the important things about the book is precisely that: it narrows the gap between great literature and the larger public.

EGB: Yes, that's very important. One writes to be read, and not only by other writers.
GGM: One writes to be read, and not only by other writers.

EGB: Because there are books that are written for writers.
GGM: Many, many books are for writers. But what's odd is how, without any intention of mine to produce a best-selling book, that's what's happened. And there's more: with the breakthrough opened up by *One Hundred Years of Solitude*, my other books have moved in, and for the last two years they've been selling, in cheap editions, at an average of ten thousand copies every three months. Books, that, as I said to you, had sold a thousand each in ten, twelve years. What I'm trying to say is that I think those other books were written under the same formula . . .

EGB: With a bit more immaturity . . .
GGM: Probably with a bit more immaturity.

EGB: Those books were sort of a preparation for the high point of *One Hundred Years of Solitude*, no? Some say, for instance Vargas Llosa, that in those books you hadn't yet set your imagination free, you hadn't given all of yourself, even though you already showed a craft, a facility for expression.
GGM: Well, that's what I realized after writing *One Hundred Years of Solitude*. That is, the other ones I wrote with the same suppleness, that's clear and I realize it now. And I remember how I worked on the other books: they all responded to an approach, a plan that was rigid and well established before I'd started to write the book.

EGB: Don't you think it would be interesting if you explained that process that takes you to *Leaf Storm*, to *One Hundred Years of Solitude*, going through *No One Writes to the Colonel*, *In Evil Hour*, the practice stories, a bit as a block? But there are appreciable differences between them, and together they comprise your career as a writer.

GGM: At first it seemed a bit unfair that my works were known in reverse order. Yes, the impression readers might get, after they know *One Hundred Years of Solitude*, is that they're reading previous works. But if they'd read them in order, what one sees is a progression, a quest through all of the books. What's difficult is to know which is the book one is writing. In my case it *is* the book of Macondo, which has the most to say. But if you think on it carefully, you'll see that the book I'm writing isn't the book of Macondo, but of solitude.

EGB: Solitude as the other side of love, of solidarity, as you said at lunchtime?

GGM: Exactly. I don't see why the reviewers don't seem to have taken much notice, but the only books of mine that take place in Macondo are *Leaf Storm* and *One Hundred Years of Solitude*, and some of the stories in *Big Mama's Funeral*. *Colonel* and *In Evil Hour* occur in a town that is not Macondo. The fact is that some of the characters in those volumes have lived previously in Macondo and now they're in that book.

Specifically, the Colonel whom no one writes to, as seen in *One Hundred Years of Solitude*, was a young treasurer in the wars of Colonel Aureliano Buendía, who, after the Treaty of Neerlandia was signed, showed up and placed on the table the seventy-two golden bricks that were his mission. And Colonel Aureliano Buendía signed and sealed a receipt that allowed him to prove his status as war veteran so he could apply for the pension that he's always waiting for in the book.

In *No One Writes to the Colonel* you'll find the date and the time when this man left Macondo, because the banana odor upset his innards and he went off to live to another town. A town completely different from Macondo, with no railroad and a dirty and overflowing river where every Friday a boat arrives. It's the same town where *In Evil Hour* happens.

And there's the theme of solitude: the solitude of the Colonel who, with his wife and his rooster, tries waiting for a pension that never arrives. It doesn't arrive because of social injustices, because of infinite red tape.

In Evil Hour also unfolds in that town that isn't Macondo. There's a character, Father Ángel, who had been the priest in Macondo and who's transferred to that town. He's the only link to Macondo. And once again the major drama is the solitude of the mayor who came to conquer the town and starts to sink and finds himself conquered by it. Which was, clearly, a reflection of the situation of the entire country.

And there's another clear difference: that town can be placed in immediate history, in the context of Colombia; you can almost set the dates. You've seen how I worry about obscuring dates, but in those books they can be identified. This doesn't happen in Macondo—where *Leaf Storm* and *One Hundred Years of Solitude* take place—because in Macondo there's always a mythic dimension.

Now then, in all those books there's a constant feature: Colonel Aureliano Buendía has something to do with some character or place. The doctor in *Leaf Storm* arrives in the house with a letter written in Panama. The Colonel of the novel had been a treasurer for the revolution. In *In Evil Hour* there's a line, a quick one, about a house where Colonel Aureliano Buendía spent a night while passing through.

EGB: Is that deliberate? Did you somehow want to connect one book with another?
GGM: I now realize that I did. I always had in mind that Colonel from the previous century's civil wars, who'd fought in thirty-two uprisings and lost them all. But I was afraid of the warrior's false biography because I thought it could turn out boring. But in each book I'd write . . .

EGB: . . . the character would find his way in.
GGM: That's it, he'd find his way in. Even in *One Hundred Years of Solitude* I thought that Colonel Aureliano Buendía would be as marginal a character as in the other books, that he'd simply be passing through Macondo. But that was at the beginning, and I didn't know a lot of the things that happened later in the book.

EGB: Well, so we have the constant theme: solitude. But now tell me about your search for its expression in the different books, its literary treatment.
GGM: You see, I started out well, started out where I should've. The same mythic treatment in *One Hundred Years of Solitude* is in *Leaf Storm*. It was the right path. But there arose in Colombia what happens to be known as *La Violencia*, an expression I accept simply for convenience's sake, because violence stretches across the history of Colombia from end to end. And in

that period of political violence, which was organized by those in power, the Conservatives annihilated towns, entire populations, armed the police and the army and their supporters to terrorize the Liberals, who were the majority. That's how they could stay in power.

That time of violence had so large an impact on those who weren't yet writers in Colombia—many of whom witnessed terrible dramas of violence—that they felt the need to tell about it. And so in four or five years you had more than fifty novels, which is what is now called the Novel of *La Violencia* in Colombia.

Actually, more than novels they're immediate, shocking testimonials, mostly badly written, written in haste, with very slight literary value. But they have the advantage of being there as material and at any time, once it settles in, it'll be very useful for knowing that whole period.

Back then I was twenty-two or twenty-three years old. I'd written *Leaf Storm* and had in my head the inchoate nebula for *One Hundred Years of Solitude*. And I said to myself, "How can I depict what we're experiencing by using mythic treatment and terrain? Seems like escapism." It was a mistaken, political decision, I now believe.

I decided to approach the current situation in Colombia and wrote *Colonel* and *In Evil Hour*. I didn't write exactly what one would call novels of *la Violencia* for two reasons: one, because I hadn't lived it directly—I lived in cities. And two, because I felt that what mattered, for literature, wasn't an inventory of the dead and the description of violent methods—which was what other writers did. Rather what counted for me was the motives and root causes of that violence, and above all the consequences of that violence for the survivors.

That's why you'll find that in *In Evil Hour* there are no massacres. The critical period of *la Violencia* is practically over. What you see in the book is that the pause is patched with cobwebs and that the violence will come back, that it's not over because the causes aren't gone.

Then I confronted an official change of language. Because the technique and language are determined by the subject of the book. And I couldn't deal with those problems via the language that I'd used in *Leaf Storm* and that I wished to use in what would be called *One Hundred Years of Solitude*. That's why there's such a basic difference in language.

So the books that have a language in common are *Leaf Storm* and *One Hundred Years of Solitude* on one hand, and on the other, *No One Writes to the Colonel* and *In Evil Hour*. In the book of stories, *Big Mama's Funeral* there's both, because the stories are a bit like leftover materials that I put together a book with.

You'll find that the language in *Colonel* and *In Evil Hour* is more concise, drier, direct, picked up right from journalism, because I was trying to write reports with literary qualities, I was taking literary time to write them. I was a writer-reporter who, besides, was a reporter in real life.

EGB: And what made you change and take up again, in *One Hundred Years of Solitude*, the language and treatment of your first book?

GGM: Because I felt that path was leading me nowhere. I had to write a book every time the situation changed, just as one does in reporting. I think I was more mature politically and realized it wasn't true that the mythic treatment was escapist. And then I took the plunge and did *One Hundred Years of Solitude* the way I did.

EGB: It would be interesting if you explained why you arrive at the conclusion that the mythic treatment didn't involve escapism, and why you say you did it with greater political maturity.

GGM: You see, what happened was that I hit upon a clearer idea of the concept of reality. The immediate realism of *No One Writes to the Colonel* and *In Evil Hour* has a certain reach. But I realized that reality is also the myths, beliefs, and legends of the people. These are their everyday life and they intervene in their victories and defeats. I realized that reality isn't just the police who arrive and shoot people, but also the entire mythology, all the legends, everything that comprises people's lives. And all of that needs to be included.

EGB: As does Glauber Rocha, in film.

GGM: Exactly. The Brazilians are doing it in film in a marvelous way. When you use that larger range for measuring Latin American reality, you realize it reaches absolutely fantastical levels. And at this time I've come to believe there's something we can call "parareality," which isn't less metaphysical, doesn't have to do with superstitions or imaginative speculations, but which exists as a result of deficiencies or limits in scientific research, and so we still can't call it "real reality."

I'm speaking of omens, therapies, those many premonitory beliefs in which Latin American folk live every day, giving superstitious interpretations to objects, things, events. Interpretations, moreover, that go back to our most remote ancestors.

Look: one night, three years ago I'm in a car from Barranquilla to Cartagena, which is two hours away. It was two in the morning. I fell asleep in the back seat and midway the driver woke me up and said to me, "Hey, d'you know something about mechanics? 'Cause the car is stalled and actually, it's not mine. It belongs to my brother, who loaned it to me for the trip. And I don't know how to fix it." There was no light, and almost no traffic on the road. But, well, as it turns out, a couple of hours later we found out it was the transmission belt. We fixed it somehow and went on. At my family's house, in Cartagena, they didn't know I was coming that night. But they're Buendías! Aside from there being twelve of us, they all have the same surname. The fact is I arrived almost at dawn, I knocked, they opened the door, and at that very moment one of my brothers, who came out wrapped up in a sheet, says, "Boy, what a coincidence. I dreamed that Gabo was on the road and that he needed our help."

I don't give metaphysical explanations for that, you understand, but I believe they're things that are part of a reality we don't know. And exploring that reality at this point interests me as much as the other kind.

That's why I tell you that I think I had enough political maturity so as not to get some inferiority complex. I could say: my commitment is to all reality, to a literature that refers to all reality.

EGB: That's the consideration, I believe, that leads you to Magical Realism.
GGM: Exactly. It's why I took up once again in *One Hundred Years of Solitude* the path of *Leaf Storm*.

EGB: Now compared with *Leaf Storm* there is in *One Hundred Years* a flowering of imagination through language . . .
GGM: Well, wait, between *Leaf Storm* and *One Hundred Years of Solitude* there are some fifteen years of hard knocks, of living a lot and being aware of this every day, trying to see how things were. Fifteen years of life experience and of writing apprenticeship.

I believe that writing is learned by writing, and journalism taught me to write every day for lots of years. And now I write my novels as if I worked at a newspaper. I arrive at my newspaper at nine in the morning, I sit down, I write about the day's business, which I already know what it is with my work plans. And at three o'clock I quit, put on my hat, and leave.

EGB: But in any case you must have had to do some grunt work as far as enriching your language was concerned, because in *One Hundred Years* there's a luxuriant handling of the prose.

GGM: If it didn't sound pretentious, I'd tell you that I'd already known that Spanish prose. I simply hadn't needed it before. What you call richness of language I hadn't needed either in journalism or in my three previous books.

I conclude that *One Hundred Years of Solitude* had to be written that way because that's how my grandmother talked. I tried to find the language that was most suitable for the book, and I remembered that my grandmother used to tell me the most atrocious things without getting all worked up, as if she'd just seen them. I then realized that that imperturbability and that richness of imagery with which my grandma told stories was what gave verisimilitude to mine. And my big problem with *One Hundred Years of Solitude* was credibility, because I believed it. But how was I going to make my readers believe it? By using my grandmother's same methods.

You'll notice that in *One Hundred Years of Solitude*, especially in the beginning, there are a huge amount of deliberate archaisms. Later, halfway through the book, I was sailing like a fish in water and in the last parts there aren't only archaisms, there are neologisms and invented words and whatever. 'Cause I believe that the final part reflects the joy I felt at having found the book.

EGB: Well, we've arrived, on purpose or not, at the jaws of the monster. Let's discuss *One Hundred Years* and avoid the millions of things that have been said about the book in this world. What do you think of the criticism you've read about *One Hundred Years*? Do any of them get it right?

GGM: About *One Hundred Years of Solitude*, as you say, tons and tons of papers have been written. One finds stupid things, important things, consequential things. But no one has touched on the point that most interested me as I wrote the book, which is the idea that solitude is the opposite of solidarity, and I believe that is the essence of the book.

That's what explains the frustration of the Buendías, one by one, the frustration of their environment, the frustrations of Macondo. And I believe there's a political concept here: solitude as the negation of solidarity is a political concept. And an important one. And nobody has seen it, or at least nobody has said it.

The Buendías' frustration comes from their solitude, that is, their lack of solidarity. The frustration of Macondo comes from there, and the frustration of everything, everything, everything.

It's the lack of love. Aureliano Buendía's incapacity to love is written in all his words in the book. At the end, when the Aureliano with the tail of a pig is born, it reads, "The only one in a century who had been engendered with love."

EGB: And it's he who brings an end to the lineage.
GGM: It's he who brings an end to the lineage.

EGB: Where has the best criticism of *One Hundred Years of Solitude* appeared?
GGM: It's unfortunate to have to say so, but the best criticism has been done in the United States. They're professional, conscious readers, well trained, some of them progressive, others as reactionary as they're supposed to be, but as readers they're fantastic.

EGB: The enemy knows us.
GGM: And besides, we still give them facts so that they'll know us.

EGB: Was it a lot of work to organize the material for the book?
GGM: It was very tedious. You've got to organize it in your head. Otherwise you'll drown in paper.

EGB: You don't keep notes?
GGM: No, only daily notes, for working. That is, making sure to go this way, that way, and not forget this. When I finished *One Hundred Years of Solitude*, when I made the finished copy and my publisher acknowledged receipt of the original, I called on my wife and we destroyed a box of papers that was this big, where the notes for the book were. 'Cause whoever found these notes would have known how it was put together, what's true and what's false, what's genuine and what's gruesome, would know that it didn't come from

true literary necessity but that it was merely a technical device. All that would be known. So, buddy, it's going with me to the grave!

EGB: Well, but admit you had to make a Buendía family tree so you wouldn't get lost in that tangle. Some of us, more or less, have started to make one.
GGM: Yes, I made it. But really the family tree is easier than it seems. There's a simple trick. The José Arcadios are the ones that continue the family line, not the Aurelianos, except for José Arcadio Segundo and Aureliano Segundo. But they were identical twins who probably got mixed up in their infancy and went on being mixed up throughout the book. And there are clues: one is that they have the traits that correspond to the Aurelianos and the José Arcadios, switched around. Another clue is when they're buried. Since they died at the same time and were put in identical coffins, the little drunkards who bury them get it wrong and mix up the graves. It seems that all their lives they were wrong, but in death the whole thing was set straight.

Yes, I made a family tree to avoid getting tangled up as I wrote. You can imagine: if reading it is tough, how it must have been to write it!

EGB: Why "Buendía"?
GGM: Because it seemed right to me. Besides, it's been Buendía since *Leaf Storm*. And Colonel Aureliano Buendía flits through the other books like a ghost until, at last, he takes on life in *One Hundred Years of Solitude*.

EGB: When starting the book, had you decided that you would tell the story of the life of the Colonel and the thirty-two wars?
GGM: No, I felt that the Colonel should be as marginal a character as in my other books, that he'd simply pass through Macondo. But I didn't know that Colonel Buendía had been born in Macondo, and didn't know that he was the son of José Arcadio Buendía and Úrsula Iguarán. They had two sons, and at some point I realized that one of them was the Colonel, but I didn't know which of the characters—whether José Arcadio of the tattoos who goes around the world seventy-five times, or the other one, that solitary goldsmith, Aureliano—would end up being the Colonel.

EGB: What about the repeated names?
GGM: Well, that's very Latin American. I'm named after my father. You're probably named after yours.

EGB: Yeah.

GGM: Back home we're twelve and the last one also is called Gabriel, like me. I'd already left for my studies, and my mother said that she wanted to have another Gabriel in the house. So she gave my name to the last brother. It's very Latin American. It wasn't my aim to complicate things.

EGB: How did you work through *One Hundred Years of Solitude*? How did you structure the novel?

GGM: Starting with the sentence that says, "Many years later, as he faced the firing squad, Colonel Aureliano Buendía was to remember that distant afternoon when his father took him to discover ice." You know that's true; I'll explain. The original idea I had of *One Hundred Years of Solitude*, the opening image—because the first thing I'll have for a book is an image, not an idea or concept but an image—is that of an old man who takes a kid to discover ice.

EGB: Was it your grandfather?

GGM: It's the image from an occasion when my grandfather took me to see the dromedary at a circus. But at the same time, in Aracataca, where we lived, I'd never had the chance to see ice. And once the banana company commissioner received some frozen snapper. And I was struck by those red snappers that looked like rocks, so I asked my grandfather. And my grandpa, who always explained everything to me, said they looked like rocks because they were frozen. And I asked him what "frozen" meant, and he took me by the hand and took me to the commissioner and asked them to open up a box of frozen snapper, and I got to discover ice. And of course, when I had to decide between dromedary and ice, I stayed with ice because, from a literary standpoint, it was much more suggestive. What's incredible now is that all of *One Hundred Years of Solitude* started from that all-so-simple image.

EGB: When did you start writing it?

GGM: At age eighteen, and at the time it was called *The House*, because I thought the story would never go outside the Buendía home. But I lacked the drive, the life experience, and the literary resources to write a work like that, and I quit. I wrote *Leaf Storm*. It was chance.

EGB: And when you wrote it . . .

GGM: It was a fiesta for me, especially at the end of the book, when I had it in my hands. I pull people's legs, throw in private jokes and secret messages for my friends. I knew the book wouldn't escape me and I got around to playing out of sheer joy.

EGB: There's one thing I'd like to clarify. I read a statement of yours where you said that it was a mistake for the critics to take *One Hundred Years of Solitude* seriously because it was a novel without any seriousness. And since I believe it's profoundly serious and believe you do too, I'd like you to tell me how to interpret that statement of yours.

GGM: You see, it should be taken this way. There are few things that scare me more than solemnity. And buddy, I come from the most solemn country in the world, which is Colombia. And the only place that's not solemn in Colombia is the Caribbean fringe. We Caribbeans see the rest of Colombia, especially the guys from Bogotá, as terrifyingly solemn. On the coast, we josh, we take on the most serious and bothersome things as if we weren't taking them seriously, out of fear of solemnity. Sort of, if you wish, Cuban style, which is the same, since the Caribbean is one country.

That's what I want to tell the critics who interpret the novel solemnly. What bothers me is the solemnity of those very serious critics who sit down and start pontificating about a novel that is anti-solemn.

Of course, and that's when I tell them not take it seriously, in the sense that they should approach the book the same way it was written. 'Cause they've been dressing it up with the hat and robe of a bishop, and that is truly terrible.

EGB: The new book you're writing, *The Autumn of the Patriarch*, is it written in the same tone?

GGM: No, it's completely different. When I sat down to write *The Autumn of the Patriarch*, I realized it was coming out like *One Hundred Years of Solitude*. My arm was still warm and it was too easy. From there I concluded that I had to take fully apart the style of *One Hundred Years of Solitude* and start from elsewhere. How to start from elsewhere? From scratch. How to start from scratch? I'll write children's stories. So I wrote five of them. You must have read one in the magazine *Casa de las Américas*. Roberto Fernández Retamar asked me to send him something, and I sent it to him, it was unpublished. And then he asked me for the others and I sent them on. But they weren't written with publication in mind. They were like piano exercises to look for the style I'd use in the new book. Until I got to the fifth story and said: that's what it's like, the book I'm going to write.

EGB: But does *The Autumn of the Patriarch* start out, like *One Hundred Years of Solitude*, with a key paragraph?
GGM: Nope. Owing to its structure, the first chapter is half-done because I need information from the rest of the novel, which is still unfinished.

EGB: Does it start out from a simple image, like all your other books?
GGM: It starts out from the image of an inconceivably old dictator who is all alone in a palace filled with cows.

EGB: How was that image generated? Do you know?
GGM: I knew . . . I knew, I think I forget. I know where I got the idea to write a book about a dictator. In Caracas, at the start of 1958, when Pérez Jiménez fell.

Pérez Jiménez had already left. The government junta was meeting in a chamber at Miraflores Palace. And in the anteroom there we were, all the journalists in Caracas, at four A.M., waiting the whole night for an announcement about the fate of the country which was being played out in that chamber.

At a certain moment the door opened the first time, and out came an officer in combat fatigues, his boots all muddy, pointing toward the room with a submachine gun. Pointing in, where Larrazábal and others were deciding Venezuela's lot. And he moved backwards among us journalists, with those boots of his, down the carpeted stairway. He got into a car and left.

I don't know who that soldier was. I do know he got asylum in Santo Domingo. But at that moment, and I can't say how, I had an insight about what power is. How that guy who was taking off—via an infinitely delicate contact—lacked power, and how, if that contact hadn't failed him, the story of that guy and of the whole country would have changed.

And so, what is the spark that generates power? What is power? It's so mysterious! The dictator in my book says it's like "a living Saturday."

Now I'm trying to remember what you asked me, about where the image comes from of a dictator alone in his palace, surrounded by cows . . .

EGB: Why cows?
GGM: Well, cows, yes, that's obvious. It's about Latin American dictators, who're feudal, cattle-raising dictators, they're into livestock. Besides I think the image of the cow inside the palace is beautiful. There's even a scene in the

book where a cow sticks its head over the balcony, and the people who're down on the street say, "Oh, shit. A cow in the presidential palace." Dictators in Latin America are like cattle ranchers.

EGB: Is the novel a monologue of the dictator?
GGM: No, but it's as if it were, because the narrator never becomes detached from the character of the dictator, which is the only character in the book, since all others exist through him and through the contacts they have with him. And since he's a very ill-informed man, the reader will always be as ill-informed as he is.

EGB: Can you pinpoint the country where the book takes place?
GGM: A country in the Caribbean. The sea that it faces—at the start of the book, because afterwards the dictator sells it to a foreign power and what remains is a nitrate desert—is the Caribbean, which can be seen from all the windows of the palace. But it's a mixture of Spanish and English Caribbean, because the architecture has to it a lot of Santo Domingo, Puerto Rico, and Cartagena. But at the same time there are Hindu stores, there are Dutch people, and pirates.

EGB: So you don't care at all about time as a concept?
GGM: Not at all. Here's an example: one day, the dictator wakes up. He's a dictator installed by the Marines who one day take off, after having signed a treaty guaranteeing to them the administration in perpetuity of customs and the right to return and occupy the country in case the yellow fever flares up again. They split and leave the Navy destroyer rotting in the port. One day, the dictator wakes up and gets out of bed, and finds out that everyone in the palace is wearing red bonnets, the maids who're sweeping, the milkmen, the orderlies who're unloading green produce. And then he asks, "What's going on with all these people and their red bonnets?"

They say, "Well, you see, some strange guys have arrived with shipments of red bonnets, and they'll barter anything for red bonnets: iguana eggs, alligator grease and leather, tobacco, chocolate, everything, everything you've got they'll exchange you for a red bonnet."

And then the dictator, who never says anything without thinking and mulling it over first, wonders, "What is this?" He opens the window that looks out on the sea and he sees the ocean, he sees the Marines' destroyer, and, behind the ship he sees the three caravels at anchor. Christopher Columbus has arrived.

So you can say how I'm dealing with the problem of time. What's important to me is that all this has been a single moment. Chronological order doesn't matter to me one bit.

With objects I follow the same criterion. If it suits me poetically that the dictator go out in an armored Cadillac, he'll go in an armored Cadillac. If poetically I care more that he ride in a nineteenth-century carriage, he'll ride in a nineteenth-century carriage. It doesn't matter much, and it provides a lot of literary devices.

EGB: Is it a difficult book to write?
GGM: It's a very difficult book to write.

EGB: Why?
GGM: Because I want it to be a long poem about the solitude of power. So I have to write it as one writes poetry: word by word, word by word.

EGB: How much are you advancing per day?
GGM: Now I'm happy. Now I'm at almost two pages a day. I've been at it three years, but—oh, man!—there were times when I'd spend a week on a single line. Until I got used to the method, which, whatever you call it, is different from anything I'd done earlier.

EGB: Don't you let stand, temporarily, a line that you're not completely satisfied with?
GGM: No. Do you know why? Because at the moment I'm writing it, that line is important to me. If I let it stand temporarily to look at it afterwards, within the context of the book it loses importance and will stay that way. That's why I don't pass over a line, any single line with which I'm not completely satisfied. Besides, readers pay me to do it.

EGB: What did you write today?
GGM: Ah, an episode I like a lot. The episode of the children.

EGB: Let's hear it.
GGM: It's the last thing I'm going to tell you about the novel.

EGB: Why? Do you think I won't read it otherwise?

GGM: Neither you nor anybody's going to read it!

The dictator has been sold a system for winning the lottery. A guy shows up who says, "I've got the infallible system for winning the lottery." And he explains it to him, and it's so simple the dictator keels over. It's a lottery for two million pesos with only three digits, and the drawing is done in public on the Palace balcony.

The Plaza de Armas, which is in front, fills up with people who're going to witness the drawing. The crowd is asked to pick out at random three innocent children, between ages five and seven. And the crowd sends them up to the balcony to draw the three numbers.

And the figures on the balls always coincide with the dictator's ticket. He hits the jackpot.

Everything goes well. Months and months go by. Until one day the dictator is approached and asked, "Well, general, sir, what shall we do with the children?" He answers, "What children?" They say, "The lottery children. 'Cause the security services, for your own good, decided to keep watch over them, and not release them so they wouldn't blab. We've got two thousand of them and we've said we don't, and the parents have rebelled and we've sprayed them with bullets. And all that music you hear at night is so you won't hear the shots we're taking at the parents who're calling for their kids."

And the dictator thinks and says, well, why? And he starts to investigate and he finds that the guy who's sold him the system, and who takes a fourth of the first prize, has also sold the second prize to the head of security, and the rest to the Joint Chiefs of Staff. The whole Joint Chiefs are involved in the affair, and that's why, every time the dictator would ask them what's he like, that guy, he'd get impeccable reports about some saint. And it turns out the guy had a chain of whorehouses and gambling outfits. So the Dictator faces a great problem: there are telegrams from the Organization of American States, from the Pope. The dictator calls in the Joint Chiefs, and the minute he brings them together he realizes they're scared and capable of anything. And he feels alone against them all, and tells them not to worry, nothing's happened here, I'll take the rap, keep on working as ever, and now what matters is the good name and the honor of the Armed Forces. I'll take the blame, and you guys just leave well enough alone.

And they tell him, "Yes, general, sir, you'll assume responsibility, but, what do we do with the kids?"

"Yes, what do we do with the kids?" says he.

You get a Commission from the OAS, from the Red Cross, from the parents. He says, "Well, get hold of the kids and take them to the far South." The Commission comes, searches everywhere and comes to the conclusion that there are no kids, that the desirable thing is to hold elections within a reasonable time frame, for the sake of democracy. And the dictator agrees, and they leave.

Fine, on to other stuff. But they say, "Yes, general, sir, but, what do we do with the kids?" "Take them to the North." The dictator gets worried, gives orders to airlift them toys. But, what do we do with the kids? It's a refrain.

The best counsel the dictator has is his mother, a former bird breeder who'd paint other colors onto birds and then sell them as rare species. She lives in a room in the palace and still paints birds, paints their feathers, and they're strange creatures, she disguises the orioles as parrots and the roosters as . . . So . . . The dictator has concealed from her the matter of the children and the lottery, it's one of the few things he's hidden from her. Until one day he can't take it any longer and tells her, "I've got this problem." And his mother answers him, "Let's see, tell me exactly how it's all happened." And he tells her everything, and when he's finished, his mother says to him, "Don't you realize? You've got no choice but to have them killed." Says he, "But it's two thousand kids." And she says, "They're going to die in a war, anyway." Then the dictator gives the order to kill them. They're put in a huge ship and made to sing so they won't cry. And they sink.

That's where I'm at now.

(*The tape recorder keeps spinning in silence.*)

The problem with the children gets pretty prolonged.

EGB: So far as to constitute an important aspect of the book?
GGM: No, you see, that's precisely where the problem lies. There are many, many stories like this in the book. All this I've just told you takes up five pages in the novel! And with more minute detail than I've told you. It's an episode that's not important in the book; it's a book that has a capacity to devour material . . .

EGB: Well, *One Hundred Years of Solitude* devours . . .
GGM: . . . but this one devours more. It's got me all bothered, because there's a large amount of material I have high hopes for, and they get gobbled up in three or four pages.

EGB: Obviously because you want it to get gobbled up.

GGM: Sure, I want it that way. Just to avoid delighting in descriptions and stuff like that, I always want to get to the bottom of the matter. I'm not interested in the episode of the children, nor in the cleverness of the lottery. I'm interested in the way the dictator reacts to and deals with these issues.

EGB: And do you already have a complete idea of the novel?

GGM: Ah, yes, I've got it as if I had read it!

EGB: So the problem is one of writing.

GGM: The problem is one of writing, and I've found that grammar is like a corset.

EGB: And what have you done about?

GGM: I sent it to hell a while ago.

EGB: And in the course of the writing, have you modified the plan you'd worked out previously?

GGM: Well, this book is different, because it's been shaped in the course of the writing.

EGB: The solution you chose, definitively, for the novel, was it the same one you handled from the start?

GGM: You know, among the many forms I'd had for writing the book, there's one I discarded, which was the trial of Sosa Blanco in Cuba. I was at that trial and I wanted to imagine my dictator in the same circumstances as Sosa Blanco, and, through the trial, provide the reality of the character. But it didn't work because it didn't give me the subjectivity of the dictator, how he thinks, how he reacts—which is what interests me.

Later I thought it could be a monologue of the accused dictator on the dock, but that created another problem for me: the dictator would have to speak in a language not his own. The dictator can't read or write. He learns later, but since the days of the Marines he has signed with his thumbprint, and when he got tired he had a rubber stamp of his thumbprint made and he'd sign with the stamp. But he's illiterate and he would have had to speak with the literary language of the narrator, which would've been false.

Besides, what most matters to me isn't what the dictator knows, but rather what he *doesn't* know. And he couldn't say that in a monologue, since the dictator can't talk about what he doesn't know.

EGB: Yet you were saying that the narrator doesn't follow the other characters when they stray away from the dictator. So how can you present what the dictator doesn't know?

GGM: There's information flow that comes to him, at times. Other times, he does a personal investigation as in the affair of the lottery. But the more he consolidates his power, the more he becomes isolated, because the entire apparatus starts perfecting itself, and when the machinery reaches such a degree of perfection that he attains absolute power, he is completely isolated, and nothing arrives his way any longer.

EGB: The Dominicans used to explain to me a characteristic of Trujillo: the absolute unpredictability of the repression he wielded. The insecurity of the people was all that much greater when the repression turned out to be capricious and unpredictable. Is there something of this in your dictator?

GGM: Yes, there is. He has a sentence: "The less the people understand, the more they'll be scared."

EGB: Is there a point where he loses contact with reality to such an extreme degree that he believes his own lies?

GGM: That's one of the problems I face now, because, at heart, my dictator isn't that way . . . but the . . .

EGB: . . . but the same game he's involved in seems to lead him . . .

GGM: Yeah, but he never becomes fully convinced, because he's a really cowardly sort, very hesitant, always filled with great uncertainties, and he's always in permanent crisis. That is to say, the life of this guy is limited to conjuring up a crisis only to fall into another one, and there are two hundred-some years of permanent crisis.

What I don't know exactly is up to what point he thinks he's his own character. But a novelist has an advantage over an historian. An historian has to dispense with the magical aspect of the dictator, and for me that is the most interesting aspect.

The thing is, I'm learning a lot from this book just by writing it. This stuff I'm telling you today I couldn't have said three months ago, and a year and a half ago I was completely in the clouds. All I had was faith, faith in the image and faith that some day I could arrive at the point where the incredibly old man ends up alone with the cows in his palace. And now I do have it perfectly planned and I know the moment when it's going to arrive.

EGB: You trust that you've created a living character that in its own life he'll be explaining to you what he is?
GGM: Well, that happens in every novel I've written. As I explained earlier, I didn't know that Colonel Aureliano Buendía had been born in Macondo, and when I did find out I didn't know which of the sons of the founders of Macondo would be the Colonel.

EGB: And they themselves decided?
GGM: They decide. Look, when I say it this way it sounds a lot like writer's theatrics, but Remedios, the Beauty, according to my notes, eloped with a guy, and the Buendías kept up appearances by saying she'd risen to heaven bodily. But when the moment of truth came, I thought it better if she did rise to heaven bodily.

EGB: I don't know up to what point you had the right to take away that marvelous girl from this world.
GGM: What's simply tremendous about writing is exactly that: to discover the book, discover the characters, see how they create themselves.

EGB: Your dictator, from the start, is he old, really old?
GGM: Always. I was interested in the image of the dictator as old, I wasn't interested in his evolution: what he was like at twenty, thirty, forty years of age. That could get me into historian-type complications that I didn't want to enter into.

EGB: Is there any serious problem that still needs working out?
GGM: Finding a difficult balance in the book. The novel is a meditation on power; power for power's sake. Right now, I've got a big problem of conscience, the concern that all that meditation could absolve the dictator, in the sense

that he might come off as the victim of some apparatus and of a set of circumstances, something I don't believe to be historically true. So that equilibrium is the one I need to find.

EGB: Isn't it the dictator who determines the course of events?
GGM: Yes, he always determines, but he determines by basing himself on bad information.

EGB: What's his criterion for deciding?
GGM: His decisions lead solely and exclusively to staying in power.

EGB: Does he ever take the people's interests into account?
GGM: Nope. There's a moment when he's told he could do such and such in order to improve the situation of the poor, and he says that's bull shit, there's no hope for the poor, and he says a sentence, "The day that shit's worth something, the poor will be born without assholes."

EGB: So it's clear why he wants power: he wants power itself and nothing else.
GGM: Power for power's sake.
   (*Another brief silence on the tape recorder, with the sounds of cigarette lighters and ice cubes in glasses.*)
   What else have you got there?

EGB: A question I was saving for when we'd spoken enough about your books. I'd like to know the personal decalog of García Márquez, his values, his principles.
GGM: Well, look. After one makes those decisions that are of a literary nature but that aren't determined, as we've said, by one's political background, one then finds oneself in a situation like mine at this moment—sought out by journalists, by publishers, in sum, by everything that we know is prompted by a situation such as this.
   And then there arises a problem that I didn't know was going to arise: the conduct of a progressive but non-militant writer who lives in the capitalist world.
   That is, it forces you to create an ethic that you need to create slowly on your own, because you don't learn it in school. You learn it gradually from

daily life and that ethic, to me, is closely related to money. I believe in the corrupting power of money, and I live watching over and taking care of myself in that regard.

I don't have monetary ambitions, or I have monetary ambitions only to the extent that I allow myself to buy my time as a writer. And I believe that, in a capitalist system, the only clean money I can earn is that which I get from the sales of my books. I'm not interested in money, but I won't allow publishers to rob me of a penny, because, do you know how the money that a book produces gets distributed?

EGB: Not very well.
GGM: We writers are cows for milking, old man. Everyone lives off us. I sit down right now to write this book and I don't know how many people are going to live off it. The one who's working is me, but there are some gentlemen who're sitting about waiting for me to write it so they can print it, distribute it, and sell it, and the book price goes up because of that. Books are expensive.

Ninety percent of the book, I don't know exactly how, is divided among the publisher, the jobber, and the retailer. There remains a ten percent, from which the writer's taxes are withheld and you've got to pay your agent ten percent of that sum. So, figure it out. *One Hundred Years of Solitude* in Spain costs 180 pesetas. I earn—in round figures—eighteen pesetas. Deducting for the agent, let's say sixteen pesetas. How much is admission to the movies if I want to take my wife and two kids? Fifty pesetas per person, 200 pesetas. I make sixteen pesetas per book. How many books do I need to sell in order to take them to the movies? I don't know: twelve or thirteen books. You understand? And I've still got to pay for everything else: housing, a thousand things. Meanwhile, how much do the publisher and other middlemen make? Look: everything comes down to this statement, which is unbeatable: all publishers are rich, and all writers are poor.

So I don't let them cheat me. Because it's my own, clean product. I watch over my sources of money. I'm against all subsidies for writing, of any sort: whether foundation grants, or aid, even prizes. I think that in any case such money will condition and compromise the writer. And I've believed this for a long time. And it's been a long time since I ever, at any moment, accepted a writing grant or an official or diplomatic post.

EGB: You recently rejected the offer to be Colombian consul in Barcelona.

GGM: Yes, I was offered the job by telegram. I replied with my own, rejecting the offer and saying something about being too busy. I didn't want to get into debating other stuff. I thought it was over, but shortly thereafter the Colombian government publicized the matter and I realized that the offer wasn't as innocent as I'd thought and that it could seem as if I might accept when I'd finished writing my novel. And then I wrote an open letter explaining that my turning down the post had political motives: that what I rejected was the length and breadth and depth of my country's anachronistic structure. Naturally, it was interpreted as fame having gone to my head and a Consulate in Barcelona being too little. I couldn't care less, because what I believe, and have no hesitation in saying so, is that one Miguel Angel Asturias is enough for Latin America. I feel that, when you're not actively militant, you need to be very scrupulous in your passive militancy. I'm not allowed to enter the United States, and I don't want the visa. I think that the fact of my being denied a visa to the U.S. is part of my political capital, precisely because I was a correspondent for Prensa Latina while the Cuban exiles landed at Bay of Pigs.

EGB: But I've led you astray from what you were explaining: your preoccupation with the sources of money.

GGM: I realized that what I had to do was keep working at related jobs till I could live off my books. I worked in journalism, publicity, TV, film, without accepting any help that was offered me. What I'm doing now with my royalties is buying time to dedicate myself exclusively to writing.

And then comes the interesting part: I'm concerned about how, in a socialist society, this problem of the writer's independence is to be solved, because I believe it continues under socialism. The Soviet solution is dangerous, that of the writer who lives on a State salary solely to write. First, there's already a conditioning of the writer, because that writer probably does everything possible to please the officials whom he depends on to keep receiving his salary. Or he writes what he feels he should write and it turns out it doesn't please the official, and then he ceases to be a writer, even though he probably still is one. It's the same problem in some socialist countries.

Now the case of Cuba is most interesting, because I've got the impression, from the little information I have at my disposal, that there still isn't a well-defined policy in that regard, which probably will start soon and which can rely on the experiences of other socialist countries. 'Cause I believe that Cuba is where there's a magnificent opportunity to hit upon a positive solution to the problem.

EGB: I believe, as you do, that the solution will be found in Cuba. But money certainly won't matter. In Cuba there's a tendency to eradicate money as a measure of value. What would matter will be the vocation, work, and output of a writer who, integrated with the Revolution and with his freedom to create guaranteed, won't have to worry about the way his basic necessities are provided. But frankly I don't believe this is an immediate problem. Writers in Cuba who are committed to the Revolution can scarcely contemplate dedicating all their time to literature. They divvy it out among the other pressing tasks they need to perform and their work. I would say that there's too much noise out in the street to set out to write like that, without further ado. But this business we're discussing prompts me to ask you about the militancy of the writer. Do you think the militancy of a writer ends with his writing?
GGM: That, precisely, is a problem of conscience. I don't believe so. I believe that, in any case, there's time for other kinds of militancy. But this brings us to another problem, the conflict between vocation and conviction. So I'm of the conviction that a writer's political activism doesn't end with this literary work, rather he can give more. But my vocation is to dedicate myself completely to literature, and I do so. Perhaps the solution to this conflict depends on each individual case.

EGB: You recently stated in an interview that the things that most interest you in the world are the music of the Rolling Stones, the Cuban Revolution, and four friends. Give me a summary of your relationship to the Cuban Revolution.
GGM: I believe in the Cuban Revolution every day.

EGB: Which aspect of the Revolution is the most important to you?
GGM: What matters to me is that its socialism gets created by taking into account its own conditions, a socialism that looks like Cuba and only Cuba: humane, imaginative, joyful, without bureaucratic rustiness. This is wonderful for all of Latin America, where conditions closely resemble those of Cuba.

EGB: When do you go to Cuba?

GGM: At any time. I'll have the draft for my book done by December, and I hope to go to Cuba during the first months of the following year. If I haven't gone to Cuba before, it's for purely practical reasons: I had to finish my novel.

EGB: Well, I think we've covered everything. Now I ask you: anything else?

GGM: There's something else. I'm not going to write any more novels.

EGB: How is that?

GGM: I'm out of fuel, guy. *The Autumn of the Patriarch* closes the cycle of solitude: an old dictator alone in his palace, among his cows. There's no more solitude to be asked for. I haven't any subject in mind for new novels.

EGB: What will you write?

GGM: Stories. I have about a hundred ideas. I'll write lots of them. And there's something else I want to do: novelized reports. A bit the way Truman Capote has done them, but—how can I say?—less elaborated, less theatrical. Mine will be to take a real fact and give it an entire history, a mythology, the people . . . Look, last time I was in Colombia, in a town near Bogotá, a lot of people got poisoned by bread. Do you realize what an amazing subject that is? Following the true story point by point: how the bread got poisoned, who ate it, who didn't, death thus choosing at random, the life in that town, its legends and the bread, the poison in the bread . . .

All done once again. We start over. And the tape recorder is up in smoke. And one wants to keep listening to this prestidigitator of images and words. But at some point one needs to stop, because the interview, contrary to appearances, only took twenty-four days and nights. In the form of cigars, cigarettes, snuff, and pipe tobacco we consumed the entire tobacco shipment of three caravels that arrived a few days ago in Barcelona from an uncertain port in the Caribbean, and we used up some ten miles of tape imported from the Netherlands.

When, at nightfall the last day, Colonel Aureliano Buendía said good-bye to us because he'd left a little gold fish unfinished, and Remedios, the Beauty, picked up her sheets to take flight through the window, and all that was left was a few cows looking for leftover grass amid the armchairs, Mercedes, the wife of García Márquez, entered, and I sighed with relief because, on the outside, she doesn't resemble Ursula Iguarán. She is a serene beauty who looks at you from Macondo. And the couple's two sons, Rodrigo and Gonzalo, their arms tattooed with animals and flowers and names they told me, and I wanted to believe they were decals. And I too departed, yet indeed, as I left, carelessly, I looked at the seats of their pants and I can testify: they do not have pig's tails. Happily, the family line continues.

Gabriel García Márquez

Rita Guibert / 1971

Interview conducted 3 June 1971. Reprinted from *Seven Voices: Seven Latin American Writers Talk to Rita Guibert*, by Rita Guibert, Alfred A. Knopf, Inc., 1973, pp. 305–37. Copyright © 1973 by Rita Guibert. Reprinted by permission. Translated by Frances Partridge.

The fact of the matter is that my pursuit of García Márquez—a special trip from Paris to Barcelona, a two-week wait in a Catalonian hotel, long-distance calls and cables and letters from New York to Spain—actually started only after I handed over to him, during our second and last meeting in the Barcelona Ritz, the questionnaire I had prepared at his own suggestion. You see, García Márquez is well known for his resistance to reporters, and he was at that time only willing to grant a written interview. Over a cup of tea he promised to have his answers ready in a couple of days, suggesting that if I wait there I could follow through my interview with new questions based on his written statements. But from then on I was unable to reach García Márquez, although before I left, he did get word to me through his wife that he would mail me the manuscript—which I never received.

Six months later, when García Márquez came to New York to receive the honorary degree given to him by Columbia University, he answered my telephone call without delay. The following morning we met at his hotel, the Plaza, where we had an early breakfast after persuading the maître d' to let us in—not because of García Márquez's mafioso mustache, but because he was tieless. Then we borrowed the deserted Persian Room, and this time, with a whirling tape, we finished in less than three hours the long-awaited interview.

Gabriel García Márquez (Gabo to his friends) was born in 1928 in Aracataca, a very small Colombian town close to a banana plantation in a place called Macondo, an even tinier town in the middle of nowhere, which García Márquez used to explore when he was a child.

Years later, he named the mythical land where some of his stories take place after Macondo, and closed the cycle with *One Hundred Years of Solitude*, the novel he began when he was eighteen. But as a young writer he had "neither the vital experience nor the literary means" to complete such a work (then called "The House") and decided instead to write *Leaf Storm*, his first book. Only in 1967, after many years of struggle and frustration in writing it, *One Hundred Years of Solitude* (his fifth book) was published in Buenos Aires, provoking—as the Peruvian novelist Mario Vargas Llosa wrote—"a literary earthquake throughout Latin America. The critics recognized the book as a masterpiece of the art of fiction and the public endorsed this opinion, systematically exhausting new editions. . . . Overnight, García Márquez became almost as famous as a great soccer player or an eminent singer of boleros." In 1969, the book's translation was selected by the Académie Française as the best foreign book of the year and other translations earned an equally enthusiastic response. But, according to the author, the best reviews he received came from the United States: "They are professional readers . . . some are progressive, others so reactionary, as they are supposed to be; but as readers, they are wonderful."

García Márquez doesn't consider himself an intellectual but "a writer who rushes into the arena like a bull and then attacks." For him, literature is a very simple game and "in a literary panorama dominated by Julio Cortázar's *Hopscotch*, Lezama Lima's *Paradiso*, Carlos Fuentes's *A Change of Skin*, and Guillermo Cabrera Infante's *Three Trapped Tigers*," writes Emir Rodríguez Monegal, "all experimental works to the limit of experimentation itself; all hard and demanding on their readers," García Márquez, in his *One Hundred Years of Solitude*, "with an olympian indifference to alien technique, sets himself free to narrate, with an incredible speed and apparent innocence, an absolutely lineal and chronological story . . . with its beginning, middle and end." And, as García Márquez himself says, it is the "least mysterious" of his books because "I tried to lead the reader by the hand so as not to get him lost at any moment."

Similarly, in a way, García Márquez had been led to success by his friends—because it was his friends who took the manuscript of *Leaf Storm* (1955) to the printer when they found it on his desk after he has gone to Italy in 1954 as a reporter for the Colombian daily *El Espectador*. Then in Paris, in 1957, after the dictator Rojas Pinilla had shut down the newspaper, García Márquez, who was living on credit in a Latin Quarter hotel, finished *No One*

Writes to the Colonel; but considering his work a failure, he buried the manuscript, "tied with a colored ribbon in the bottom of a suitcase." Subsequently, he returned to Colombia to marry his fiancée, Mercedes—the same Mercedes of the "sleepy eyes" engaged to Gabriel in *One Hundred Years of Solitude*—and moved for a couple of years to Venezuela where, while working as a journalist, he wrote *Los funerales de Mamá grande*. From Caracas he went to New York as the correspondent for Prensa Latina—revolutionary Cuba's news agency. Resigning after several months, and traveling by land through the south of the United States, he arrived in Mexico in 1961, where he settled for several years. And there, again, it was García Márquez's friends who arranged for his two recent books to be published in 1961–2, the same period in which his novel *La mala hora*, written in Mexico, was published after winning a Colombian literary contest. His friends had forced him to submit the manuscript to the competition after persuading him to change the original title, "Este pueblo de mierda." "The truth is," says Mario Vargas Llosa, "that without the obstinacy of his friends, García Márquez would perhaps still today be an unknown writer."

Today García Márquez can allow himself to live as a "professional writer" on the success earned mainly from *One Hundred Years of Solitude*—the saga of Macondo and the Buendías, which starts in a world "so recent many things lacked names and in order to indicate them it was necessary to point," a world where carpets fly; the dead are resuscitated; a rain lasts exactly four years, eleven months, and two days; the first Buendía spends his last years tied to a chestnut tree in his orchard muttering in Latin; tiny yellow flowers fall from the sky when he dies; Ursula, his wife, lives through generations and generations; Aureliano discovers that literature is the best toy ever invented to mock the public . . . and the chronicle ends when, after more than one hundred years of the family's struggles to avoid the fulfillment of an old prophecy, the line of the Buendías comes to an end when out of incestuous union a boy born with a pig's tail is devoured by an army of ants. And with this saga the author confirms what he said some time ago: "Everything is permitted to the writer, as long as he is capable of making it believable."

Postscript: Before leaving New York, García Márquez, who after our interview moved from his previous hotel to an undisclosed address, called to send me "a kiss as a gesture of tenderness." I then asked him how he spent the days in the city. "Great, Mercedes and I spent three delicious days shopping in New York." "Did you visit the museums? Did you go to the country?" "Of course not, and you can add to everything I told you that I don't like either art or nature."

RG: Your resistance to journalists is well known, and in the present case a lot of persuasion and several months of waiting have been necessary to overcome it.

GGM: Look, I've got absolutely nothing against journalists. I've done the job myself and I know what it's like. But if at this stage of my life I were to answer all the questions they want to ask me, I shouldn't be able to work. Besides, I should also be left with nothing to say. You see I realize that just because I have a fellow feeling for journalists, interviews have in the end become a form of fiction for me. I want the reporter to go away with something new, so I try to find a different answer to the same old questions. One no longer tells the truth, and the interview becomes a novel instead of journalism. It's literary creation, pure fiction.

RG: I don't object to fiction as a part of reality.

GGM: That could make a good interview!

RG: In *Relato de un náufrago* (The Story of a Castaway)—a journalistic report written in 1955 for Bogotá's newspaper *El Espectador* and published as a book in Barcelona in 1970—you narrate the odyssey of a sailor who lived for ten days adrift on a raft. Is there any element of fiction in that story?

GGM: There's not a single invented detail in the whole account. That's what's so astonishing. If I had invented that story I would have said so, and been very proud of it too. I interviewed that boy from the Colombian navy—as I explain in my introduction to the book—and he told me his story in minute detail. As his cultural level was only fair he didn't realize the extreme importance of many of the details he told me spontaneously, and was surprised at my being so struck by them. By carrying out a form of psychoanalysis I helped him remember things—for instance, a seagull he saw flying over his raft—and in that way we succeeded in reconstructing his whole adventure. It went like a bomb! The idea had been to publish the story in five or six installments in *El Espectador* but by about the third there was such enthusiasm among the readers, and the circulation of the paper had increased so enormously, that the editor said to me, "I don't know how you're going to manage, but you must get at least twenty installments out of this." So then I set about enriching every detail.

RG: As good a journalist as a writer . . .
GGM: It was my bread and butter for many years, wasn't it? . . . and now as a writer. I've earned my living at both professions.

RG: Do you miss journalism?
GGM: Well, I do feel a great nostalgia for my journalist days. As things have turned out I couldn't be a hard-nosed reporter now, which was what I used to prefer . . . going wherever the news was, whether it was a war, a fight, or a beauty contest, landing by parachute if necessary. Although my work as a writer, particularly as I do it now, derives from the same source as my journalism, the elaboration is purely theoretical, whereas the other was done on the spot. Today, when I read some of the things I wrote as a journalist I'm full of admiration, much more than for my work as a novelist, although I can give all my time to that now. Journalism was different; I used to arrive at the newspaper office and the editor would say, "We've got just an hour before this piece of news must be handed in." I think I should be incapable of writing one of those pages nowadays, even in a month.

RG: Why? Have you become more conscious of language?
GGM: I think one needs a certain degree of irresponsibility to be a writer. I was about twenty at that time and I was hardly aware what dynamite I held between my hands and in every page I produced. Now, particularly since *One Hundred Years of Solitude*, I've become very conscious of it because of the enormous interest the book has aroused . . . a boom of readers. I no longer think of what I write as if it would only be read by my wife and my friends, I know that a lot of people are waiting for it. Every letter I write weighs me down, you can't imagine how much! Then I nearly die of envy of my old journalist self, and the days when I used to dispatch the business so easily. It was terrific to be able to do that. . . .

RG: How has the success of *One Hundred Years of Solitude* affected your life? I remember your saying in Barcelona, "I'm tired of being García Márquez."
GGM: It's changed my whole life. I was once asked, I can't remember where, how my life differed before and after that book, and I said that after it "there

are four hundred more people." That's to say before the book I had my
friends, but now there are enormous numbers of people who want to see
me and talk to me—journalists, academics, readers. It's strange . . . most of
my readers aren't interested in asking questions, they only want to talk about
the book. That's very flattering if you consider case by case, but added up
they begin to be a problem in one's life. I would like to please them all, but
as that's impossible I have to act meanly . . . you see? For instance, by saying
I'm leaving a town when all I'm really doing is changing my hotel. That's
how vedettes behave, something I always hated, and I don't want to play the
vedette. There is, besides, a problem of conscience when deceiving people
and dodging them. All the same I have to lead my own life, so the moment
comes when I tell lies. Well, that can be boiled down to a cruder phrase than
the one you mentioned. I say, "I've had it to the balls with García Márquez!"

RG: Yes, but aren't you afraid that attitude may end by isolating you in an
ivory tower, even against your will?
GGM: I'm always aware of that danger, and remind myself of it every day.
That's why I went to the Caribbean coast of Colombia a few months ago, and
from there explored the Lesser Antilles, island by island. I realized that by
escaping from those contacts I was reducing myself to the four or five friends
I make wherever I live. In Barcelona, for instance, we always mix with about
four couples, people with whom we have everything in common. From the
point of view of my private life and my character, that's marvelous—that's
what I like, but a moment came when I realized that this life was affecting
my novel. The culmination of my life—to be a professional writer—had
been achieved in Barcelona, and I suddenly became aware that it was a
terribly damaging thing to be. I was leading the life of the complete
professional writer.

RG: Could you describe what the life of a professional writer is like?
GGM: Listen, I'll tell you what a typical day is like. I always wake very early, at
about six in the morning. I read the paper in bed, get up, drink my coffee
while I listen to music on the radio, and at about nine—after the boys have
gone to school—I sit down to write. I write without any sort of interruption
until half past two, which is when the boys come home and noise begins in
the house. I haven't answered the telephone all morning . . . my wife has been

filtering calls. We lunch between half past two and three. If I've been to bed late the night before I have a siesta until four in the afternoon. From that time until six I read and listen to music—I always listen to music, except when I'm writing because I attend to it more than to what I'm writing. Then I go out and have a coffee with someone I have a date with and in the evening friends always come to the house. Well . . . that seems to be an ideal state of things for a professional writer, the culmination of all he's been aiming at. But, as you find out once you get there, it's sterile. I realized that I'd become involved in a completely sterile existence—absolutely the opposite of the life I led when I was a reporter, what I wanted to be—and that this was having an effect on the novel I was writing—a novel based on cold experience (in the sense that it no longer interested me much), whereas my novels are usually based on old stories combined with fresh experiences. That's the reason I went to Barranquilla, the town where I was brought up and where all my oldest friends live. But . . . I visit all the islands in the Caribbean, I take no notes, I do nothing, I spend two days here and then go on somewhere else . . . I ask myself, "What did I come for?" I'm not very clear what I'm doing, but I know I'm trying to oil some machinery that has ground to a halt. Yes, there's a natural tendency—when you have solved a series of material problems—to become bourgeois and shut yourself in an ivory tower, but I have an urge, and also an instinct, to escape from that situation— a sort of tug-of-war is going on inside me. Even in Barranquilla—where I may be staying for a short period of time, which has a lot to do with not being isolated—I realize that I'm losing sight of a large area that interests me, out of my tendency to confine myself to a small group of friends. But this isn't me, it's imposed by the medium, and I must defend myself. Just another argument, as you see, which makes me say without dramatization but for the sake of my work—"I've had it to the balls with García Márquez."

RG: Your awareness of the problem should make it easier to deal with this crisis.
GGM: I feel as if the crisis had lasted longer than I thought it would, much longer than my publisher thought, much longer than the critics thought. I keep on meeting someone who is reading my book, someone who has the same reaction that readers had four years ago. Readers seem to emerge from caves like ants. It's really phenomenal. . . .

RG: Which doesn't make it any less flattering.

GGM: Yes, I do think it's very flattering, but the difficulty is how to deal with this phenomenon in practice. It's not only the experience of meeting people who have read the book, and hearing what it meant to them (I've been told amazing things), it's the experience of being popular. Those books have brought me a popularity more like that of a singer or film star than a writer. All this has become quite fantastic, and strange things happen to me: since the time I was on night shift at the newspaper I have been very friendly with the taxi drivers of Barranquilla, because I used to go and drink coffee with those parked at the cab stand across the street. Many of them are still driving, and when I take their taxis today they don't want to be paid; but the other day one who obviously didn't know me took me home, and when I paid him he said to me confidentially: "Did you know that García Márquez lives here?" "How do you know?" I asked him. "Because I've often taken him in my cab," he replied. You notice that the phenomenon is being reversed, and the dog is biting its own tail . . . the myth has caught up with me.

RG: Anecdotes for a novel . . .

GGM: It would be a novel about a novel.

RG: The critics have written at length about your work. Which of them do you agree with most?

GGM: I don't want my answer to seem unappreciative, but the truth is—and I know it's difficult to believe—that I don't pay much attention to the critics. I don't know why, but I don't compare what I think with what they say. So I don't really know whether I agree with them or not. . . .

RG: Aren't you interested in the critics' opinions?

GGM: They used to interest me a lot at first, but now rather less. They seem to have said very little that's new. There was a moment when I stopped reading them because they were conditioning me—in a way they were telling me what my next book ought to be like. As soon as the critics began rationalizing my work I kept on discovering things that were not convenient for me to discover. My work stopped being intuitive.

RG: Melvin Maddocks of *Life*, said of *One Hundred Years of Solitude*, "Is Macondo meant to be taken as a sort of surrealistic history of Latin America?

Or does García Márquez intend it as a metaphor for all modern men and their ailing communities?"

GGM: Nothing of the sort. I merely wanted to tell the story of a family who for a hundred years did everything they could to prevent having a son with a pig's tail, and just because of their very efforts to avoid having one they ended by doing so. Synthetically speaking, that's the plot of the book, but all that about symbolism . . . not at all. Someone who isn't a critic said that the interest the novel had aroused was probably due to the fact that it was the first real description of the private life of a Latin American family . . . we go into the bedroom, the bathroom, the kitchen, into every corner of the house. Of course I never said to myself, "I shall write a book that will be interesting for that reason," but now that it's written, and this has been said about it, I think it may be true. Anyway it's an interesting concept and not all that shit about a man's destiny, etc. . . .

RG: I think the theme of solitude is a predominant one in your work.

GGM: It's the only subject I've written about, from my first book until the one I'm working on now, which is an apotheosis of the theme of solitude. Of absolute power, which I consider must be total solitude. I've been writing about that process from the first. The story of Colonel Aureliano Buendía— the wars he fought and his progress to power—is really a progress toward solitude. Not only is every member of his family solitary—as I've repeated often in the book, perhaps more than I ought—but there's also the anti-solidarity, even of people who sleep in the same bed. I think the critics who most nearly hit the mark were those who concluded that the whole disaster of Macondo—which is a telluric disaster as well—comes from this lack of solidarity—the solitude which results when everyone is acting for himself alone. That's then a political concept, and interests me as such—to give solitude the political connotation I believe it should have.

RG: When you were writing it, were you consciously intending to convey a message?

GGM: I never think about conveying messages. My mental makeup is ideological and I can't get away from it—nor do I try or want to. Chesterton said that he could explain Catholicism starting from a pumpkin or a tramway. I think one could write *One Hundred Years of Solitude*, or a story about sailors, or the description of a football match, and still keep its ideological content.

It's the ideological spectacles I wear that explain—not Catholicism in this case—but something else which I can't define. I have no preconceived intention to say this or the other thing in a book of mine. I'm solely interested in the behavior of the characters, not whether that behavior is exemplary or reprehensible.

RG: Are you interested in your characters from a psychoanalytical point of view?
GGM: No, because that would need a scientific training which I don't possess. The opposite happens. I develop my characters and work on them, in the belief that I'm only making use of their poetical aspects. When a character has been assembled, some of the experts tell me that this is a psychoanalytic analysis. And I'm confronted then with a series of scientific assumptions that I don't hold and have never even dreamed of. In Buenos Aires—a city of psychoanalysts, as you know—some of them held a meeting to analyze *One Hundred Years of Solitude*. They came to the conclusion that it represented a well-sublimated Oedipus complex, and goodness knows what else. They discovered that the characters were perfectly coherent from a psychoanalytic point of view, they almost seemed like case histories.

RG: And they talked about incest too.
GGM: What interested me was that the aunt should go to bed with her nephew, not the psychoanalytic origins of this event.

RG: It still seems strange that, although *machismo* is one of the typical features of Latin American society, it's the women in your books who have strong, stable characters—or, as you've said yourself, they are masculine.
GGM: This didn't happen consciously, the critics made me see it, and set me a problem by so doing, because I now find it more difficult to work on that material. But there's no doubt that it's the power of women in the home—in society as it's organized, particularly in Latin America—that enables men to launch out into every sort of chimerical and strange adventure, which is what makes our America. This idea came to me from one of the true stories my grandmother used to tell about the civil wars of the last century, which can be more or less equated with Colonel Aureliano Buendía's wars. She told me that a certain man went to the war and said to his wife, "You'll decide what to do with your children." And for a year or more the wife was the one who kept the

family going. In terms of literature, I see that if it weren't for the women taking responsibility for the rearguard, the evil wars of the last century, which are
so important in the history of our country, would never have taken place.

RG: That shows that you're not antifeminist.
GGM: What I most definitely am is anti*machista. Machismo* is cowardly, a
lack of manliness.

RG: To return to the critics . . . you know that some of them have insinuated
that *One Hundred Years of Solitude* is a plagiarism of Balzac's *La Recherche de
l'absolu.* Günther Lorenz suggested this at a writer's conference in Bonn in
1970. Luis Cova García published an article called "Coincidence or Plagiarism?"
in the Honduran review *Ariel*, and in Paris a Balzac specialist, Professor
Marcelle Bargas, made a study of the two novels and drew attention to the
fact that the vices of one society and period, as depicted by Balzac, had been
transferred to *One Hundred Years of Solitude.*
GGM: It's strange; someone who had heard these comments sent me Balzac's
book, which I had never read. Balzac doesn't interest me now, although he's
sensational enough and I read what I could of him at one time—however, I
glanced through it. It struck me that to say one book derives from the other
is pretty light and superficial. Also, even if I were prepared to accept the fact
that I had read it before and decided to plagiarize it, only some five pages of
my book could possibly have come from *La Recherche*, and in the final analysis a single character, the alchemist. Well . . . I ask you, five pages and one
character against three hundred pages and some two hundred characters that
don't come from Balzac's book. I think the critics ought to have gone on and
searched two hundred other books to see where the rest of the characters
came from. Besides which, I'm not at all afraid of the idea of plagiarism. If I
had to write *Romeo and Juliet* tomorrow I would do it, and would feel it was
marvelous to have the chance to write it again. I've talked a lot about the
Oedipus Rex of Sophocles, and I believe it has been the most important book
in my life; ever since I first read it I've been astonished by its absolute perfection. Once, when I was at a place on the Colombian coast, I came across a
very similar situation to that of the drama of *Oedipus Rex*, and I thought of
writing something to be called *Oedipus the Mayor.* In this case I wouldn't
have been charged with plagiarism because I should have begun by calling
him Oedipus. I think the idea of plagiarism is already finished. I can myself

say where I find Cervantes or Rabelais in *One Hundred Years of Solitude*—not as to quality but because of things I've taken from them and put there. But I can also take the book line by line—and this is a point the critics will never be able to reach—and say what event or memory from real life each comes from. It's a very curious experience to talk to my mother about such things; she remembers the origin of many of the episodes, and naturally describes them more faithfully than I do because she hasn't elaborated them as literature.

RG: When did you start writing?
GGM: As far back as I can remember. My earliest recollection is of drawing "comics" and I realize now that this may have been because I couldn't yet write. I've always tried to find ways of telling stories and I've stuck to literature as the most accessible. But I think my vocation is not so much to be a writer as a story-teller.

RG: Is that because you prefer the spoken word to writing?
GGM: Of course. The splendid thing is to tell a story and for that story to die there and then. What I should find ideal would be to tell you the story of the novel I'm now writing, and I'm sure it would produce the same effect I'm trying to get by writing it, but without so much effort. At home, at any time of day, I recount my dreams, what has happened to me or not happened to me. I don't tell my children make-believe stories, but about things that have happened, and they like that very much. Vargas Llosa, in the book he's doing on the literary vocation, *García Márquez, historia de un deicidio*, takes my work as an example and says I'm a seedbed of anecdotes. To be liked because I've told a good story: that's my true ambition.

RG: I've read that when you finish *El otoño del patriarca* (*The Autumn of the Patriarch*) you're going to write stories instead of novels.
GGM: I've got a notebook where I'm jotting down the stories that occur to me and making notes for them. I've already got about sixty, and I fancy I shall reach a hundred. What is curious is the process of internal elaboration. The story—which may arise from a phrase or an incident—either occurs to me complete in a fraction of a second or not at all. It has no starting point; a character just arrives or goes away. I'll tell you an anecdote which may give you some idea how mysteriously I arrive at a story. One night in Barcelona when we had visitors, the lights suddenly went out. As the trouble was local

we sent for an electrician. While he was putting the defect right and I was holding a candle for him to see by, I asked him, "What the devil's happened to the light?" "Light is like water," he said, "you turn a tap and out it comes, and the meter registers it as it comes through." In that fraction of a second, a complete story came to me:

In a city away from the sea—it might be Paris, Madrid, or Bogotá—there live on the fifth floor a young couple and their two children of ten and seven. One day the children ask their parents to give them a rowboat. "How can we give you a rowboat?" says the father. "What can you do with it in this town? When we go to the seaside in the summer we can hire one." The children obstinately persist that they want a rowboat, until their father says: "If you get the top places in school I'll give you one." They get the top places, their father buys the boat, and when they take it up to the fifth floor he asks them: "What are you going to do with it?" "Nothing," they reply, "we just wanted to have it. We'll put it in our room." One night when their parents are at the cinema, the children break an electric light bulb and the light begins to flow out—just like water—filling the whole house three feet deep. They take the boat and begin rowing through the bedrooms and the kitchen. When it's time for their parents to return they put it away in their room and pull up the plugs so that the light can drain away, put back the bulb, and . . . nothing has happened. This becomes such a splendid game that they begin to let the light reach a greater depth, put on dark glasses and flippers, and swim under the beds and tables, practicing underwater fishing. . . . One night, passersby in the street notice light streaming out of the windows and flooding the street, and they send for the fire brigade. When the firemen open the door they find that the children had been so absorbed in their game that they had allowed the light to reach the ceiling, and are floating in the light, drowned.

Can you tell me how it was that this complete story, just as I've told you, occurred to me within a fraction of a second? Naturally, as I've told it often, I find a new angle every time—change one thing for another or add a detail—but the idea remains the same. There's nothing deliberate or predictable in all this, nor do I know when it's going to happen to me. I'm at the mercy of my imagination, and that's what says *yes* or *no*.

RG: Have you written that story yet?
GGM: I've merely made a note: #7 "Children drowning in light." That's all. But I carry that story in my head, like all the rest, and I revise it from time to

time. For instance, I take a taxi and remember story #57. I completely revise it and realize that in an incident that had occurred to me the roses I visualized aren't roses at all but violets. I incorporate this change in my story and make a mental note of it.

RG: What a memory!
GGM: No, I only forget what has no literary value for me.

RG: Why don't you write it when you first think of it?
GGM: If I'm writing a novel I can't mix other things with it, I must work at that book only, even if it takes me more than ten years.

RG: Don't you unconsciously incorporate these stories in the novel you're writing?
GGM: These stories are in completely separate compartments and have nothing to do with the book about the dictator. That happened with *Big Mama's Funeral*, *La mala hora* (*In Evil Hour*) and *No One Writes to the Colonel*, because I was working on the lot of them at practically the same time.

RG: Have you never thought of becoming an actor?
GGM: I'm terribly inhibited in front of cameras or a microphone. But in any case I would be the author or director.

RG: On one occasion you said, "I've become a writer out of timidity. My real inclination is to be a conjuror, but I get so confused when I try to perform a trick that I've had to take refuge in the solitude of literature. In my case, being a writer is a stupendous task, because I'm a numbskull at writing."
GGM: What a good thing to read me! The bit about my real vocation being to be a conjuror corresponds exactly with what I've told you. It would delight me to have success telling stories in salons, like a conjuror pulling rabbits out of a hat.

RG: Is writing a great effort for you?
GGM: Terribly hard work, more so all the time. When I say I'm a writer out of timidity, it's because what I ought to do is fill this room, and go out and tell my story, but my timidity prevents me. I couldn't have carried on this conversation of ours if there had been two more people at this table; I should have

felt I couldn't control my audience. Therefore when I want to tell a story I do it in writing, sitting alone in my room and working hard. It's agonizing work, but sensational. Conquering the problem of writing is so delightful and so thrilling that it makes up for all the work . . . it's like giving birth.

RG: Since you first made contact in 1954 with the Experimental Cinema in Rome, you've written scripts and directed films. Doesn't this expressive medium interest you any more?
GGM: No, because my work in the cinema showed me that what the writer succeeds in putting across is very little. So many interests, so many compromises are involved that in the end very little of the original story remains. Whereas if I shut myself in my room I can write exactly what I want to. I don't have to put up with an editor saying, "Get rid of that character or incident and put in another."

RG: Don't you think the visual impact of the cinema can be greater than that of literature?
GGM: I used to think so, but then I realized the limitations of the cinema. That very visual aspect puts it at a disadvantage compared to literature. It's so immediate, so forceful, that it's difficult for the viewer to go beyond it. In literature one can go much further and at the same time create an impact that is visual, auditory, or of any other sort.

RG: Don't you think the novel is a disappearing form?
GGM: If it disappears it'll be because those who write it are disappearing. It's difficult to imagine any period in the history of humanity when so many novels have been read as at present. Whole novels are published in all the magazines—both for men and for women—and in the newspapers, while for the almost illiterate there are comic strips which are the apotheosis of the novel. What we could begin to discuss is the quality of the novels that are being read, but that has nothing to do with the reading public, only with the cultural level the state has given them. To return to the phenomenon of *One Hundred Years of Solitude*—and I don't want to know what caused it, nor to analyze it, nor for others to analyze it at present—I know of readers, people without intellectual training, who have passed straight from "comics" to that book and have read it with the same interest as the other things they have been given, because they underestimated it intellectually. It's the publishers,

who, underestimating the public, publish books of very low literary value; and the curious thing is that that level also consumes books like *One Hundred Years of Solitude*. That's why I think there's a boom in novel readers. Novels are read everywhere, at all times, all over the world. Story-telling will always be of interest. A man comes home and starts telling his wife what's happened to him . . . or what hasn't happened so that his wife believes it.

RG: In your interview with Luis Harss you say: "I've got fixed political opinions . . . but my literary ideas change with my digestion." What are your literary ideas today at eight o'clock in the morning?
GGM: I've said that anyone who doesn't contradict himself is a dogmatist, and every dogmatist is a reactionary. I contradict myself all the time and particularly on the subject of literature. My method of work is such that I would never reach the point of literary creation without constantly contradicting myself, correcting myself, and making mistakes. If I didn't I should be always writing the same book. I have no recipe. . . .

RG: Have you a method for writing a novel?
GGM: Not always the same, nor do I have a method for looking for a novel. The act of writing is the least important problem. What's difficult is assembling the novel and solving it according to my view of it.

RG: Do you know whether analysis, experience, or imagination controls that process?
GGM: If I were to try and make such an analysis I think I should lose a great deal of spontaneity. When I want to write something it's because I feel that it's worth saying. Still more . . . when I write a story it's because I should enjoy reading it. What happens is that I set about telling myself a story. That's my method of writing, but although I have a hunch which of these—intuition, experience, or analysis—plays the greater part, I avoid inquiring deeply into the question because either my character or my system of writing makes me try to prevent my work becoming mechanical.

RG: What is the starting point of your novels?
GGM: A completely visual image. I suppose that some writers begin with a phrase, an idea, or a concept. I always begin with an image. The starting point of *Leaf Storm* is an old man taking his grandson to a funeral, in *No One*

Writes to the Colonel it's an old man waiting, and in *One Hundred Years*, an old man taking his grandson to the fair to find out what ice is.

RG: They all begin with an old man. . . .
GGM: The guardian angel of my infancy was an old man—my grandfather. My parents didn't bring me up, they left me in my grandparents' house. My grandmother used to tell me stories and my grandfather took me to see things. Those were the circumstances in which my world was constructed. And now I'm aware that I always see the image of my grandfather showing me things.

RG: How does that first image develop?
GGM: I leave it to simmer . . . it's not a very conscious process. All my books have been brooded over for a good many years. *One Hundred Years* for fifteen or seventeen, and I began thinking about the one I'm writing now a long while ago.

RG: How long do you take writing them?
GGM: That's rather quicker. I wrote *One Hundred Years of Solitude* in less than two years—which I think is pretty good. Before, I always used to write when I was tired, in my free time after my other work. Now that I'm not under economic pressure and I have nothing to do but write, I like indulging in the luxury of doing it when I want to, when I feel the impulse. I'm working differently on the book about the old dictator who lived for 250 years—I'm leaving it alone to see where it goes.

RG: Do you correct your writing much?
GGM: As to that, I keep on changing. I wrote my first things straight off without a break, and afterwards made a great many corrections on the manuscript, made copies, and corrected it again. And now I've acquired a habit which I think is a vice. I correct line by line as I work, so that by the time a page is finished it's practically ready for the publisher. If it has a blot or a slip it won't do for me.

RG: I can't believe you're so methodical.
GGM: Terribly! You can't imagine how clean those pages are. And I've got an electric typewriter. The only thing I am methodical about is my work, but it's

an almost emotional question. The page that I've just finished looks so beautiful, so clean, that it would be a pity to spoil it with a correction. But within a week I don't care about it so much—I only care about what I'm actually working on—and then I can correct it.

RG: And the galley proofs?
GGM: In *One Hundred Years* I only changed one word, although Paco Porrúa, literary editor of *Sudamericana*, told me to change as many as I liked. I believe the ideal thing would be to write a book, have it printed, and correct it afterwards. When one sends something to the printers and then reads it in print one seems to have taken a step, whether forward or backward, of extreme importance.

RG: Do you read your books after they are published?
GGM: When the first copy arrives I cut everything I have to do, and sit down—at once—and read it straight through. It has already become a different book from the one I know because a distance has been established between author and book. This is the first time I'm reading it as a reader. Those letters before my eyes weren't made by my typewriter, they aren't my words, they are others that have gone out into the world and don't belong to me. After that first reading I've never again read *One Hundred Years of Solitude*.

RG: How and when do you decide on the title?
GGM: A book finds its title sooner or later. It's not a thing I consider very important.

RG: Do you talk to your friends about what you're writing?
GGM: When I tell them something it's because I'm not quite sure about it, and I generally don't let it remain in the novel. I know from the reaction of my listeners—by means of some strange electric current—whether it's going to work or not. Although they may say sincerely, "Marvelous, terrific," there's something in their eyes that tells me it won't do. When I'm working on a novel I'm more of a nuisance to my friends than you can possibly imagine. They have to put up with it all, and afterwards when they read the book they get a surprise—as happened to those who were with me when I was writing *One Hundred Years*—because they don't find in it any

of the incidents I told them about. What I had talked about was rejected material.

RG: Do you think about your readers when you write?
GGM: I think of four or five particular people who make up my public when I'm writing. As I consider what would please or displease them, I add or subtract things, and so the book is put together.

RG: Do you generally keep the material that has accumulated while you are working?
GGM: I don't keep anything. When the publishers notified me that they had received my first manuscript of *One Hundred Years of Solitude*, Mercedes helped me throw away a drawerful of working notes, diagrams, sketches, and memoranda. I threw it out, not only so that the way the book was constructed shouldn't be known—that's something absolutely private—but in case that material should ever be sold. To sell it would be selling my soul, and I'm not going to let anyone do it, not even my children.

RG: Which of your writings do you like best?
GGM: *Leaf Storm*, the first book I ever wrote. I think a lot of what I've done since then springs from it. It's the most spontaneous, the one I wrote with most difficulty and with fewer technical resources. I knew fewer writers' tricks, fewer nasty tricks at that time. It seems to me a rather awkward, vulnerable book, but completely spontaneous, and it has a raw sincerity not to be found in the others. I know exactly how *Leaf Storm* went straight from my guts onto the paper. The others also came from my guts but I had served my apprenticeship. . . . I worked on them, I cooked them, I added salt and pepper.

RG: What influences have you been conscious of?
GGM: The notion of influence is a problem for the critics. I'm not very clear about it, I don't know exactly what they mean by it. I think the fundamental influence on my writing has been Kafka's *Metamorphosis*, although I don't know whether the critics who analyze my work discover any direct influence in the books themselves. I remember the moment when I bought the book, and how as I read it I began to long to write. My first stories date from that time—about 1946, when I had just gotten my baccalaureate. Probably as

soon as I say this to the critics—they've got no detector, they have to get certain things from the author himself—they'll discover the influence. But what sort of influence? He made me want to write. A decisive influence, which is perhaps more obvious, is *Oedipus Rex*. It's a perfect structure, wherein the investigator discovers that he is himself the assassin . . . an apotheosis of technical perfection. All the critics have mentioned Faulkner's influence. I accept that, but not in the sense they think when they see me as an author who read Faulkner, assimilated him, was impressed by him and, consciously or unconsciously, tries to write like him. That is more or less, roughly, what I understand by an influence. What I owe to Faulkner is something entirely different. I was born in Aracataca, the banana-growing country where the United Fruit Company was established. It was in this region, where the Fruit Company was building towns and hospitals and draining some zones, that I grew up and received my first impressions. Then, many years later, I read Faulkner and found that his whole world—the world of the southern United States which he writes about—was very like my world, that it was created by the same people. And also, when later I traveled in the southern states, I found evidence—on those hot, dusty roads, with the same vegetation, trees, and great houses—of the similarity between our two worlds. One mustn't forget that Faulkner is in a way a Latin American writer. His world is that of the Gulf of Mexico. What I found in him was affinities between our experiences, which were not as different as might appear at first sight. Well, this sort of influence of course exists, but it's very different from what the critics pointed out.

RG: Others speak of Borges and Carpentier, and think they see the same telluric and mythological approach as that of Rómulo Gallegos, Evaristo Carrera Campos, or Asturias. . . .
GGM: Whether I follow the same telluric line or not I really don't know. It's the same world, the same Latin America, isn't it? Borges and Carpentier, no. I read them when I had already written quite a lot. That's to say I would have written what I did anyhow, without Borges and Carpentier, but not without Faulkner. And I also believe that after a certain moment—by searching for my own language and refining my work—I have taken a course aimed at eliminating Faulkner's influence, which is much in evidence in *Leaf Storm* but not in *One Hundred Years*. But I don't like making this sort of analysis. My position is that of a creator, not of a critic. It's not my job, it's not my vocation, I don't think I'm good at it.

RG: What books do you read nowadays?
GGM: I scarcely read at all, it doesn't interest me. I read documentaries and memoirs—the lives of men who have held power, memoirs and revelations by secretaries, even if they aren't true—out of professional interest in the book I'm working on. My problem is that I am and have always been a very poor reader. As soon as a book bores me I give it up. As a boy I began reading *Don Quixote*, got bored and stopped in the middle. I've read it and reread it since, but only because I enjoy it, not because it's obligatory reading. That has been my method of reading and I have the same concept of reading while I'm writing. I'm always in terror lest at some page the reader may get bored and throw down the book. Therefore I try not to bore him, so that he shan't treat me as I treat others. The only novels I read now are those by my friends because I'm curious to know what they're doing, not out of literary interest. For many years I read, or devoured, quantities of novels, particularly adventure stories in which a lot happened. But I was never a methodical reader. Since I didn't have the money to buy books, I used to read what fell into my hands, books lent me by friends who were almost all teachers of literature or concerned with it. What I have always read, almost more than novels, is poetry. In fact I began with poetry, although I've never written poetry in verse, and I'm always trying to find poetical solutions. I think my last novel is really an extremely long poem about the loneliness of a dictator.

RG: Are you interested in concrete poetry?
GGM: I've lost sight of poetry altogether. I don't know precisely where poets are going, what they are doing, or even what they want to do. I suppose it's important for them to make experiments of every description and look for new ways of expressing themselves, but it's very difficult to judge something in the experimental stage. They don't interest me. I've solved the problem of my own means of expressing myself, and I can't now be involved in other things.

RG: You mentioned that you are always listening to music. . . .
GGM: I enjoy it much more than any other manifestation of art, even than literature. With every day that passes I need it more, and I have the impression that it acts on me like a drug. When I travel I always take along a portable radio with headphones, and I measure the world by the concerts I can hear—from Madrid to San Juan in Puerto Rico one can hear Beethoven's nine

symphonies. I remember that when I was traveling by train in Germany with
Vargas Llosa—on an extremely hot day when I was in a very bad mood—
how I suddenly, perhaps unconsciously, cut myself off and listened to music.
Mario said to me afterwards, "It's incredible, your mood has changed,
you've calmed down." In Barcelona, where I can have a fully equipped set,
in times of great depression I have sometimes listened to music from two
in the afternoon until four in the morning, without moving. My passion for
music is like a secret vice, and I hardly ever talk about it. It's a part of my
most profoundly private life. I'm not at all attached to objects—I don't consider
the furniture and other things in my house as mine, but as belonging to
my wife and children—and the only objects I'm fond of are my musical appa-
ratuses. My typewriter is a necessity, otherwise I would get rid of it. Nor
do I possess a library. When I've read a book I throw it out, or leave it
somewhere.

RG: Let's come back to your statement that you "have fixed political opinions." Can you say exactly what they are?
GGM: I think the world ought to be socialist, that it will be, and that we
should help this to happen as quickly as possible. But I'm greatly disillu-
sioned by the socialism of the Soviet Union. They arrived at their brand of
socialism through special experiences and conditions, and are trying to
impose in other countries their own bureaucracy, their own authoritarian-
ism, and their own lack of historical vision. That isn't socialism and it's the
great problem of the present moment.

RG: When the Cuban poet Heberto Padilla was imprisoned and made a
signed "confession," international intellectuals—who have always supported
the Cuban Revolution—sent two letters of protest to Castro in the course of
a month. After the first letter—which you also signed—Castro said in his May
Day speech that the signatories were pseudo-revolutionary intellectuals who
"gossip in Paris literary salons" and pass judgment on the Cuban revolution;
Cuba, he said, does not need the support of "bourgeois intrigue-mongers."
According to international commentaries this showed a rupture between
intellectuals and the Cuban regime. What's your own position?
GGM: When all this came to light, international and Colombian news agencies naturally began to press me to give my opinion, because in a way I was
involved in all this. I didn't want to do so until I had complete information

and could read the shorthand reports of the speeches. I couldn't give an
opinion on such an important matter merely on the versions put out by the
information agencies. Besides, I knew at the time that I was going to receive a
Doctorate of Letters at Columbia University. For anyone who didn't know
that this decision had been made previously, it might lead them to believe
that I was going to the United States because I had broken with Castro. I
therefore made a statement to the press, completely clarifying my position
toward Castro, my doctorate, and my return to the United States after twelve
years, during which time I had been refused a visa:

(Summary of García Márquez's statement to the Colombian press, May 29, 1971):

Columbia University is not the government of the United States, but a strong-
hold of nonconformism, of intellectual integrity . . . of those who will annihilate
the decrepit system of their country. I understand that I am being granted this dis-
tinction principally as a writer, but those who grant it are not unaware that I am
infinitely hostile to the prevailing order in the United States. . . . It is good for you
to know that I only discuss these decisions with my friends, and especially with
the taxi drivers of Barranquilla, who are champions of common sense. . . . The conflict between a group of Latin American writers and Fidel Castro is an ephemeral
triumph for the news agencies. I have here the documents relevant to this matter,
including the shorthand report of Fidel Castro's speech, and although it does in
fact contain some very stern passages, none of them lend support to the sinister
interpretations given them by the international news agencies. Certainly we have to
do with a speech in which Fidel Castro makes fundamental proposals about
cultural matters, but the foreign correspondents said nothing about these; instead
they carefully extracted and put together again as they chose certain loose phrases
so as to make it seem that Fidel Castro had said what in fact he had not said . . . I
didn't sign the letter of protest because I was not in favor of their sending it. The
truth is that I believe such public messages are valueless as a means to the desired
ends, but very useful for hostile propaganda. . . . However, I will at no time cast
doubt on the intellectual integrity and revolutionary sincerity of those who signed
the letter, who include some of my best friends. . . . When writers wish to take part
in politics they are actually being moral rather than political, and those two terms
aren't always compatible. Politicians, for their part, resist writers meddling in their
affairs, and on the whole accept us when we support them and reject us when we
are against them. But that's hardly a catastrophe. On the contrary, it's a very useful,
very positive dialectic contradiction, which will continue until the end of mankind,

even if politicians die of rage and writers are skinned alive. . . . The only pending matter is that of the poet Heberto Padilla. Personally, I haven't succeeded in convincing myself that Padilla's self-criticism was spontaneous and sincere. I don't understand how after so many years of contact with the Cuban experiment, living daily through the drama of the revolution, a man like Heberto Padilla could not have taken before the stand he suddenly took in prison. The tone of his confession is so exaggerated, so abject, that it seems to have been obtained by ignominious means. I don't know whether Heberto Padilla is doing harm to the revolution by his attitude, but his self-criticism certainly is doing a great deal of harm. The proof of this is to be found in the way the text divulged by Prensa Latina was splashed in the hostile Cuban press. . . . If a germ of Stalinism really exists in Cuba we shall see it very soon, it will be proclaimed by Fidel Castro himself. . . . In 1961 there was an attempt to impose Stalinist methods, and Fidel Castro denounced it in public and eradicated it in embryo. There is no reason to think that the same wouldn't happen today, because the vitality, the good health of the Cuban Revolution cannot have decreased since that time. . . . Of course I am not breaking with the Cuban Revolution. Moreover: none of the writers who protested about the Padilla case has broken with the Cuban Revolution so far as I know. Mario Vargas Llosa himself commented on this in a statement subsequent to his famous letter, but the newspapers relegated it to the corner for invisible news. No: the Cuban Revolution is an event of fundamental importance to Latin America and the whole world, and our solidarity with it can't be affected by a blunder in cultural politics, even when the blunder is as large and as serious as the suspect self-criticism of Heberto Padilla. . . .

RG: Are the hopes of intellectuals being accomplished by the Cuban Revolution?
GGM: What I believe to be really grave is that we intellectuals tend to protest and react only when we are personally affected, but do nothing when the same thing happens to a fisherman or a priest. What we ought to do is look at the revolution as an integral phenomenon, and see how the positive aspects infinitely outweigh the negative ones. Of course, manifestations such as the Padilla case are extremely dangerous, but they are obstacles that it shouldn't be hard to surmount. If not it would indeed be grievous, because everything that has been done—making people literate, giving them education and economic independence—is irreversible and will last much longer than Padilla and Fidel. That is my position and I won't budge

from it. I'm not prepared to throw a revolution on the rubbish heap every ten years.

RG: Do you agree with the socialism of the Chilean Popular Front?
GGM: My ambition is for all Latin America to become socialist, but nowadays people are seduced by the idea of peaceful and constitutional socialism. This seems to be all very well for electoral purposes, but I believe it to be completely utopian. Chile is heading toward violent and dramatic events. If the Popular Front goes ahead—with intelligence and great tact, with reasonably firm and swift steps—a moment will come when they will encounter a wall of serious opposition. The United States is not interfering at present, but it won't always stand by with folded arms. It won't really accept that Chile is a socialist country. It won't allow that, and don't let's be under any illusions on that point.

RG: Do you see violence as the sole solution?
GGM: It's not that I see it as a solution, but I think that a moment will come when that wall of opposition can only be surmounted by violence. Unfortunately, I believe that to be inevitable. I think what is happening in Chile is very good as reform, but not as revolution.

RG: You said of imperialist cultural penetration—in your interview with Jean-Michel Fossey—that the United States was trying to attract intellectuals by giving them awards and creating organizations where a lot of propaganda went on. . . .
GGM: I have a profound belief in the power of money to corrupt. If a writer, particularly at the start of his career, is given an award or a grant—whether it comes from the United States, the Soviet Union, or from Mars—he is to some extent compromised. Out of gratitude, or even to show that he hasn't been compromised, this help affects his work. This is much more serious in the socialist countries where a writer is supposed to be working for the state. That in itself is the major compromise of his independence. If he writes what he wants, or what he feels, he runs the risk that some official—almost certainly a failed writer—will decide whether it can be published or not. So that I think that as long as a writer can't live by his books he ought to take on some marginal work. In my case it was journalism and advertising, but no one ever paid me to write.

RG: Neither did you accept the office of Colombian consul in Barcelona.
GGM: I always refuse public office, but I rejected that particular post because I don't want to represent any government. I think I said in an interview that one Miguel Angel Asturias was enough for Latin America.

RG: Why did you say that?
GGM: His personal behavior sets a bad example. Winner of the Nobel Prize and the Lenin Prize, he goes to Paris as ambassador representing a government as reactionary as Guatemala's. A government fighting against the guerrillas who stand for everything he says he has stood for all his life. Imperialists don't attack him for accepting the embassy of a reactionary government, because it was prudent, nor does the Soviet Union because he's a Lenin Prize winner. I've been asked recently what I thought of Neruda becoming an ambassador. I didn't say that a writer shouldn't be an ambassador—though I never would myself—but representing the government of Guatemala is not the same thing as representing the Chilean Popular Front.

RG: You must often have been asked how you manage to live in a country with such a dictatorship as Spain's.
GGM: It seems to me that if you give a writer the choice of living in heaven or hell, he chooses hell . . . there's much more literary material there.

RG: Hell—and dictators—also exist in Latin America.
GGM: I'd like to clear this matter up. I'm forty-three years old and I've spent three of them in Spain, one in Rome, two or three in Paris, seven or eight in Mexico, and the rest in Colombia. I've not left one city merely in order to live in another. It's worse than that. I don't live anywhere, which causes some anguish. Also I don't agree with an idea that has arisen—and been much discussed lately—that writers live in Europe so as to live it up. It's not like that. One doesn't go in search of that—anyone who wants to can find it anywhere—and often life is very difficult. But I haven't the smallest doubt that it's very important for a Latin American writer to view Latin America from Europe at some given moment. My ideal solution would be to be able to go back and forth, but (1) it's very expensive, and (2) I'm restricted by the fact that I dislike air travel . . . although I spend my life in airplanes. The truth is that at the moment I don't care where I live. I always find people who interest me, whether in Barranquilla, Rome, Paris, or Barcelona.

RG: Why not New York?

GGM: New York was responsible for withdrawing my visa. I lived in this city in 1960 as correspondent for Prensa Latina, and although I did nothing except act as correspondent—collecting news and dispatching it—when I left to go to Mexico they took away my resident's card and entered me in their "black book." Every two or three years I've asked for a visa again, but they went on automatically refusing it. I think it was mainly a bureaucratic matter. I've received one now. As a city, New York is the greatest phenomenon of the twentieth century, and therefore it's a serious restriction of one's life not to be able to come here every year, even for a week. But I doubt if I have strong enough nerves to live in New York. I find it so overwhelming. The United States is an extraordinary country; a nation that creates such a city as New York, or the rest of the country—which has nothing to do with the system or the government—could do anything. I believe they will be the ones to create a great socialist revolution, and a good one too.

RG: What have you to say about the solemn title conferred on you by Columbia University?

GGM: I can't believe it. . . . What I find completely puzzling and disconcerting is not the honor nor the recognition—although such things can be true—but that a university like Columbia should decide to choose me out of twelve men from the whole world. The last thing I ever expected in this world was a doctorate of letters. My path has always been anti-academic; I never graduated as doctor of law from the university because I didn't want to be a "doctor"—and suddenly I find myself in the thick of the academic world. But this is something quite foreign to me, it's off my beat. It's as if they gave the Nobel Prize to a bullfighter. My first impulse was not to accept it, but then I took a plebiscite among my friends and none of them could understand what reason I had for refusing. I could have given political reasons, but they wouldn't have been genuine, because we all know, and we have heard declared in university speeches, that imperialism is not their prevailing system. So that to accept the honor wouldn't involve me politically with the United States, and there was no need to mention the subject. It was rather a moral question. I always react against ceremonies—remember that I come from the most ceremonious country in the world—and I asked myself, "What should I be doing in a literary academy in cap and grown?" At my friends' insistence I accepted the title of *doctor honoris causa* and now I'm delighted, not only at having accepted it, but also on behalf of my country and Latin America. All this patriotism one pretends not to care about suddenly does become important. In these last days, and more still during the ceremony, I thought about the strange things that were happening to me. There was a moment when I thought that death must be like that . . . something that happens when one least expects it, something that has nothing to do with me. Also I have been approached to publish an edition of my complete works, but I emphatically refused this in my lifetime, since I have always thought of it as a posthumous honor. During the ceremony I had the same feeling . . . that such things happened to one after death. The type of recognition I have always desired and appreciated is that of people who read me and talk to me about my books, not with admiration or enthusiasm but with affection. What really touched me during the ceremony in the university, and you can't imagine how deeply, was when during the return procession the Latin Americans who had practically taken over the campus came unobtrusively forward saying "Up with Latin America!" "Forward, Latin America!" "Go ahead, Latin America!" At that moment, for the first time, I felt moved and was glad I had accepted.

The Yellow Trolley Car in Barcelona: An Interview

William Kennedy / 1973

"Do you speak English?" I asked him.

"Nada," he said on the phone. "Nada, nada."

Well, it isn't true, but he likes to insist that it is, and so I dug up some rusty Spanish and asked when we'd get together and where he lived. "In a house," he said, and added he'd pick me up at five at my hotel on La Rambla, the great thoroughfare of Barcelona's old city. I told him my wife, Dana, was a *puertorriqueña*, so we could get through the fine points of language in either direction and he said *bueno* and that was that.

Ten minutes later he'd changed his mind and said he'd come by at noon. And at precisely noon on the Day of the Book, Gabriel García Márquez came down the crowded, noisy Rambla in a double-breasted navy-blue sports jacket, gray slacks, an open-collared blue shirt with a brown and white paisley design, a full head of curly black hair, and with a less than lush goatee, begun recently when he'd gone away for a month and forgotten his razor.

Hallo, hello, greetings, how are you, *cómo está*, a pleasure, handshakes, and then he asked: "Have you bought a book yet?"

"Of course. Yours."

His book means his big book, *Cien Años de Soledad* (*One Hundred Years of Solitude*), the semi-surreal saga of a hundred years of life among the Buendías, a family of mythical achievements and absurdities in the mythical South American town of Macondo. García's dramatic comedy of Macondo's century, acclaimed a masterpiece again and again, seems to suggest every human high and low point from post-Genesis to the air age. The *Times Literary Supplement* described it as "a comic masterpiece and certainly one of Latin America's finest novels to date." It won the Prix du Meilleur Livre

Étranger in France in 1969 and won Italy's Premio Chianciano the same year. It has been published in twenty-three countries, has sold a million copies in the Spanish language during twenty-one printings since Editorial Sudamericana in Buenos Aires brought it out in 1967. It has been translated into eighteen languages, sold sixty thousand copies in Brazil, fifty thousand in Italy, thirty thousand in Hungary, 18,650 in hardcover and 46,650 in paper in the United States, where it made the best-seller list. All of this gives him the economic and literary freedom he long sought, but also burdens him with what he now sees as a "persecution" by newsmen and editors.

In a letter to a friend he bemoaned the waste of two hours of self-revelation to reporters who reduce it to a page and a half of copy. As for the editors, one came and asked García's wife, Mercedes, for his personal letters. A girl appeared with the idea for a book called "250 Questions to García Márquez." Wrote García to his friend: "I took her for coffee and explained that if I answered 250 questions the book would be mine." Another editor asked him to write a prologue to the diary of Che Guevara in the Sierra Maestra and García answered he would gladly do it but it would take him eight years, because he wanted to do it right.

And so when any outlander calls, he does not invite him home but meets him elsewhere, in front of a hotel on Las Ramblas, for instance, stays long enough to be civil, then excuses himself. If the interview goes well, he might keep it going. His problem, he says, is to see as few people as possible. Even friends are a complication at times. He accepts a luncheon date with a friend and finds twenty strangers invited to meet him.

"Then I can't make jokes," he said. "I have to be intelligent for them. This is horrible."

But life in Barcelona is not out of control, despite these pressures. "I have accomplished one thing," he said. "I have not become a public spectacle. I know how to avoid that."

As we walked inconspicuously along the crowded Rambla, seeing flowers everywhere, García had another question: "Did you buy a rose when you bought the book?"

Dana showed him a rose to prove we had. It is the custom on the Day of the Book for the city's publishing houses and bookstores to sell books in temporary wooden stalls on the main streets. By tradition, you buy a rose for your lady and she buys you a book.

"We ought to go someplace where it's quiet," I said, barely able to hear García above crowd noises.

"It's hard to find a place like that in Spain," he said, but then he pointed. "Look, we could go to that bar. It's American. Nobody goes there."

So at a Formica-topped table in a bar-restaurant memorable now for its plainness and near emptiness, García ordered coffee for himself and red wine for the visitors, specifying Imperial 1956 to the waiter so that our taste would not be offended by the ordinary *tinto*, which he does not drink. He apologized for not having wine himself. Too early. He likes to drink when it's dark. Also, he had only one coffee in the two hours we talked. Weight-watching. And balancing values.

"Coffee now," he said, "less whiskey tonight."

I told him the last writing I had done before leaving for a European trip was a short review of his last book published in the United States, *Leaf Storm* (*La Hojarasca*), actually his first short novel, published in Colombia in 1955. I explained that even though another short novel and many short stories had been published in the United States, very little personal information about him was available. He agreed.

Moreover, despite a critical reception in this country that for a Latin has been second only to the Borges boom of the 1960s, the literary magazines have been rather unconcerned with the man who wrote a masterwork. This is less strange than it seems. I remember a conversation in an Irish bar in Albany, New York, some years ago, when revolutions were erupting in two Latin American nations. The bored bartender ended a discussion of both upheavals with the observation that "neither of them countries is worth a cat's titty," and this has stood ever since in my mind as a most lucid summary of United States attitudes—literary, political, military, it doesn't matter—toward the lands and people of the subcontinent.

It has been suggested that this less than enthusiastic reception of García as a literary personage has a political basis: the consequence of his work as a Communist newsman from 1959 to 1961 for Fidel Castro's *Prensa Latina* in Bogotá, Havana, and New York. He left the United States in 1961, and not until he was given an honorary degree by Columbia University in 1971 was he allowed to return. But if his Communist past ever did percolate down to the level of assignment editors, which is doubtful, it is likely that the Cat's Titty syndrome, rather than anticommunism, was the dampening agent. Another literary Latin leftist. Ho-hum.

The Spanish-speaking literary world behaves differently toward García. At Columbia University last April, Pablo Neruda referred to *Cien Años* as "perhaps the greatest revelation in the Spanish language since the *Don Quixote* of Cervantes." García is already the subject of an excellent critical biography, *Historia de un Deicidio* ("The Story of a Deicide") by Mario Vargas Llosa, published in 1971 by Barral Editores, Barcelona. Vargas, a teacher and novelist (*The Time of the Hero, The Green House*), wrote the book with García's full cooperation, and García says it is the best book about him to date; and there are several. But he vouches for the authenticity of only the first eighty-four biographical pages, paying Vargas the compliment of being afraid to read the rest.

"Mario's book may have the key to me," he said.

Why should he be afraid of somebody else's analysis?

"It's a gamble," he said, "a game. It's possible I would not be harmed by change if I read it. But why should I take the risk?"

There are instructive literary ironies in García's becoming both a critical success and a best-seller. ("If I hadn't written *Cien Años*," he said, "I wouldn't have read it. I don't read best-sellers.") He had given up writing and for more than five years did not write a word. This was overreaction to his negative feeling about his early books, to a disorienting change he'd made in his style and approach to his material, and to the influential but frustrating hold that film had on him.

He says he was always a writer, for as long as he can remember. He was born on March 6, 1928, in the small northern Colombian town of Aracataca, which is the prototype in García's imagination for the mythical village of Macondo, where life rages and sighs for one hundred years in his master-piece. His first published stories did not appear until 1947, when he was at the University of Bogotá, studying law and hating it. Political violence closed the university and he transferred his studies to Cartagena and continued writing. Then during a visit to Barranquilla, he became involved with a small group of other writers and newsmen who knew his work. He quit law school, moved to Barranquilla, and took a job as a newspaper columnist. In 1954 he returned to Bogotá as a film critic and reporter for *El espectador.*

"As a reporter," he said, "I was the lowest on the paper and wanted to be. Other writers always wanted to get to the editorial page, but I wanted to cover fires and crime."

His biographer compares his career as journalist-into-novelist to Ernest Hemingway's, and there are similarities. But there are also substantial differences. Hemingway was the realistic, impressionistic, serious-minded reporter. García, much less solemn about his job, more inclined to see it as a source of experience rather than as an outlet for opinion, seems to have had as much Ben Hecht as Hemingway in him. At least that is the impression one gets after reading a letter García wrote to a friend, recollecting a story he once covered in the Colombian town of Quibdó. An *El espectador* correspondent had cabled reports of wild fighting in Quibdó, and García and a photographer traveled far and with great difficulty to reach the action, only to find a sleepy, dusty village, and no fighting whatsoever. They did discover the correspondent beating the heat in a hammock. He explained that nothing ever happened in Quibdó and that he'd sent the cables in protest. Unwilling to go back empty-handed after such an arduous trip, García, his photographer, and the correspondent, with the help of sirens and drums, gathered a crowd and took action photos. García sent back action stories for two days, and soon an army of reporters arrived to cover it all. García then explained the Quibdó scene to them and directed the creation of a new and even larger demonstration they could report on.

A high point of his newspaper career came in 1966 when a sailor named Luis Alejandro Velasco came to *El espectador* with the offer to tell the whole story of his famous survival at sea.

Velasco had lived ten days on a life raft after a Colombian naval destroyer, en route home from New Orleans, was struck by a storm. Eight sailors were lost overboard and only Velasco survived. This had already made him a national hero, and quite wealthy. But only the newspapers favored by Colombian dictator Gustavo Rojas Pinilla had been allowed to talk to him. His offer to *El espectador* to tell the tale anew, long after public interest had peaked, was first received, says García, as "una noticia refrita"—a rehashed story—but one editor had second thoughts, and turned Velasco over to García.

The result was a fourteen-chapter, first-person narration, signed by the twenty-year-old seaman, which revealed that the destroyer had not encountered a storm at all—and meteorologists verified this—but had been carrying contraband cargo, badly packed on the deck. The vessel almost keeled over in some high winds, the cargo broke loose, and the eight crewmen were knocked overboard. The public found this story delicious and *El espectador*'s circulation climbed. The embarrassed dictatorship denied all, but the paper subsequently proved its case with photos from other crewmen, showing men standing on the destroyer's deck alongside clearly labeled boxes of TV sets, refrigerators, and washing machines from the United States. The Rojas Pinilla government initiated reprisals against the paper and months later, when García was in Paris as *El espectador*'s roving European correspondent, closed it down.

The articles were republished in paperback in Barcelona under García's name in early 1970, the first time he was publicly connected with them. He entitled the book: *The Tale of a Shipwrecked Sailor who was adrift ten days on a life raft without food or water, who was proclaimed a hero of the nation, kissed by beauty queens and made rich by publicity, and then loathed by the government and forgotten forever.* In a prologue to the unaltered reprint, García credits Velasco with a natural gift for narrative and an astonishing memory for detail, and adds: "It depresses me that editors are not interested in the merits of the text as much as they are in the name of the author, for much to my regret, this makes me out to be a fashionable writer. Fortunately, there are books that belong not to those who write them but those who suffer them and this is one of those." And he states that the rights of the book belong to Velasco, not García.

It was Hemingway who argued against journalism, adjudging it a good training ground if you get out in time, but one that could spoil a writer who stayed at it too long. García could not accept such a dictum, for he was writing journalism to live, and he stayed at it from 1948 to 1961. He was much more in tune psychologically with William Faulkner, who felt that nothing could destroy a good writer. Like so many serious writers at mid-century, García was deeply influenced by the work of Faulkner, and so much has been made of this that he now draws the curtain on extended talk about the relationship. Nor can he read Faulkner anymore, perhaps because of this, although he ascribes it to the effusion of Faulknerian rhetoric that put him off when he went back to him in 1971. But in the late 1940s, when García was writing *Leaf Storm*, Faulkner was of major importance to him.

Leaf Storm was finally published in 1955, the same year as the shipwreck articles, after almost seven years of searching for an editor who would accept it. One critic rejected the book for an Argentinian publisher, advising García that he was not talented as a writer and ought to dedicate his life to something else. The story of *Leaf Storm* is told alternately by a father, his daughter, and his grandson, who are the only mourners at the burial of a doctor who once lived with them. The doctor later became a recluse and by a single act earned the enmity of the whole town, which now wants to humiliate his corpse. Faulknerian phrasing is evident and the doctor bears some resemblance to Reverend Gail Hightower of *Light in August.*

But despite Faulkner's influence, *Leaf Storm* is not a derivative work. Its own language is rich, dense, but without the difficulty that goes with much of Faulkner. It is occasionally surreal in a way that Faulkner's work is not. And though it establishes Macondo in emulation of Faulkner's Yoknapatawpha County, it does so with such originality and relevance to Latin American life that by the time Macondo matured into the fully appointed village in *Cien Años,* multitudes of Latin readers recognized it as the dwelling place of their communal spirit.

The world García imagines is always solidly grounded in the real world, but it is deceptive, for the real is also frequently surreal.

In *Leaf Storm*, the old doctor sits down to a pretentious, bourgeois dinner and startles everybody by saying to a servant: "Look, miss, just start boiling a little grass and bring that to me as if it were soup." "What kind of grass, doctor?" the servant asks. "Ordinary grass, ma'am," the doctor says. "The kind that donkeys eat."

Surreal? Not to García. "A man said that in my house," he said.

He believes that Faulkner differs from him on this matter in that Faulkner's outlandishness is *disguised* as reality.

"Faulkner was surprised at certain things that happened in life," García said, "but he writes of them not as surprises but as things that happen every day."

García feels less surprised. "In Mexico," he says, "surrealism runs through the streets. Surrealism comes from the reality of Latin America."

About two weeks before we talked, a newsman had called to ask García for his reaction to an occurrence in a rural Colombian town. About ten in the morning at a small school, two men pulled up in a truck and said, "We came for the furniture." Nobody knew anything about them, but the schoolmaster nodded, the furniture was loaded onto the truck and driven off, and only much later was it understood that the truckmen were thieves.

"Normal," says García.

"One day in Barcelona," he continued, "my wife and I were asleep and the doorbell rings. I open the door and a man says to me, 'I came to fix the ironing cord.' My wife, from the bed, says, 'We don't have anything wrong with the iron here.' The man asks, 'Is this apartment two?' 'No,' I say, 'upstairs.' Later, my wife went to the iron and plugged it in and it burned up. This was a reversal. The man came before we knew it had to be fixed. This type of thing happens all the time. My wife has already forgotten it."

García likes the principles of surrealism but not the surrealists themselves. Given a choice, he prefers the painters to the poets, but he does not think of himself as being like any of them. And it is true that his work is based more in the anecdote than in the symbolic or random flow of events so important to the surrealists; true also that his aim is to be accessible, not obscure. And yet, a surreal quality, a rendering of the improbable and impossible as real, pervades his work. And its importance to him has obviously intensified since the tepidly surreal grass-eating of *Leaf Storm*. In *Cien Años* he made the leap to earth-eating, to a plague of insomnia, to ghosts that grow old, to a young woman who ascends bodily into heaven and takes two bedsheets with her. His improbability usually extends an everyday reality. In *Cien Años*, for instance, José Arcadio, son of Úrsula, enters his bedroom, closes the door, and a pistol shot is heard. Then:

> A trickle of blood came out under the door, crossed the living room, went out into the street, continued on in a straight line across the uneven terraces, went down steps and climbed over curbs, passed along the Street of the Turks, turned a corner to the right and another to the left, made a right angle at the Buendía house, went in under the closed door, crossed through the parlor, hugging the walls so as not to stain the rugs, went on to the other living room, made a wide curve to avoid the dining-room table, went along the porch with the begonias, and passed without being seen under Amaranta's chair as she gave an arithmetic lesson to Aureliano José, and went through the pantry and came out in the kitchen, where Úrsula was getting ready to crack thirty-six eggs to make bread.
>
> "Holy Mother of God!" Úrsula shouted.
>
> She followed the thread of blood back along its course, and in search of its origin she went through the pantry, along the begonia porch where Aureliano José was chanting that three plus three is six and six plus three is nine, and she crossed the dining room and the living rooms and followed straight down the street, and she turned first to the right and then to the left to the Street of the Turks, forgetting that she was still wearing her baking apron and her house slippers, and she came out onto the square and went into the door of a house where she had never been,

and she pushed open the bedroom door and was almost suffocated by the smell of burned gunpowder, and she found José Arcadio lying face down on the ground on top of the leggings he had just taken off, and she saw the starting point of the thread of blood that had already stopped flowing out of his right ear.

We talked of this passage in connection with the surreal aspect of the book, but García all but dismissed the improbable quality of it, saying only: "It is the umbilical cord." And we moved on to something else.

After *Leaf Storm*, García encountered some heady influences that would change his fictional style and bring him as close to socialist realism as he would ever come. The Communists in Bogotá wooed him after *Leaf Storm* was published; but while they wanted him as a writer and a mind, they rejected his style as too artistic to convey the stringent socialist realities. On this point Mario Vargas Llosa writes: "Although he never fell into the coarse conceptions of socialist realism, García Márquez nevertheless reached a similar conclusion about his narrative language some months later, at the beginning of his second novel." The change in his writing that followed could hardly be adjudged a bad one, for working in his new style García produced three highly regarded works. But he was not satisfied, because the change restricted his imagination.

He had a flurry of party militancy in Bogotá, but it faded quickly and he then went to Europe for *El espectador*. He found himself in Rome covering Pope Pius XII's hiccups, and he enrolled at the Centro Sperimentale de Cinematografía, with plans to become a director and film his own version of *Leaf Storm*. After some months of study, he moved to Paris and learned there that the Rojas dictatorship had closed his paper and that he was out of a job.

He stayed in Paris, beginning a short story about some violence he remembered from childhood, changing the locale from Macondo to "El Pueblo" (the town), a shift which has generated confusion about the settings of his various works. His language became more staccato, with dialogue playing a larger role. The short story he had begun expanded quickly and took shape as a novel, then two novels. The last offshoot he completed first and it became *El Coronel No Tiene Quien Le Escriba* (*No One Writes to the Colonel*), the story of an old military man who waits endlessly for his military pension, long after he and the war that he fought in have been forgotten by the government.

"He had written a small masterwork," Vargas Llosa writes, "but not only did he not know it, he also experienced the same sensation of failure as when he finished *Leaf Storm*."

He then completed his novel about violence in the same small town, the violence provoked by *pasquines*—anonymous signs that appear mysteriously on the walls of public places. The book is called *La Mala Hora* ("The Evil Hour").

García's life in Paris while writing these works was memorable but not happy. He lived, he said, on "daily miracles," deeply impoverished, as a foreigner not allowed to work, unable to speak the language very well, at one point turning in empty bottles for cash. When his money ran out, his landlord let him live in an attic, where he wrote steadily. When he returned to Paris in 1968 as a success and looked back on his three years of poverty, he concluded: "If I had not lived those three years, probably I would not be a writer. Here I learned that nobody dies of hunger and that one is capable of sleeping under bridges."

My wife and I had just come from Paris to Barcelona, and we told of the extraordinary time we'd just had in the city.

"I had money when I went back there," García said. "I wanted to eat all the things I had not eaten, drink all the wine I could not afford to buy. And I hated it. I hate Paris."

He lifted himself out of his poverty there in 1957 by selling newspapers in Bogotá and Caracas on the idea of a series of ten articles about the Iron Curtain countries. A newsman who went with him on that tour, Plinio Apuleyo Mendoza, later in the year became editor of *Momento*, a Caracas magazine, and hired García immediately. It was in Caracas, confronting his fictional world only on his days off, and reporting meanwhile on the last days of the Pérez Jiménez dictatorship, that he wrote some new short stories. These he called *Los Funerales de la Mamá Grande (Big Mama's Funeral)* when he published them in Mexico in 1962. These, too, have the staccato quality, except for the title story, which is written in dense language that satirizes Colombian political and editorial-page rhetoric. It is the only story set in Macondo, another point of confusion. The others in the collection, all set in El Pueblo, make no mention of Macondo.

The assumption by many casual readers of Garcia's work is that all his fiction is set in Macondo. But when he broke with the lush style of *Leaf Storm* and took up with the Communist party realists, he not only adopted a kind of Hemingway realism but he also left his fictional hometown. He returns to his natural style, an exalted but not overblown prose, only in the title story, in which he returns to Macondo.

García said he has a problem convincing people about El Pueblo. "*Leaf Storm* and *Cien Años* are in Macondo, nothing else," he said emphatically of his books. "The other three [*Colonel, Mala Hora, Mamá Grande*] are in El Pueblo." He opened the United States edition of the *Colonel* to page 42 and cited internal evidence where the Colonel remembers Macondo and mentions when he physically left it, in 1906.

"But some people," he said, "do not accept any evidence, and I leave them so I don't have to discuss it."

Another rumor is that he is through writing about Macondo, but of this he says, "It is a lie. I don't tamper with the future." During the past year, in fact, he completed a short novel which develops the lives of characters he created in *Cien Años*. It is called *The Incredible and Sad Tale of Innocent Eréndira and Her Heartless Grandmother*, and is now being translated into English by Gregory Rabassa, who translated both *Cien Años* and *Leaf Storm*.

García's career as a fiction writer remained publicly static during his time in Venezuela, but journalistically he took an odd turn: he left *Momento* and went to work for *Venezuela Gráfica*, a magazine commonly called *Venezuela Pornográfica* in Caracas. Solemn fictionists might be put off by such work, but García accepted it then and still accepts it.

"I'm interested in personal life," he said, explaining that at the moment in Barcelona he was reading the memoirs of Jackie Kennedy's chauffeur. "I read all the gossip in all the magazines. And I believe it all."

The Cuban revolution lifted him, for the first time in his life, out of journalistic fluff and fun and into advocacy. He opened the Bogotá office for *Prensa Latina*, went to Havana later, and in 1961 became assistant bureau chief in New York. He quit in mid-1961 during a wave of revisionism, in solidarity with his disgruntled boss; and with his wife, Mercedes, the Barranquilla girl who had waited for him for three years until he married her in 1958, and his two-year-old son, Rodrigo, he left New York, but not without a tropical memory of the city.

"It was like no place else," he said. "It was putrefying, but also was in the process of rebirth, like the jungle. It fascinated me."

The Garcías headed for New Orleans by Greyhound, passing through Faulkner country. García duly noted one sign advising DOGS AND MEXICANS PROHIBITED and found himself barred from hotels where clerks thought him Mexican. He had planned to return to Colombia, but Mexico, being a film capital, lured him, and on the urging of Mexican friends he changed plans and began slowly, and with much difficulty, a new career as a screenwriter. He wrote one short story in Mexico and then lapsed into a silence that lasted several years.

The screenwriting was partially the cause of the silence, but so was what he considered his failure as a writer of fiction. He wrote film scripts, some in collaboration with Mexican novelist Carlos Fuentes, and several became movies, memorable now mainly because he worked on them. In dry periods he worked again as an editor and at one point did publicity for the J. Walter Thompson office in Mexico City.

"It was a very bad time for me," he said, "a suffocating time. Nothing I did in films was mine. It was a collaboration, incorporating everybody's ideas, the director's, the actors'. I was very limited in what I could do and I appreciated then that in the novel the writer has complete control."

His friends remembered him as being blocked and in a period of severe self-criticism, dissatisfied with all he had done, not wanting to return to anything like it.

It was in January 1965, while driving from Mexico City to Acapulco, that he envisioned the first chapter of the book that was to become *Cien Años*. He later told an Argentinian writer that if he'd had a tape recorder, he could have dictated the entire chapter on the spot. He then went home and told Mercedes: Don't bother me, especially don't bother me about money. And he went to work at the desk he called the Cave of the Mafia, in a house at number 6 Calle de La Loma, Mexico City, and working eight to ten hours a day for eighteen months, he wrote the novel.

"I didn't know what my wife was doing," he said, "and I didn't ask any questions. But there was always whiskey in the house. Good Scotch. In that respect my life hasn't changed much since those days. We always lived as if we had money. But when I was finished writing, my wife said, 'Did you really finish it? We owe twelve thousand dollars.' She had borrowed from friends for a year and a half."

At one point, he said, his wife was given the option by the butcher shop, where she was a good client, to pay by the month. She refused, but later, when getting money every day was more difficult, she accepted the offer and paid monthly installments to the butcher. At another point there was no money for the rent, so she told the landlord she couldn't pay for six months and somehow he said all right; so they didn't have to worry about that.

"She is stupendous," García said.

We had been talking in the Rambla bar for almost two hours and now García had to leave for an appointment. But he said we should come to his home at five and continue the talk, and we did.

He and Mercedes both greeted us. She is a slender, serene beauty, her dark, shoulder-length hair parted in the middle, an Indian quality in her face that is reminiscent of some of Gauguin's Tahitian women. She speaks softly and said that the Spaniards tell her she speaks a sweet Spanish, as contrasted with the cacophonies of Castilian. She employs a day maid to help with the house-work, in notable contrast to the time when García was writing *Cien Años*. She lived those days, she said, trying not to dwell on the precarious quality of their life, for when she did, she became very nervous.

"I would not want to go through that again," she said.

It is not at all likely she will have to.

The Garcías' apartment is modern in its furnishings, with wall-to-wall car-peting, floor-to-ceiling drapes, the color scheme beige, brown, and orange. The hi-fi, which García, and no one else, operates, is a significant object in the room, and in García's life. He treats his records as if they were fine crystal, wiping each one after use. His sons Gonzalo, ten, and Rodrigo, now twelve, have their own phonograph, so that Papa's will not be disturbed. Reading as he listens to music forms the second part of his day and regularly follows his morning work period, which usually begins at ten and lasts until about two. (One page a day, of twenty-four lines, is his average output, five pages his record.) Apart from the records—he played Leonard Cohen for the visiting North Americans—a large and orderly collection of classical works on cas-settes occupies a shelf beside the sofa.

"There were no records where I grew up," he said, "and now all this on cas-settes. Imagine!"

A discussion of some of García's literary tastes was prompted by the living-room shelves which held some of his books.

"He left most of his books in Colombia when he moved to Barcelona," Mercedes said, "but the Conrad, Plutarch, and Kafka he takes with him wherever he goes. And the Virginia Woolf he always buys when he gets there, if he can find it."

The shelves had all of these, plus the complete works of Stefau Zweig and A. J. Cronin, fourteen volumes of Borges, Rabelais's works, and among other items, *The Day of the Jackal* by Frederick Forsyth. Ah ha! A best-seller.

"Literarily," García said, "it is of no importance. But things happen. It is good false reporting."

From the blue he asked: "What do you think of Graham Greene?" His manner implied that I would be judged by my response. I said I had a high opinion of Greene.

"He teaches you how to write," García remarked. "His technique of narration is so good. He also taught us to see the tropics in books like *The Power and the Glory, The Comedians*, and *A Burnt-out Case*, which is set in Africa, but which is like Latin America. People think of life in the tropics as being exuberant, happy, rich. But Greene shows its elements—the heat, the plants, the rain, the animals, the sea. And he shows life is poor and sad. And that is the truth about that place."

Greene brought to García's mind one of his prejudices. "The intellectuals would like to like Greene," he said, "but they don't think they should. He writes a good book like *A Sort of Life* and then confuses them by writing *Travels with My Aunt.* The intellectual is the worst thing there is. He invents things and then he believes them. He decides the novel is dead but then he finds a novel and says he discovered it. If you say the novel is dead, it is not the novel. It is you who are dead."

He talked of liking Ray Bradbury, but selectively. "There are two Ray Bradburys. One writes the science fiction and one is human. I don't like the science fiction."

He said that he has read no great American writers since what he called "the Lost Generation"—meaning Faulkner and Dos Passos, and Erskine Caldwell and Hemingway for their short stories. He liked none of the Hemingway novels. "*The Sun Also Rises* was a lengthened short story," he said. Of the Faulkner works, he was most captivated by *Absalom, Absalom!*, but added, only half facetiously, that he thought *The Hamlet* was "the best South American novel ever written."

"Until you're about the age of twenty," he said, "you read everything, and you like it simply because you are reading it. Then between twenty and thirty you pick what you want, and you read the best, you read all the great works.

After that you sit and wait for them to be written. But you know, the least known, the least famous writers, they are the better ones."

Of contemporary Latin American novelists, two in particular, and both of them known in the United States, were early boosters of *Cien Años*: Carlos Fuentes and the Argentine, Julio Cortázar. García sent his first three chapters to Fuentes, who was so impressed that he wrote for a Mexican magazine:

> I have just finished reading the first seventy-five pages of *Cien Años de Soledad*. They are absolutely magisterial. . . . All "fictional" history coexists with "real" history, what is dreamed with what is documented, and thanks to the legends, the lies, the exaggerations, the myths . . . Macondo is made into a universal territory, in a story almost biblical in its foundations, its generations and degenerations, in a story of the origin and destiny of human time and of the dreams and desires by which men are saved or destroyed.

Cortázar, one of the first readers of the completed book, and equally enthusiastic, said García's imagination had redeemed the South American novel from its boring ways. Cortázar's novel *Hopscotch* had won the National Book Award for its English translator, Gregory Rabassa, in 1967. García was dissatisfied with the English translation of *No One Writes to the Colonel* and, after reading Rabassa's version of *Hopscotch*, he asked his publisher to have Rabassa, a professor of Romance languages at New York's Queens College, translate *Cien Años*. The publisher found Rabassa tied up for a year.

"I'll wait," García said, a decision for which anyone attuned to the English translation must be grateful.

Rabassa describes García's Spanish as "classical, very clear. He doesn't fool around with syntax. Certain local words do creep in, in dialogue, but he is not an experimenter. He uses the right word in the right place. I would compare his language to Cervantes.'"

Rabassa will doubtlessly translate García's next major work, which Vargas has said has the title of *El Otoño del Patriarca* ("*The Autumn of the Patriarch*"). García has been working on it since before *Cien Años*, inspired by his exposure to the Jiménez dictatorship in Venezuela, and strengthened by what he learned of the Batista dictatorship during his time in Cuba, and the Rojas dictatorship in Colombia. The central figure is a Latin dictator who lives to be 270 years old.

García's alienation from right-wing politics raises the question of why he now lives in Spain under the Franco dictatorship. I asked how he felt about Spanish politics. He groaned and put his head in his hands as a reaction to a question whose public answer could jeopardize his residency in Barcelona, where he lives in apolitical peace.

"If I were to choose a country which had politics that I like," he said, "I would not live anywhere."

"A clever answer," I said. "I won't press the point."

"You are a gentleman," he said.

We talked of Barcelona as a place to live and I expressed my short-term admiration of its magnificence and the vibrancy of its life. I also told a trolley-car story: that when we crossed into Spain at Port Bou, we asked at the tourist window for some literature on Barcelona and were given a brochure which, among other things, detailed the trolley lines in the city, by number and destination. At Columbus Plaza we tried to get a trolley that would take us to Antonio Gaudí's Sagrada Familia church, one of Barcelona's wonders. A vendor of fresh coconut at the plaza explained that there hadn't been any trolley cars in Barcelona for fourteen or fifteen years. Why, then, were they still mentioning them by name in the tourist literature? The coconut vendor had no answer and so we boarded a bus instead of a trolley and rode toward Gaudí's monumental work. We stood at the back of the bus and watched the mansions and apartment buildings make splendid canyons out of the street, at times looking like I imagined Fifth Avenue must have looked in its most elegant nineteenth-century moments. And then I said to Dana: "Look, there's a trolley."

She missed it, understandably. Its movement was perpendicular to our own. It crossed an intersection about three blocks back, right to left, visible only for a second or so, then disappeared behind the canyon wall.

"What trolleys still run in Barcelona?" I asked García.

He and his wife both said there were no trolleys in Barcelona. Mercedes remembered a funicular that went somewhere.

"This one was yellow," I said, "and old-fashioned in design."

"No," she said. "The funicular is blue."

García called his agent, Carmen Balcells, on the phone. "Is there a yellow trolley car in Barcelona?" he asked. "I'm here having an interview with Kennedy and he saw a yellow trolley."

He listened, then turned to us and said, "All the trolleys were yellow in the old days."

He asked about the blue trolley, but Carmen said it was outside of town, nowhere near where we had been. In a few minutes she called back to say that about two years ago there was a public ceremony in which the last trolley car in Barcelona had been formally buried.

What had I seen? I have no idea.

"To me," García said, "this is completely natural."

Then he told of hailing a taxi in Barcelona not long before this, but when he saw someone in the back seat he pulled down his arm. The cab driver stopped anyway and García then saw no one in the back seat. He explained this to the cabbie, who was outraged. "People are always seeing somebody in the taxi with me," he told García.

We had been drinking Scotch carefully for about five hours, lost in small talk and the free-form interchange of two languages. What had begun as a meticulous quest for the translation of phraseology through the intermediacy of Dana had loosened to the point where I was asking Dana questions in Spanish and she was talking to García in English. García was popping English phrases at me more and more, and I was fluently pidgin in Spanish. There was no comprehension problem. We praised the liberating effect of whiskey, but I downgraded it as a tool for writing. García agreed but hesitated: "There is a point where it works," he said.

It was a quarter to eleven, the theater hour in Barcelona, when García decided we should go to dinner. He drove, soberly, through the old streets, parked near an alley, and then led the way to what he called "the best secret restaurant in Barcelona." I put on my steel-rimmed glasses to read the menu, but García said, "I have better glasses than those," and took out a pair of steel-rimmed half-glasses.

"Are you blind without them?" I asked.

"Not quite," he said, holding the menu as far away as he could. "My arm is still long enough."

I ordered baby squid in garlic and acceded to García's choice of *perdiz*, which we finally figured out meant partridge. He ordered French wine, Côtes du Rhône, I think, which came in a dusty, crooked-necked bottle. He chewed a piece of bread, clearing his taste buds of old Scotch, before tasting the wine for approval.

We had one more literary discussion at dinner. We had talked of politics and fiction earlier and he had mentioned a writer who, he felt, had hurt himself by overemphasizing politics, and whose work had changed. García considered this a loss. I then asked what he thought the proper place of politics was in fiction. He borrowed my pen and drew some intersecting vertical and horizontal lines in my notebook, creating twelve boxes. Beneath the boxes he wrote the word "*ficción*" and drew arrows to the left and right vertical borders. Then he wrote "*politic*" in the left central square. He paused. The vacant squares impelled him to further statement, and randomly, in two languages, he filled them in: "*tristeza*," "*love*," "*humor*," "*dinero*," "*esperanza*," "*muerte*," "*nostalgia*," "*vida*," and three question marks.

There is another García drawing in my notebook; it shows a flower blooming atop a two-leafed potted plant and an open-mouthed fish about to bite on a dangling fishhook as a one-eyed sun rises, or perhaps sets, behind an undulating horizon. In homage to Kennedy, he included in the drawing a two-wheeled trolley on a track, off to the left, denoting it as "old yellow," and he signed it in two places and included my own name with the year mentioned, 1972.

We eventually left the restaurant, around one-thirty. I discovered I'd left my copy of the Vargas biography at the García apartment, but I was told not to worry, that there would be bookstalls open on La Rambla where we could get another copy. García drove to one but it was Mercedes who leaped out and bought the book; for how would it look, García said, for him to go out and buy his own biography at one-thirty in the morning?

There was a conversation whose site I do not remember. Maybe it was the American bar, or maybe the apartment, or the best secret restaurant in Barcelona. But it has to do with García and his going back to Colombia every two or three years, and returning to Aracataca.

"Each year less," he said of the hometown, meaning each year the world he knew vanishes a little more. But there is a renewal. For each year, as the fame of *Cien Años* grows, Aracataca becomes more and more a place where tourists who have read the book go to compare its reality with the reality they have in their heads. They want to see the chestnut tree where José Arcadio Buendía, the founder of Macondo, died in beatific madness, tied to the trunk for years, seeing the ghosts of his past grow old along with him. They want to see the old Buendía house, and the plaza where thousands of striking banana workers were massacred by the army and their corpses taken on the longest train in the world to a remote point and dumped into the sea, so that not only would no evidence of their deaths remain but that the lie would be given to anyone brazen enough to suggest that a massacre had taken place.

Years later that massacre would merely be a legend, its reality as accepted, yet as unverifiable, as the Trojan horse, or my yellow trolley car. García overheard it as a legend in Aracataca when he was young and he later reinvented it, just as he reinvented most of Macondo from bits and pieces of Aracataca, from the storied or merely imagined past. The Macondo he created barely exists in Aracataca today, but that does not stop the enterprising small boys of the town from reinventing, with *their* imaginations, what the tourists want to see. For a few coins they will find José Arcadio Buendía's tree and the place where the ants devoured the last newborn in the Buendía line, the infant that had been conceived incestuously and born with the tail of a pig. The cycle of the imagination is not dependent on any reality that can be bought at the hardware store like a seventy-eight-cent screwdriver.

Writing fiction today, a friend once advised me, is about as significant as playing bridge. Possibly this is true for those who dwell in the Land of the Cat's Titty. Possibly, for them, other things have replaced it. But in the face of a primordial event like the creation of Macondo, the argument is now worth rebutting. Whatever the numbers, and the numbers never mattered, there are still those who would rather dwell there for a time, and ride the yellow trolley car that may or may not exist, and thrive on the heat of a one-eyed sun, and draw sustenance from a book full of verities and question marks. Those who feel this have no need to justify their preference.

A Bogotá journalist went to Aracataca in 1969 and found that the home of García's ancestors was being eaten to dust by ants, just as García had predicted the dust storm that would bury the Buendía house and the town forever. The journalist found ruins and solitude in the town, no doubt what he went to find, and which always exist everywhere if you look closely. But the fading of Aracataca was not the consequence of a cursed, fateful prophecy. It had been predicted by García Márquez not because he had chosen it to be that way in his godlike role as novelist, but because—like the gypsy Melquíades, who in *Cien Años* had written in the coded parchments that "The first of the line is tied to a tree and the last is being eaten by the ants"— he deciphered the key to history, and he knew that events occurred because they had to, that the turn of time was cyclical and that the vital, bloody warmth of every life held in itself not only its own dusty eventuality, but the seeds of regeneration as well.

García's nickname is Gabo, and the diminutive of that is Gabito. And in an Aracataca bar the Bogotá journalist heard a song being sung which was really a song of the rebirth of this novelist, this man:

> It was in the land of Macondo,
> Where little Gabriel was born.
> All of the people knew him,
> By the name of Gabito. . . .

Journey Back to the Source
El Manifiesto / 1977

From *El Manifiesto* (Bogotá), 1977. Reprinted in Alfonso Rentería Mantilla, ed., *García Márquez habla de García Márquez* (Bogotá: Rentería Editores, 1979), pp. 159–67. Translated by Gene H. Bell-Villada.

EM: Among critics there is a generally accepted notion that you're lacking in literary background, that you write only from your personal experiences, your imagination. What can you tell us in that regard?
(*García Márquez's eyes light up. As if we had pushed a hidden button, the character—who inevitably brings to mind the figure of Anthony Quinn in* Zorba the Greek—*manifests himself in a torrent of laughs, gestures, shouts. The magic word has been uttered. We've touched on his Achilles's heel: literature.*)
GGM: Yes. With my joshing I've probably contributed toward the idea that I lack literary education, that I write only from personal experiences, that my sources are Faulkner, Hemingway, and other foreign writers. Little is known about my knowledge of Colombian literature. No doubt, my influences, especially in Colombia, are extra-literary. More than any book, I think what opened my eyes was music, vallenato songs. I'm talking about many years ago, at least thirty years ago, when vallenato music was hardly known outside a corner of the Magdalena valley. What called my attention most of all was the form the songs used, the way they told a fact, a story . . . All quite naturally. Then, when vallenato was commercialized, what mattered more was the feeling, the rhythm . . . Those vallenato songs narrated as my grandmother used to, I remember . . . Later, when I started studying the Spanish ballads of the *Romancero*, I found that it was the same esthetic, and found it all once again in the *Romancero*.

EM: Couldn't we talk about music?
GGM: Yes, but afterwards, and not for the record . . . No, it's not that I can't talk about music. But I get caught up in a tangle that doesn't end. It's . . . something very intimate, even more of a secret when the people whom you're talking to know about music . . . For me, music is anything that makes

sound. And I change a lot . . . Bartok, for instance, who's an author I really like, is hell to listen to in the mornings. One gets more easily into Mozart in the morning. But afterwards, I'm calm . . . I've got all of Daniel Santos, Miguelito Valdés, Julio Jaramillo, and all of the singers who're so discredited among intellectuals. You see, I don't make distinctions, I recognize that everything has its value. The only thing where I'm all-embracing is in musical matters. Somehow I listen to no less than two hours of music a day. It's the only thing that relaxes me, puts me in the right mood . . . And I go through all kinds of phases.

Home is where your books are, they say, but for me it's where my recordings are. I've got more than five thousand of them.

Which of you guys listens to music? You know, as a habit? You do? For how long? How far can you go? For example, have you gotten to the Orquesta Casino de la Playa? Is Miguelito Valdés and the Casino de la Playa a reference for you?

EM: Yes, of course.
GGM: And starting out there with the boleros?

EM: Yes. Daniel Santos from 1940.
GGM: With the Cuarteto Flórez?

EM: Yeah! . . . The Farewell, at the Serranía . . .
GGM: That's the origin of *salsa*, the Casino de la Playa Orchestra. The pianist was Sacasas, who was most famous for his solos called *montunos*. It's a quarrel I've had with the Cubans, an old fight, especially with Armando Hart . . . Hey! . . . Is that thing [the tape recorder] running?

EM: Yeah . . . It's running.
GGM: Turn it off!

My literary background was basically in poetry, but bad poetry, since only through bad poetry can you get to good poetry. I started out with that stuff called popular verse, the kind that was published in almanacs or on loose sheets of paper. Some of them were influenced by Julio Flórez. When I got to high school I started out with the poetry that appeared in grammar books. I realized that what I most liked was poetry and what I most hated was Spanish class, grammar. What I liked was the examples. There were mostly

examples from the Spanish Romantics, which were probably the closest thing
to Julio Flórez—Nuñez de Arce, Espronceda. Then, the Spanish classics. But
the revelation comes when you really get into Colombian poetry—
Domínguez Camargo. At that time the first thing you learned was World
Literature. It was terrible! There was no access to the books. The professors
said that they were good because of this or that. Much later I read them and
thought them incredible. I'm referring to the classics.

But they were incredible not because of what the professor said, but
because of what went on: Ulysses tied to the mast so he won't succumb to
the sirens' song . . . All that stuff that happens. Afterwards, we'd study
Spanish literature, and Colombian literature only in the last year of high
school. So when I made it to that class I knew more than the professor did. It
was in Zipaquirá. I had nothing to do and to avoid getting bored I'd hole
up at the school library, where they had the Aldeana collection. I read the
whole thing! . . . From volume one to the last! I read *El carnero*, memoirs,
reminiscences . . . I read it all! Of course, when I reached my last year in
secondary school, I knew more than the teacher did. That's where I realized
that Rafael Núñez was the worst poet in the country . . . The National
Anthem! . . . Can you imagine that the lyrics to the National Anthem were
chosen because they were a great poem by Núñez? That it was first chosen as
an anthem you might accept, but what prompts horror is that it was chosen
as Anthem because it was poetry.

As far as literature was concerned, the Caribbean coast didn't exist. When
literature gets separated from life and seals itself off in closed circles, then a
gap appears and it's filled by the provincials . . . They save literature when it's
become rhetoric.

At age twenty I already had a literary background that was enough for me
to write everything I've written . . . I don't know how I discovered the novel.
I thought that what interested me was poetry . . . I don't know . . . I can't
remember when it was I realized that the novel was what I needed to express
myself . . . You guys can't imagine what it meant for a scholarship kid from
the Coast enrolled at the Liceo de Zipaquirá to have access to books . . .
Probably Kafka's "The Metamorphosis" was a revelation . . . It was in 1947 . . .
I was nineteen . . . I was doing my first year of law school . . . I remember the
opening sentences; it reads exactly thus: "As Gregor Samsa woke up one
morning from troubled dreams, he found himself transformed in his bed
into a monstrous vermin."! . . . Holy shit! When I read that I said to myself,

"This isn't right! . . . Nobody had told me this could be done! . . . Because it really can be done! . . . So then I can! . . . Holy shit! . . . That's how my grandmother told stories . . . The wildest things, in the most natural way."

And next day I set out, just like that, next day at eight o'clock in the morning, to try to find out what the hell had been done in the novel from the beginnings of humanity up to myself. So I latched onto the novel in rigorous order, let's say from the Bible up to what was being written at that time. Beginning then, for six years, I didn't do literature by myself; I stopped studying and dropped out of everything. I started writing a series of stories that were completely intellectual. They were my first stories, published in *El Espectador*. The chief problem I had when I began writing those stories was that of other writers: what to write about.

But after the April 9 riots in Bogotá, when I had nothing left except the clothes on my back, I left for the Coast and started work there, at a newspaper. And then the subjects started to invade me. I started encountering an entire reality I'd left behind, on the Coast, which I couldn't interpret because of a lack of literary grounding. That was the first invasion, to such an extent that I'd write as if in a fever.

I've a great deal of affection for *Leaf Storm*. Even lots of compassion for that guy who wrote it. I can see him perfectly. A twenty-two- or twenty-three-year-old kid who feels he's not going to write anything else in life, feels it's his only chance, and he tries to throw in everything he remembers, everything he's learned about literary technique and sophistication from every author he's seen. At that time I was catching up, I was into the English and North American novelists. And when the critics start finding my influences in Faulkner and Hemingway, what they find—it's not that they're not right, but in some other way—is that when I'm confronted with that whole reality on the Coast, and I start connecting with my experiences literarily . . . the best way to tell it, I realize, isn't Kafka's . . . I realize the method is precisely that of the American novelists. What I find in Faulkner is that he's interpreting and expressing a reality that looks a lot like Aracataca's, like the banana zone's. What they give me is the instrument . . .

When I re-examine *Leaf Storm*, I find exactly the readings that went into that work . . . I mean just like that! . . . It's when I leave behind all those intellectual stories, when I realize that it was in my hands, in everyday life, in the brothels, the towns, the music . . . Precisely, I rediscover the vallenato songs. That's when I met Escalona, you know. We started working together, we took one hell of a trip through La Guajira, where there were experiences I can now rediscover with the utmost naturalness. There's a journey by Eréndira that is the journey I took through La Guajira with Escalona . . . There's not a single line in any of my books that I can't tell you which experience from reality it corresponds to. Always, there's a reference to a concrete reality. Not a single book! And someday, with more time, we could verify that, we could start playing this game, to wit: this corresponds to such-and-such, that to another, and I can remember the day and all, exactly . . .

EM: It would be interesting to do that with *The Autumn of the Patriarch*.
GGM: *The Autumn* . . . is the one I can most do it with, because as a book it's completely coded.

EM: Getting back to the matter of your influences, what did the "Barranquilla Group" mean for your literary education?
GGM: It was the most important aspect because, while I'd been here in Bogotá, I studied literature in an abstract way, through books. There was no correspondence between what I was reading and what was out on the street. The minute I'd go down to the corner for a cup of coffee, I'd find a world that was completely different. When I was forced to leave for the Coast by the circumstances of April 9, it was a total discovery: that there could be a correspondence between what I was reading and what I was living and had always lived. For me, the most important thing about the "Barranquilla Group" is that I had all sorts of books available. Because Alfonso Fuenmayor, Alvaro Cepeda, and Germán Vargas were there, and they were voracious readers. They had all the books. We'd get drunk until sunrise talking about literature, and one night there might be ten books I didn't know, but next day I had them. Germán would bring me two, Alfonso, three . . . The old man Ramón Vinyes would let us get involved in all sorts of reading adventures; but he wouldn't let go of the classic anchor-line, the old guy. He'd say: "Fine, you guys might read Faulkner, the English, Russian, or French novelists, but remember—always with ties to this." And he wouldn't let you do without Homer, without the Romans, he wouldn't let us run wild. What was amazing was that those drinking binges we'd get into corresponded exactly to what I was reading. There was no gap there. So I began to live and I'd realize just what I was living, that it had literary value and how to express it. And so you find in *Leaf Storm* that I had the impression that I wouldn't have enough time,

that I needed to throw everything in there, and it's a baroque novel and all complicated and all screwed up . . . I was trying to do something that I'll later do much more serenely in *The Autumn of the Patriarch*. If you pay attention, the structure of *Patriarch* is exactly the same as that of *Leaf Storm*; they're points of view organized around a dead man's body. In *Leaf Storm* it's more systematized because I'm twenty-two or twenty-three years old and don't dare fly solo. So I adopt a little the method of Faulkner's *As I Lay Dying*. Faulkner, in fact, of course, he assigns names to the monologues. So I, simply so as not to do the same thing, I tell it from three viewpoints that are easily identifiable because they're an old man, a boy, and a woman. In *Autumn of the Patriarch* I'm cracking up with laughter throughout, at the time I can do whatever I want. I don't care who's talking and who isn't talking, I care about expressing the reality that's there. But it's not gratuitous, let me say. It's not by chance that at bottom I keep trying to write the same first book. It shows clearly in *Patriarch* how one goes back to the structure, and not just the structure but the same drama.

And that's it. It was amazing because I was living the same literature that I was trying to create. They were fantastic years because, you see . . . There's one thing that the Europeans especially hold against me—namely, that I don't manage to theorize about anything I've written, because every time they ask a question I've got to answer them with an anecdote or with a fact that fits reality. It's the only thing that allows me to support what's written and what they're asking me about.

I remember that I was working at *El Heraldo*. I'd write a piece and they'd pay me three pesos for it, and maybe an editorial for another three. The fact is I didn't live anywhere, but right near the newspaper there were some hotels for transients. There were prostitutes around the place. They'd go to some little hotels that were right above the notary offices. The notaries were downstairs, the hotels upstairs. For a peso and fifty cents they'd let someone in and that gave you admission for twenty-four hours. And then I started making the greatest discoveries: hotels for one peso fifty that were unknown! It was impossible. The only thing I needed to do was take care of the drafts in progress of *Leaf Storm*. I'd carry them in a leather bag, I'd tote them everywhere, under my arm . . . I'd arrive every night and pay a peso fifty, and the guy would give me the key. And I should mention that the doorman was a little old guy and I know where he is now. I'd arrive every afternoon, every night, and pay him the peso fifty.

Of course, after two weeks it became mechanical. He'd grab the key, always to the same room, I'd give him the peso fifty . . . One night I didn't have the peso fifty . . . I arrived and said to him, "Look, you see this here? They're some papers, it's what most important to me and it's worth much more than a peso fifty. I'll leave them with you and tomorrow I'll pay." It became almost routine, when I had the peso fifty, I'd pay, when I didn't, I'd go in . . . "Hello, good evening!" and "Splat!" . . . I'd put the folder on his desk and he'd give me the key. I spent more than a year that way. What used to surprise that guy was that once in a while the governor's chauffeur would come for me because, since I was a reporter he'd have the car pick me up. And the old guy didn't understand anything about what was going on!

I lived there, and of course, when I'd get up next day, the only other people still around were the prostitutes. We were good friends, and we'd make breakfasts that I'll never forget. They'd lend me soap. I remember that I'd always run out of soap and they'd lend it to me. And that's where I finished writing *Leaf Storm*.

The problem with all that stuff about the "Barranquilla Group" is . . . well, I've said a lot about it, and it always comes out wrong, I can't manage to get it right! For me it was a time when I was completely dazzled, it's truly a discovery . . . Not of literature, but of literature being applied to real life, which ultimately is the big problem of literature. Of a literature that truly matters, applied to a reality.

I was so much aware of what I was doing that I realized I had to take off and travel down the Magdalena River as far as Riohacha, as far as the Guajira peninsula. It was a route precisely the opposite of the one traveled by my family, because they were from Riohacha, and from La Guajira they'd moved to the banana country . . . It was like their return trip . . . like their journey back to the source. What I'd gotten into my head was to do that return journey because in it I kept finding other points of reference, all the things that spoke to me about my grandparents. It was a world that had been nebulous to me, and when I'd arrive in the towns—Valledupar, La Paz—I'd find, this is what they used talk about, that's why they used to tell me about this . . .

My grandfather had killed a man, and I remember the screwiest thing happening . . . I was in Valledupar, and suddenly a tall guy, really tall, with a cowboy hat, introduced himself to me. And he said, "Are you Márquez?" I said, "Yeah!" Then . . . he . . . stares at me like this . . . and says to me, "Your grandpa killed my grandpa!" And I shit my pants! I looked him and didn't know what to say . . . He ordered . . . I'd sort of settled in, leaning against the wall . . . and he started telling me. His name was José Prudencio Aguilar! And I'll say no more.

It was all like that. Do you know how I financed that whole trip lasting over a year, when I was roaming this way and that through the entire region? Ultimately it was on that journey that I found all the roots for *One Hundred Years of Solitude* and everything else. I was selling encyclopedias! I sold the *Enciclopedia Utea*. It has medical books. Books for everything!

When I left La Guajira I moved to *El Espectador*. What I want to say is that when I did the move, I didn't need to read any more or do anymore to write everything I've written. My education was complete. Since then I've had another kind of development, ideological, if you will . . . which is another matter, a way of digging deep into the interpretation of all that stuff. But I was completely formed. And I arrived in Paris, arrived in Europe, was in Europe . . . Holy shit! I wrote *No One Writes to the Colonel* in a Paris hotel. And that thing has all the smells, the tastes, the temperature, the heat, everything. It was written during winter, with shitloads of snow outside and cold inside and me wearing my overcoat, and that book has the heat of Aracataca. 'Cause if I didn't succeed in making it hot in the book I felt it wasn't right . . It was lots of work!"

EM: And what about your experience as journalist, as regards your literary education? What can you tell us about it? As an example, the series "La Marquesita de la Sierpe" (The Little Marchioness of La Sierpe) stands out. It's a report on a region of the country that looks completely unreal.
GGM: Well, it *is* unreal, in the sense that it's not verified, they're not proven events. They're told as if they were verified. They're things I told with utter naturalness. Don't know if I explain . . . That is . . . . I know La Sierpe, I was in La Sierpe, but of course I didn't see the "gold gourd" or the "white crocodile" or any of those things. But it was a reality that lived inside the consciousness of the people. The way they told it you felt no doubt that that's how it was. In a certain way it's the method of *One Hundred Years of Solitude*. And then you can't be a writer without having tricks. What's important is the legitimacy of those tricks, up to what point they're used and to what degree.

I remember perfectly when I was in Mexico, writing, describing Remedios the Beauty's ascent to heaven. It was one of those paragraphs. I was aware, first, that without poetry she couldn't rise. I'd say: she's got to rise to poetry—and yet, with poetry and all she wouldn't rise either. I was getting desperate because it was a reality within the book. I couldn't dispense with it because it was a reality within the guidelines I'd imposed on myself. Because arbitrariness has rigid laws. And once I impose them on myself I can't break them. I can't say the rook moves this way and then, when it suits me, make it move another way. If I established how the rook and the knight move, I was screwed!. . . Because whatever I may do they've got to continue that way. Otherwise, it all turns into a holy mess. Within the reality of the book, Remedios the Beauty rose to heaven, but she wouldn't rise even with poetry. I remember being desperate one day, 'cause I was all caught up and stuck in it. I went out to the patio, where there was a big and beautiful black woman who did the housework, who was trying to hang the sheets with one of those clothes pins . . . And there was wind . . . And so if she hung the sheet this side, the wind blew it off that side . . . And she was completely crazy with those sheets . . . until she couldn't take it any more and Aaaaahhhh! Aaaahhhh! . . . She cried out desperately! . . . Wrapped up in the sheets! . . . And up she went . . . And that's how it was with everything.

EM: " . . . Then he went to the chestnut tree, thinking about the circus, and while he urinated he tried to keep on thinking about the circus, but he could no longer find the memory. He pulled his head in between his shoulders like a baby chick and remained motionless with his forehead against the trunk of the chestnut tree . . ." —*One Hundred Years of Solitude*.
GGM: The episode was foreordained, from before I had *One Hundred Years of Solitude*. I always knew there was a character, an old general from the civil war, who died urinating under a tree. That's what I knew. I didn't know how or which way it was going to work out. That's how the personality of Colonel Buendía took shape.

There was a moment in *One Hundred Years of Solitude* when I thought Colonel Aureliano Buendía would seize power. And that would've been the dictator of *The Autumn of the Patriarch*. But it would've completely messed up the book's structure, making it into something else. Besides, within the trajectory of the character and the reality of the book, what really mattered to me was for him to sell the war, sell it . . . from . . . an ideological point of view, if you will. The guy doesn't dare keep fighting for power except because of some stuff from the Liberals, who'd shit their pants in all the last century's civil wars in this country.

And I'd keep writing the book, and suddenly I'd remember that in the middle of all those things there was a problem waiting: Colonel Buendía and his little gold fishes. And I didn't know when I'd have to kill him. I was afraid of that moment. Probably one of the toughest times I've had in my life was when I wrote the death of Colonel Aureliano Buendía. I remember perfectly . . . One day I said, "Today's when he gets it!" . . . I've always wanted to write a story that would describe, minutely, a person's every moment in an ordinary day, until he dies. I tried to give that literary solution to the death of Colonel Aureliano Buendía, but I found that if I took that path, the book would change on me. So I threw out that possibility, and I started spinning the deal of the Colonel in my mind, until . . . (*he pounds the table*).

(*Gabo turns silent. He looks at his hands and slowly, very slowly, starts saying:*)

I went up. In one of the rooms upstairs Mercedes was taking a nap . . . I lay down at her side and said to her, "He's dead!" . . . And I cried for two hours.

But there's something that's more curious about the Colonel. For five years I had boils. Do you know what boils are? Nothing would cure them. I was given all kinds of treatments. At a New York hospital they removed them, they drew blood on one side and gave me shots on another, all sorts of stuff. And never during five years could anything be done about it. The boils would be gone and then I'd get them again. Well, when I was writing *One Hundred Years of Solitude*, I got it into my head about Colonel Aureliano Buendía, a character I detested and have always detested, because the bastard could have seized power if he'd wanted to, and he didn't out of sheer pride. So I said, Well, what disease could I give this s.o.b. that'll bug him without killing him? . . . So I gave him boils. You know, from the moment when Colonel Aureliano Buendía got stuck with sores, I got cured of them. This was ten years ago, and I've never gotten them again.

The other case is Úrsula's. In my initial plans, Úrsula had to die before the civil wars. Besides, within a strict chronology, by then she was getting to be a century old. If she died then, though, the book would fall apart. So I realized I had to hold on to her until a time when the book did fall apart but it wouldn't matter because inertia would carry it to the end. That's why she had to keep at it up to hell's end. You know, I didn't dare take Úrsula out of the picture. I had to shuffle her around, do everything possible to follow her to wherever she might go.

EM: You did with the sores the same thing that Dostoevsky did with epilepsy.
GGM: Yeah, but he didn't get cured. Isn't it true that one of the most unforgettable scenes in world literature is when Smerdyakov falls down the steps? Besides, we never find out if it's true or not, or if it was a real attack or just make-believe. It's unforgettable.

EM: Since we're talking about characters, there's something that makes me uneasy. In general your works typically have clearly defined characters that seem to fill every work, yet where the common people seem diluted, filling the work but on a secondary level, like extras.
GGM: Yes, the masses would need their writer, a writer who would create their characters. I'm a petit bourgeois writer, and my point of view has always been petit bourgeois. That's my level, my perspective, even though my attitude of solidarity might differ. But I don't know that point of view. I write from my own, from the window where I happen to be. About the masses I don't know more than what I've said and written. I probably know more, but it's purely theoretical. This point of view is absolutely sincere. And at no time have I tried to force things. There's a sentence I've said and which even bugged my dad, he thought it a put-down. "What am I, ultimately? I'm the son of the telegraph operator of Aracataca." And what my dad thought so pejorative, to me, by contrast, seems almost elitist within that society. 'Cause the telegraph operator thought of himself as the chief intellectual of the town. Usually they were failed students, guys who dropped out of their studies and ended up doing that. In Aracataca, a town filled with peons.

But you're insatiable. I've been talking about literature like I haven't, oh, in years. And besides, I'm very shy when talking literature.

EM: Yes, well, the thing is, there's still *The Autumn of the Patriarch*. Sometimes it's said you're making a clean slate of your previous work.
GGM: Yes, it's what I've said.

EM: You also said in a report that it was your autobiography, secretly coded. In this regard it looks as if writing becomes more complex, less accessible to the mass public.
GGM: But over time it'll make it to the mass public. *The Autumn of the Patriarch* is just sitting around waiting for people to catch up with it. You see,

I think readers who're caught unawares, who lack literary knowledge, can read *Patriarch* more readily than readers with literary backgrounds. I've seen it in Cuba, where the book exists out there on the streets. Uninformed readers aren't put off, they're put off less. *The Autumn . . .* is a completely straightforward novel, absolutely elementary, where the only thing I've done is break certain grammatical rules for the sake of brevity and concision, that is, in order to rework the matter of time. In a certain way, so that it won't become something infinite. I don't see anything odd about it. Besides, there are lots of works like that in the history of literature. I don't see where the difficulty is.

EM: But the impression one gets is of greater complexity. It seems like a book for the initiated.
GGM: In the structure, yes, it is. But its language is the most colloquial and popular of my novels. It's more coded in the sense that it's more restricted. It's more of the people, for taxi drivers in Barranquilla, it's closer to speech than to literary language. It's filled with little phrases from songs, all sorts of proverbial expressions, tunes from the Caribbean.

EM: So the difficulty derives from the fact that most readers who haven't lived that experience lack those same references.
GGM: No, if that's the case, then the book is wrong, because it should be accessible even if the reader lacks that information. If they need that previous information, then the book is wrong. I don't feel that those who know the codes have easier access to it. Maybe they'll enjoy it more. I think the book is intelligible even without the large number of quotes from Rubén Darío that are inside it, all over the place, because the whole book is written in Rubén Darío. If you need lots of information to read the book, then it's wrong. But I don't believe you do need it.

I think of it more as a poem than a novel. It's elaborated more as a poem than as a novel. I could've written it without reading a single book, but not without having heard all the music I've listened to. That's what made the critical curve of music while I wrote it. And for an absolutely basic reason: for the first time since *One Hundred Years of Solitude* I can buy all the records I want. Before, I had to listen to borrowed music. What's more complex about *Patriarch* is the aesthetic. It's not a new aesthetic, it's much more complex.

I've worked on it more than if it were a poem. It's a luxury that a writer who's written *One Hundred Years of Solitude* can afford, who says, Well, now

I'm going to write the book I want. I can play with it, make something, confess lots of things. You see, the solitude of power is a lot like the solitude of a writer.

It's not that the book is coded, what's coded is the events that serve as its foundation, just as some of the events in *One Hundred Years of Solitude* are. The rest is experiences I've had. When my mother reads the book she's wonderful, because she goes through it saying, "This is such-and-such, this is that, that's my buddy, the one people said was queer but really wasn't."

I think the problem with reading *Patriarch* is chiefly intellectual. You critics are the ones who don't get it, because you're looking for what's there, and there's nothing. It's the most coastal of my books, the one most restricted to the Caribbean in a sectarian way, the one that's most saying, Shit! Why do you guys have us all fucked up? This is a completely different country, another culture. It's from a desire to draw from a bunch of things, that one gets the impression they don't understand. And so, that brothel where I used to live was brimful of stuff from the Caribbean. And that port tavern where we'd go for breakfast when the paper came out, at four in the morning, where amazing fights and messes would break out. And the schooners that took off for Aruba, for Curaçao, loaded with whores . . . I don't know, that left and came back with contraband . . . And Cartagena on Saturday afternoons, with the students, all that stuff. You see, I know the Caribbean, island by island, like that, island-by-island-by-island. And it can be synthesized in a single street, like the one that appears in *The Autumn*, which is the main street in Panama, in la Guaira. But above all it's the business street in Panama City, filled with hawkers.

There's an effort at trying to seize all that and synthesize it somehow. Maybe it didn't come out right. *The Autumn* is the twelve links you get on a stroll through the central avenue in Panama, or on an afternoon in Cartagena, that whole shit-pile of the Caribbean. Because it's a goddamned shit-pile, including Cuba today, what it is, what Havana was . . . I think there's a poetical effort at trying to come out at the other end. I could've kept writing *One Hundred Years of Solitude*, the sequel, II, III, IV, like *The Godfather*. But it couldn't be. If I wanted to go on writing I needed to see what the hell I could do—something that doesn't worry me as much since *Patriarch*.

If I write stories again, the model now is Somerset Maugham. They're quiet, autumnal stories, by a man who's telling a series of things he lived and saw, in a form that's . . . let's not say "classical" because definitions screw everything up, let's say "academic, formal." 'Cause Maugham wrote very good stories. Probably the best ones I know have a certain tone, they make no noise. They're a good model for writing stories . . . So! . . . What else shall we say about *The Autumn*?

EM: Which ones in the book are your personal experiences?
GGM: That's harder to say. They're all dissolved. Some day we could sit down and read a fragment and talk about it . . . .

EM: About Rubén Darío, for instance.
GGM: Yeah, well, Rubén Darío is the poet of the era, that is, the era of the book. You know, it's sad, the difficulties that all the translators have had with him. He hasn't been translated as he should, as a great poet. He's not known anywhere. And there are other problems that put the translators into a fucking mess. The translators of *The Autumn of the Patriarch* are going completely crazy. For example, they'll ask, "What does 'la manta de la bandera' mean?" [Literally "the blanket of the flag." —Ed.] And on the coast, I don't know about here, "manta" means the cigarette paper that's sold for rolling a marihuana joint. But at one time it came with the American flag. On the coast, it's very simple. Whoever sees the phrase "manta de bandera" knows right off that it's the paper with the U.S. flag for smoking pot. You can imagine the footnote that the translator has to put in in order to explain "la manta de bandera." What's needed is to forget the antecedents' connotations and find a formula.

There's yet another wonderful item: it's the "salchichón de hoyito." [Literally "sausage with a little hole."—Ed.] That's a phrase totally for cab drivers in Barranquilla.

EM: And what is it?
GGM: It's a sausage that has a little hole on the tip. In Spain they say "la polla," in other countries they say "la pinga" . . . But what the Barranquilla drivers say is "the sausage with a little hole." So, every translator asks, "What does 'sausage with a little hole' mean?" What's hermetic, then, isn't the whole book, but all that stuff, right? The Caribbean stuff. For instance, in Cuba they don't know what "salchichón de hoyito" is, but when a Cuban reads it, when a Dominican or a Puerto Rican reads it, they know immediately what it is. They figure it out because they know the mechanisms, the contexts, they know how you get there.

Playboy Interview: Gabriel García Márquez

Claudia Dreifus / 1982

The Nobel Prize is at once the most prestigious and the least predictable of honors, so it was an unexpected pleasure for us when it was announced that the 1982 winner for literature was the Latin-American novelist Gabriel García Márquez. Not only has *Playboy* published his fiction for more than a decade but we had recently sent a reporter abroad to engage him in the most extensive interview of his career. So when it was announced that he would be making the traditional journey to Stockholm in early December to receive his award, we had the satisfaction of offering our readers a fortuitously timed interview. The world's literary community, however, may claim that the announcement was not unexpected. For years, critics had been waxing ecstatic about the author of *One Hundred Years of Solitude*, hailing him as one of the world's great living novelists, comparing his work to that of William Faulkner and James Joyce. Indeed, among the literati, García Márquez—"Gabo," as he's known to his friends—has long been talked of as a Nobel contender. The only question was *when*, not *if*.

A few basic facts about García Márquez: He is the foremost practitioner of Latin America's "magic realist" literary style, a form in which fantasy and reality are blended into a uniquely New World form of storytelling; his masterly novel of life, love and revolution in a Latin-American village, *One Hundred Years of Solitude*, has sold more than 6,000,000 copies in more than 30 languages; the book is a cult classic on American college campuses; before garnering his Nobel, García Márquez won every international prize worth having.

Beyond his literary accomplishments, García Márquez is a political activist, an advocate of social revolution in the Third World and in Latin America in particular. He is a close friend of many world leaders, including

Cuba's Fidel Castro and France's Socialist President François Mitterrand. His leftist views and background have made him a controversial figure in the U.S.

When *One Hundred Years of Solitude* was published in the United States in 1970, critics fell over one another to pronounce García Márquez a genius. That was followed in 1975 with *The Autumn of the Patriarch*, a wildly surreal work about a Latin-American dictator who's been in power so long that no one remembers how he got there. This April, Knopf will be bringing out his latest, *Chronicle of a Death Foretold*, a story of sex, murder and retribution.

Born in the Colombian coastal village of Aracataca in 1928, the writer grew up in an atmosphere that made him a natural storyteller. Aracataca, he always said, was a wonderful place of "bandits and dancers." His grandfather told young Gabriel true tales of war, injustice and politics. His grandmother recited bed-time stories of the supernatural.

Since the age of 18, García Márquez knew that a big book about Latin America brewed inside him. As a young man, he studied law at the University of Bogotá—a pursuit he continued until, in the late Forties, he quit to eke out a living as a writer and a journalist. During the Fifties and Sixties, he lived the itinerant life of a reporter in Paris, Rome and Caracas, including a stint as a correspondent for Prensa Latina, revolutionary Cuba's news agency. On one brief trip back home in 1958, he married his childhood sweetheart, Mercedes Barcha. When not writing for newspapers, García Márquez wrote fiction: *Leaf Storm, No One Writes to the Colonel, In Evil Hour* and *Big Mama's Funeral,* works that some scholars now consider first drafts of *One Hundred Years of Solitude*. By 1965, free-lancer García Márquez found himself in Mexico City, supporting his wife and two sons. It was there that the idea for *One Hundred Years of Solitude* was crystallized.

In the years since its publication in 1967, García Márquez has found himself catapulted to wealth, political influence and the international renown reserved for movie stars and statesmen. The García family now maintains elegant residences in Paris and Mexico City, and he has used his influence to become an unofficial ambassador for leftist Latin America. He has tried unsuccessfully to ignore his fame, saying, "I detest being converted into a public spectacle."

Last year, *Playboy* gave journalist Claudia Dreifus the green light to try to question this unusual writer. Her report:

"To describe García Márquez as elusive is understatement. He does not answer letters, fearing that his correspondence may be sold at auction. His telephone seems to be perpetually out of order. I wrote to him at various addresses in Paris and periodically telephoned his agent in Spain. Nothing happened. Then, one afternoon in New York, Gregory Rabassa, the author's English-language translator, telephoned: 'Gabo is in New York, just for the afternoon. If you rush, you might catch him.'

"In a flash, I contacted García Márquez at his Park Avenue hotel. 'Mr. García Márquez, there's so much that's been written about you and so little of it is true,' I said. 'With a "Playboy Interview," you could clear up all the fiction. What's more, with the situation in Central America being what it is, North Americans would be interested in hearing a different voice speak on Latin-American realities. Why don't you tell us *your* side of the story?'

"García Márquez was intrigued. In March of 1981, he'd suffered the experience of having to flee his native Colombia after the military there tried to link him with a Castroite guerrilla organization. In the United States, he was having problems with the State Department, which, because of his Castro connection, would grant him only a limited U.S. entry visa. Yes, he would like to talk about all of that. Did I speak Spanish? he asked me.

"No.

"Did I speak French?

"A little.

"Well, what did I speak?

"My heart sank as I spoke the name of the most unlikely language for this situation—German. Both of us giggled at the ridiculousness of my answer. 'We'll figure something out,' García Márquez said. 'I'll see you in either Paris or Barcelona—your choice.'

" 'I prefer Paris,' I said.

" 'Ah, yes,' he laughed; then he added, 'This conversation is beginning to sound like a scene from a Dos Passos novel.'

"Two months later, we met at his charming modern apartment in a high-rise that towered over Paris. For nine days, we talked, argued and parried, with the nimble assistance of Patricia Newcomer, who did the translating chores from Spanish to English. Sometimes, the author's wife, Mercedes, a dark woman with a quiet manner, sat in on the sessions.

"Incidentally, our conversations about Latin-American politics occurred when El Salvador was in the headlines and before the outcome of last summer's Falklands conflict and the renewed tensions in Nicaragua. These discussions should be read within that context.

"Oddly enough, the playful black humor that is the trademark of García Márquez' writing came out only after lengthy coaxing. Gabriel García Márquez was giving an interview for posterity and, God, he was serious about it. Once, in a fruitless attempt to make him laugh, I took him a box of truffles from Paris' best chocolatier. In *One Hundred Years of Solitude,* there's a priest who levitates every time he drinks chocolate. 'Will you levitate with these?' I asked.

" 'It only works with liquid chocolate!' he said glumly. And then he tossed the chocolates to a far corner of the room.

"Nonetheless, when García Márquez goes to Stockholm to receive his Nobel, he'll receive something he will doubtless appreciate more—$157,000 in cash, great acclaim and a certified place in the history of letters. It must be a delicious journey for García Márquez, the fabulist who began his writing in Aracataca, drawing cartoons of his grandmother's occult tales, the man who writes because he wants 'to be loved more.' "

PLAYBOY: You have received numerous literary honors since the publication of *One Hundred Years of Solitude.* You've been mentioned in connection with the Nobel Prize, and John Leonard of *The New York Times* once said, "The great American novel has been written by a Latin American." In view of that, do you find it ironic that because of your problem with the U.S. State Department, you have difficulty getting a visa every time you want to visit the U.S.?

GARCÍA MÁRQUEZ: First of all, the great American novel was written by Herman Melville. As to my problem, as you politely call it, it has to do with my political thinking, which is no secret. It is unpleasant. It's as if I had a mark on my forehead, and it shouldn't be that way. I am one of the great propagandists for North American literature. I have said to audiences everywhere in the world that the North American novelists have been the giants of the century. Moreover, great cultural changes are taking place in the United States because of the influence of Latin America—and my work is part of that influence. I *should* be able to participate more freely.

PLAYBOY: Why can't you?

GARCÍA MÁRQUEZ: The whole business stems from the fact that in 1961, I worked for the Cuban news agency in New York. I wasn't even a bureau chief. From that time on, my wife and I were told that we were "ineligible for entry" when we wanted to visit the U.S. That went on until 1971, when Columbia University awarded me an honorary degree. Since then, I have had some sort of conditional visa that makes me feel insecure. It's a game established by the State Department. What is frightening is that the State Department can end the game whenever it wants to and exclude me from the United States forever. No cultured man can exist today without traveling frequently to the U.S.

PLAYBOY: Despite your visa problems and your reported leftist views, it's clear that you have a real affection for Americans and American culture.
GARCÍA MÁRQUEZ: Yes, the people of the United States are one of the peoples I most admire in the world. The only thing I don't understand is why a country that manages to do so many things so well cannot do better in choosing its Presidents. But we can talk about that later. I notice you haven't asked me the one question all interviewers start with.

PLAYBOY: What question is that?
GARCÍA MÁRQUEZ: You haven't asked me if I'm a Communist.

PLAYBOY: We thought we would let the readers make up their own minds. Asking someone that question has ugly connotations in America, because of the McCarthy period.
GARCÍA MÁRQUEZ: Yes, but the readers of PLAYBOY will wonder why you didn't ask it anyway.

PLAYBOY: OK. *Are* you a Communist?
GARCÍA MÁRQUEZ: Of course not. I am not and have never been. Nor have I belonged to *any* political party. Sometimes I have the impression that in the United States, there is a tendency to separate my writing from my political activities—as if they were opposites. I don't think they are. What happens is that, as an anticolonial Latin American, I take a position that annoys many interests in the United States. And so, simplistically, some people say I am an enemy of the United States. What I'd like to correct is the problems and errors in the Americas as a whole. I would think the same way if I were a North American. Indeed, if I *were* North American, I would be even more of a radical, because it would be a matter of correcting the faults in my own country.

PLAYBOY: Incidentally, why do you always use the words North America to describe the United States?

GARCÍA MÁRQUEZ: It bothers me that the people of the United States have appropriated the word America as if *they* were the only Americans. America, in fact, begins at the South Pole and ends at the North Pole. When residents of the United States call themselves Americans, they are telling us they think of themselves as the *only* Americans. Actually, those people are residents of a country without a name.

PLAYBOY: What do you mean?

GARCÍA MÁRQUEZ: No name. They should find a name, because right now they have none. We have the United States of Mexico, the United States of Brazil. But the *United States*? The United States of *what*? Now, remember, that is said with affection. As I mentioned, I love North American literature. The only academy of letters I belong to is that of the United States. Critics in the United States are those who best understand my works.

But as a Latin American, as a partisan for Latin America, I can't help but feel resentful when North Americans appropriate the word America for themselves. As I see America, it is like a boat—with a first class, a tourist class, a hold and sailors. We Latin Americans don't want to be in the hold of the boat and we don't want the North Americans to be in first class. Nor do we want to sink the first class, because if we do, the entire boat sinks. Our historical destiny—Latin America's and North America's—is to navigate this entire boat together. For another thing, Cuba is very much a part of this American ship. Sometimes I think it would be safer for the Cuban revolution if its people could get a tugboat and tow themselves elsewhere—somewhere other than 90 miles from Florida.

PLAYBOY: Since we're playing God with geography, what else can we move?

GARCÍA MÁRQUEZ: If one could do this, perhaps one could move rivers and oceans to where they are needed. Things are so unfair. In any case, it's already been done, no? Half of Mexico was taken and moved over to the United States. The United States did the same with Puerto Rico—for which we feel great nostalgia, because it is a Latin-American country. The same thing happens to many countries of Eastern Europe. I don't want to appear sectarian.

PLAYBOY: Didn't you take a bus trip through the U.S. South in 1961 as a fairly broke reporter?
GARCÍA MÁRQUEZ: Yes. I had recently read Faulkner and greatly admired him, so I made this trip by—what do you call it?—Greyhound, from New York down to the Mexican border. I traveled by bus because I wanted to see the country from the small, dusty roads that Faulkner described—and also because I had almost no money.

PLAYBOY: How did the region look?
GARCÍA MÁRQUEZ: I saw a world very similar to my home town of Aracataca in Colombia. As a company town built by United Fruit, Aracataca had the same wooden shacks with roofs made of zinc and tin. In Faulkner's country, I remember seeing the small stores along the roadway with people seated out front with their feet up on railings. There was the same kind of poverty contrasting with great wealth. In some ways, it seemed to me that Faulkner was also a writer of the Caribbean, because of the great influence the area has had on the Gulf of Mexico and on Mississippi.

PLAYBOY: We'll be talking extensively about your work, but let's pursue this question of literature and politics a bit further. You *are* fascinated by the relationship between the two subjects, aren't you?
GARCÍA MÁRQUEZ: I'm fascinated by the relationship between literature and *journalism*. I began my career as a journalist in Colombia, and a reporter is something I've never stopped being. When I'm not working on fiction, I'm running around the world, practicing my craft as a reporter. It will interest you to know that I do every kind of journalism—except interviews. With interviews, the interviewer has to work *much* too hard. But to return to your question, what has happened is that I have, as a result of the success of my novels, this huge reputation—and, yes, I am a Latin American, and considering all that is going on in Latin America, it would be a crime not to be interested in politics. If I came from a part of the world that didn't have Latin America's enormous political, economic and social problems, I could ignore politics and live, very happily, on a Greek island. However, I am, indeed, Latin American, and so the only choice I have is to be an emergency politician.

PLAYBOY: What does an emergency politician do?
GARCÍA MÁRQUEZ: In my case, first of all, I am not a militant for any party. Nor am I involved in the politics of a single country. I feel myself *Latin American* in the broadest sense. As such, I use my international reputation to conduct what might be called extraofficial diplomacy. I have friends, at high levels, in governments in Europe and Latin America.

PLAYBOY: Let's talk about one of your famous friendships—with Fidel Castro. It *is* a close friendship, isn't it?
GARCÍA MÁRQUEZ: We are good friends. Ours is an intellectual friendship. It may not be widely known that Fidel is a very cultured man. When we're together, we talk a great deal about literature. Fidel is a fantastic reader. As a matter of fact, the friendship really began after he'd read *One Hundred Years of Solitude*, which he liked very much.

PLAYBOY: Castro once said of you, "García Márquez is the most powerful man in Latin America." If that is an accurate quote, how do you think he meant it?
GARCÍA MÁRQUEZ: The phrasing doesn't sound like Fidel, but if he did say that, I'm sure he was referring to me as a writer, not as a political man.

PLAYBOY: Are you saying you don't talk about politics with him?
GARCÍA MÁRQUEZ: Well, it would be hard not to. But we don't really talk about politics *that* much. Most people find it difficult to believe that my friendship with Fidel Castro is almost totally based on our mutual interest in literature. Very few of our conversations concern the fate of the world. More often, we talk about what good books we've read.

Whenever I go to Cuba, I always take Fidel a stack of books. Usually, upon my arrival in the country, I leave them with one of Fidel's aides and then I go about my business. A few weeks later, when Fidel and I finally get a chance to talk, he's read everything and there are 1000 things to talk about. Once, I remember, I left him a copy of Bram Stoker's *Dracula*, which is really an absolutely fantastic book but one that intellectuals consider unworthy. Well, I took that book to Fidel one night—about two in the morning. One always gets to see Fidel at that kind of odd hour. That's what his life is like. That night, he had many important state documents to read and consider. Well, we talked for about an hour, and then we met again the next day at noon.

"Gabriel, you screwed me!" he said. "That book; I couldn't get a minute's sleep." He'd read *Dracula* from four in the morning till 11 A.M. And *this* is an aspect of his personality that few people know, and it is because of this that the friendship has developed. Contrary to what is said about us, we have never conspired on political subjects. Fidel thinks writers are meant to write their books and not to conspire.

PLAYBOY: But people think you do, as you say, conspire with Castro, don't they?

GARCÍA MÁRQUEZ: There are some in the government of Colombia, my own country, who think that. But let me really tell you about my friendship with Fidel, because perhaps this is the place to clear up the misunderstandings about it. I'll begin with a story I think is typical.

In 1976 and 1977, I went to Angola to do a series of articles that was published in *The Washington Post*. On the way back from Angola, I stopped in Cuba. Well, in Havana, reporters from Reuters and Agence France Presse asked me for an interview. I told them that I had a seven o'clock plane to Mexico but that they should come by the hotel at four. Around 3:30, Fidel unexpectedly arrived for a talk. So when the journalists dropped by at four, the hotel staff told them they couldn't see me because I was with Fidel.

I told Fidel my impressions of Angola for ten minutes, and then, I don't know why—perhaps because we were discussing the food shortages in Angola—he asked me if I'd eaten poorly there. "It wasn't bad for me," I said. "I managed to find a tin of caviar somehow and I was very happy." So Fidel asked if I liked caviar. And I said, "Very much." He told me that that was a purely cultural, intellectual prejudice and that he didn't think caviar was such an exquisite dish. Well, one thing led to another, and we continued talking for hours about food—lobsters, fish, fish recipes. The man knows *everything* there is to know about seafood. So when it came time for me to leave for my plane, he said, "I'll take you to the airport." At the airport, Fidel and I sat in the VIP lounge and talked more about fish—while the plane was held up.

PLAYBOY: A VIP lounge at Havana's airport? Doesn't sound very socialist.

GARCÍA MÁRQUEZ: It *is* socialist. There are *two* VIP lounges, as a matter of fact. Anyway, the reporters caught up with us at the airport and apparently said to each other, "If García Márquez has just come from Angola and Fidel has taken him to the airport, then they must be having an extremely important conversation!" So, when I left, the journalists came to the door of the plane and said, "Don't leave without telling us: What were you talking to Fidel about for all these hours?" I said, "I'd better not answer you. If I told you the truth, you'd never believe me."

PLAYBOY: How do you go about maintaining a personal relationship with someone like Castro?
GARCÍA MÁRQUEZ: It's difficult, obviously, because it is a friendship with limitations. Fidel is a man with few personal friends. It's inevitable, of course, given his job and his power. Once, someone asked him—in front of me—if he didn't feel the solitude of power. He said no. However, I wonder if those who have power really feel how alone they are.

PLAYBOY: One of the rumors about you is that you give Castro a first look at your novels—before you submit them to your publishers. True?
GARCÍA MÁRQUEZ: Well, with my most recent book, *Chronicle of a Death Foretold*, I sent him the manuscript, yes.

PLAYBOY: Did he like it?
GARCÍA MÁRQUEZ: Fidel? Yes! The reason I showed it to him is because he is a very good reader with a really astonishing capacity for concentration— and also because he's so careful. In many of the books he reads, he quickly finds contradictions from one page to another. *Chronicle of a Death Foretold* is structured as carefully as clockwork. If there had been an error in the works, a contradiction, it would have been very serious. So, knowing about Fidel's quick eye, I showed him the original manuscript hoping he might catch any contradictions.

PLAYBOY: So you use the president of Cuba as a literary muse?
GARCÍA MÁRQUEZ: No, as a good first reader.

PLAYBOY: Knowing Castro as you do, do you have any insight into what the United States might do—or might have done—to change its relations with Cuba?
GARCÍA MÁRQUEZ: Yes. I am absolutely convinced that in Jimmy Carter's plans for a second term was a solution for the problem of Cuban—U.S. relations. He would have lifted the blockade, restored normal relations, ended the

harassment of Cuba by counterrevolutionary groups. Reagan, the instant he got into office, did the opposite. I'm sure that Carter would have solved the problem of those hostilities in the same manner John Kennedy wanted to when they killed him. Without a doubt, Kennedy was seeking a solution for Cuba.

PLAYBOY: Why, in your opinion, have so many American Presidents—Kennedy included—had such an obsession with Cuba?
GARCÍA MÁRQUEZ: For two reasons. The first is that Cuba, until the revolution, was practically a part of the United States. It was completely, completely United States territory. It was an incredible loss for the North American financial interests that controlled the country when the Cuban revolution proved a true revolution—both national and social. And that's the second reason for this obsession. Before Cuba, all revolutions in Latin America offered the possibility of sooner or later falling under the control of the United States. Cuba changed Latin-American history.

PLAYBOY: Perhaps, but it also merely switched its dependency from the United States to the Soviet Union.
GARCÍA MÁRQUEZ: A lot of that was artificial and caused by the U.S. economic blockade. The Cubans were very lucky that the Soviet Union provided aid when it did, because the United States was trying to starve them to death. But that doesn't mean that the situation isn't artificial. It is not possible for a country like Cuba to have all its energy sources 14,000 kilometers away indefinitely—an oil supertanker arrives there every 32 hours. Well, that has to change. It could change if the United States recognized that the Cubans are entitled to their own revolution in their own style—that they're entitled to it.

What many in North America don't realize is that Cuba has great affection for the people of the United States. If the blockade ended, there would be good relations. In the United States, for instance, one hears a lot of propaganda regarding Soviet cultural influence on Cuba. I believe the cultural influence of the United States on Cuba is quite a bit stronger. I remember, one night, sitting in a bar in Havana with a European journalist, and he was talking about the incredible Soviet domination of Cuba while a man played music on the piano in the bar. At the end of the two-hour conversation, I said to the journalist, "Did you notice the music the man at the piano has been playing?" Curiously, he hadn't played a single Soviet tune—it was all North American music. I wish Americans realized that kind of thing.

PLAYBOY: For three years, you were writing a nonfiction book about Cuba. Rumor has it that you've decided to withhold publication of the book. Why?

GARCÍA MÁRQUEZ: It's a long story. I've been working on that book for many years. Each time I go to Cuba, I find that my previous work has become outdated. Reality moves very fast in Cuba. Finally, I decided to cease work on the book and wait for the Cuban situation to become normal before I complete and publish it.

PLAYBOY: You're quoted in the May 22, 1980, *New York Times* as telling a reporter that you'd decided not to publish the work because it was too critical of Cuba.

GARCÍA MÁRQUEZ: All right. What I wrote is a very harsh, very *frank* book. It would be very easy for someone to quote out of context sentences that seem against Cuba. I don't want that to happen. But that's not my reason for withholding the book; I'm waiting for an event—perhaps the lifting of the U.S. blockade—before finishing it.

PLAYBOY: Another friend in a high place is France's president. François Mitterrand. Is it true that you serve as an unofficial advisor for him on Latin-American affairs?

GARCÍA MÁRQUEZ: Did you use the word advisor? No. President Mitterrand doesn't need advice on Latin America. Sometimes he needs information. Then we talk.

PLAYBOY: Paris had a confrontation some time back with Washington when it decided to send military aid to the left-wing *Sandinista* regime in Nicaragua. Is that the sort of thing you talk about?

GARCÍA MÁRQUEZ: The decision to sell them the arms? No. Discussions on that matter, apparently, were very, very secret. But in the case of the commercial and economic help the Nicaraguans were seeking, that I knew about. The people now in power in Nicaragua, they're good friends. We worked together during the years they were fighting the Somoza regime. If you want to know what I told President Mitterrand about Nicaragua and, indeed, about the entire Central American situation, I'll be glad to repeat what I said.

PLAYBOY: Please do.

GARCÍA MÁRQUEZ: It's my view that the big problem in Latin America, in Central America in particular, is that the Reagan Administration interprets everything as a result of Soviet-American dynamics. Which is ridiculous. And also unrealistic. The Reagan Administration sees any nonconformity by the people of Latin America not as the end product of the miserable conditions in those countries but as some kind of Soviet operation. In believing that, the Reagan Administration is creating a self-fulfilling prophecy—just as Kennedy did with Cuba in the early Sixties. I happen to know the *Sandinistas* very well, and I *know* they are making great efforts to work out their own system—independent of any world power. Unfortunately, the Nicaraguans are now facing all kinds of internal conspiracies and raids from the old Somoza forces operating out of Honduras and attempts to destabilize the government by elements funded by the United States. At the same time, the Nicaraguans have a desperate need for funds for food, development and self-defense. If the West refuses them that, they will be forced to seek it from the only government that will give it to them—the Soviet Union.

PLAYBOY: How do you see the situation in El Salvador? Do you think Reagan sees it purely as evidence of more Soviet activity?

GARCÍA MÁRQUEZ: I think what the United States Government wants in Central America are governments it can control. Fortunately—or, depending on what you believe, unfortunately—the U.S. can't get that without war. It's hard to know what Reagan's motives are. He must know that the case he makes—that El Salvador is the victim of a Soviet conspiracy—can't be true. If he doesn't know that, we're in a very dangerous situation, because it means that the President of the United States is completely misinformed. No, I prefer to think that Reagan and his advisors are playing some political game.

PLAYBOY: Do you believe that the Soviet Union is expansionistic?

GARCÍA MÁRQUEZ: I believe that the Soviet Union will take advantage of situations—especially when the United States refuses to support the nonconformist side. But to get back to El Salvador, it's a very dangerous situation. When you contemplate possible scenarios, you think that the world might be coming to a very great conflagration. First of all, we're not talking about a war in El Salvador alone. If the United States intervened there as it did in Vietnam, the war would soon spill over to all of Central America—perhaps all of Latin America. Yes, the United States might go into Central America militarily, because that is a weak place. Then, as a next step, the U.S. might create a Naval blockade to prevent the Cubans from helping the Central Americans. While I don't think that Cuba would do anything as preposterous as provoke a war with the United States, it certainly would defend itself against a North American invasion—which would also be a possibility.

PLAYBOY: You are obviously negative about Reagan's foreign policy, but do you think it's very different from that of his predecessor?

GARCÍA MÁRQUEZ: Very different. When it came to Latin America, Carter was extremely well informed, and during the last few years of his office, he was greatly influenced by the late General Omar Torrijos, the former leader of Panama. Torrijos was one of my closest friends, and I know of many of the things that were said between them. I know, for instance, that Carter and Torrijos together were trying to work out a negotiated political solution for the problems of El Salvador. Carter's policy on signing the Panama Canal treaties was a major step in improving relations between the United States and Latin America. The treaties, for which he fought hard, proved to be the most important of all Carter's international policies. When he signed them, he showed that the United States was beginning to deal with Latin America in a fair way. And, also, Carter's human-rights policies were often commendable. I admit that when he was in power, I thought his human-rights campaign was a façade, window dressing. However, with the advent of Reagan, I've changed my mind.

Under Carter, for purely psychological reasons, the Latin-American dictators felt watched, uncertain. In the United States, the power structure has never been monolithic. So, during Carter's term of office, you had the Pentagon and the CIA telling the dictators not to worry. You also had the State Department, at the same time, telling them that they had to respect the human rights of their citizens. The double message made the dictators feel insecure. As a result, those of us who are involved in human-rights work were able to rescue many people. However, since Reagan's election, you have Jeane Kirkpatrick running off to Chile and telling Augusto Pinochet that his is the kind of "authoritarian democracy" Latin America needs. Since her visit, it's impossible to get *one prisoner* out of Pinochet's jails! Nor can we get answers from the Argentine government about the 15,000 Argentine citizens who've disappeared. Carter took away support from the dictators to the greatest possible extent; Reagan gives them more support than should be possible.

PLAYBOY: You mentioned your friendship with Torrijos, who died in a plane crash in 1981. Is it true that you've developed an ulcer since his death?
GARCÍA MÁRQUEZ: Who told you about that?

PLAYBOY: It's just a report we heard. Why does the question upset you?
GARCÍA MÁRQUEZ: Because it's impossible for me to have any privacy anymore. Absolutely *nothing* is private!

PLAYBOY: Well, *did* Torrijos' death cause you to get an ulcer?
GARCÍA MÁRQUEZ: Yes and no. I have a chronic problem in my duodenum that is affected by stress. Some years ago, the ulcer hemorrhaged, but it was fine for the longest time. But then, when Torrijos died, I was terribly upset. He was a dear friend of mine. No, he was *more* than that. I considered myself one of his closest friends. Aside from that, he was an extremely important man for Latin America. Moreover, I barely missed joining him on the fatal flight. As you can well imagine, all that taken together caused my ulcer to hemorrhage.

PLAYBOY: You almost took the fatal flight?
GARCÍA MÁRQUEZ: Yes. Several days before the crash, it struck me that I hadn't seen Torrijos in the longest time. That bothered me. Thinking it was time to talk and catch up with things, I called him and ended up joining him on Contadora Island. We stayed, in fact, in the house where the shah had lived.

PLAYBOY: The house the shah hated so much?
GARCÍA MÁRQUEZ: Yes. I'd never seen Torrijos in a better mood. He was working a lot on the problems of El Salvador. He was convinced that a negotiated political solution was possible and that the only obstacle was that the United States might not cooperate. Carter, he said, would have accepted a negotiated settlement, but things were different with Reagan. So, after spending some time at Contadora, we flew to Panama City. We spent some time together, and then he left for an unknown place and left word that a plane would be sent shortly for me to join him. Another day passed, he was still

gone and I decided to go back to Mexico. I left a message for him saying I'd come back another time and we could finish our conversation. Two days later, he was killed in the crash. Now, if I hadn't gone back to Mexico, I would have been on that plane, too—Torrijos had very specifically invited me on that trip.

PLAYBOY: You don't think the crash was anything but an accident, do you?
GARCÍA MÁRQUEZ: There is as much probability for it to have been an accident as not. But I would like to say I have many doubts.

PLAYBOY: Torrijos may have been a friend of yours, but in the American press, he was often described as a military strong man, which is a code phrase for military dictator. There are some who think it odd for the author of *The Autumn* of the *Patriarch* and a military strong man to be best friends.
GARCÍA MÁRQUEZ: Well, a great many things are said in the U.S. press— some good, some bad, some right, some wrong. In the case of General Torrijos, he was one of Latin America's greatest nationalist leaders. His place in Latin-American history will be very high. Torrijos was, above everything, his own man. No one could ever accuse him, unlike so many others, of being a tool for North American interests. He had made the recovery of the canal the most important thing in his life, and his success with it will make him a major figure in Latin-American history. People loved him. After he died, his funeral and the emotion it caused in Panama showed that he was even more loved than he himself had imagined. I'm sure that those in North America who called him a dictator had to reconsider when they saw the enormous public outcry over his death.

PLAYBOY: You are surely aware that there is a feeling among some Americans and Europeans that Latin-American politics are hopeless and a certain brutality will always prevail in your political affairs.
GARCÍA MÁRQUEZ: Yes, it is a notion I encountered when I first traveled to Europe in the Fifties and when I was asked, "How can you live in such savage countries as exist in South America, where people kill one another for political reasons?"

PLAYBOY: And how did it make you feel?
GARCÍA MÁRQUEZ: Furious. To some extent, it is an unfair analysis. Our countries are only 170 years old; European countries are much older than

that and have gone through far more atrocious episodes than what we in Latin America are going through. That we should seem savage to them now! We have never had as barbarian a revolution as the French Revolution! The Swiss—cheese makers who consider themselves great pacifists—were Europe's bloodiest mercenaries in the Middle Ages! Europeans had to go through long periods of bloodshed and violence to become what they are today. When we are as old as the European countries, we'll be much more advanced than Europe is now, because we will have both our experience and theirs to draw upon.

PLAYBOY: You haven't lived in Colombia regularly since 1955. Why? Is it that writers simply never can go home again?

GARCÍA MÁRQUEZ: No, no, no. That hasn't happened by any great design. It's more by a series of accidents in my life. Yes, it's true that I now live half the year in Mexico and the other half in Europe. This began in 1955, when I left Colombia during the dictatorship of [Gustavo] Rojas Pinilla. When I left, it was to work in Europe as a journalist. But then Rojas Pinilla closed down my newspaper, and I found myself stranded in Paris—where I stayed for three years. After that time, I returned to South America and married Mercedes, and we moved to Venezuela, where I worked as a journalist. Then, after the triumph of the Cuban revolution, I worked for the Cuban news agency Prensa Latina in New York. Later, the family lived in Mexico, where I worked on movie scripts and, eventually, on *One Hundred Years of Solitude*. Well, one thing led to another, and I just never found myself returning to Colombia for more than a few months. After the success of *One Hundred Years of Solitude*, I had the resources to live anywhere in the world I wanted. But then Colombia became a problem for me. In Colombia, I am national property, national patrimony. All Colombians act accordingly. I have not one ounce of privacy. Nevertheless, until that recent mishap I had, I returned to Colombia periodically—for a few months, for a year, to live.

PLAYBOY: What "recent mishap"?

GARCÍA MÁRQUEZ: Well, the Colombian government—like several other governments—refuses to believe that I talk with Fidel Castro only about fish and sea-food. So, when I was in Colombia in 1981, there was a very unpleasant incident. I had just seen Fidel in Cuba two or three weeks earlier. One day, while I was in Colombia, a left-wing guerrilla group, M-19, staged a

landing in the southern part of the country. After the guerrillas were captured, the government tried to get them to declare that *I* had coordinated the
landing with Fidel Castro. *Me, personally!* Fortunately, I have many friends in
Bogotá, and whenever anything is said in front of more than three people,
one of them tells me. Three sources told me of attempts being made to link
me to M-19. There was, apparently, a dinner at the presidential palace, where,
in the presence of the president and the top military chiefs, my alleged
involvement with that group was discussed. The guerrillas, meanwhile, were
being held, tortured and told to sign confessions implicating me.

Well, when I heard that, I was alarmed, to say the least. My sources told me
not to worry—the government wouldn't dare touch me, because I was too
important. But it seemed to me that it might like to make an example out of
me to show that it had no respect for *anyone.* What I did was go immediately
to the Mexican embassy and ask for diplomatic protection in order to leave
Colombia.

Now, that caused a great scandal for the Colombian government. It offi-
cially stated there was nothing against me and that I was just probably trying
to get publicity for my new book. There has since been a trial of the guerrillas, and several of them said they were tortured and asked to sign those confessions. One did sign. What I've done, as a result, is sue the Colombian
military for abuse of authority. It's a little difficult for me to talk about this,
because by the time this interview appears, the political situation in
Colombia may well be completely changed.

PLAYBOY: When you had to flee Colombia, were you frightened? Death
squads, after all, seem to have become a major South American institution.
GARCÍA MÁRQUEZ: Not at all. The government just wanted to make a gesture at my expense—it was nothing more than that. If it wanted to kill me, it
could have just done it on any street corner. No, what it wanted was something different. The Reagan Administration and its allies in Latin America
would like to revert to the situation of the early Sixties when Cuba was completely isolated. If the government could prove that a personal friend of Fidel's
had coordinated a guerrilla landing, then it could justify breaking diplomatic
relations with Cuba. Which is what it did, anyway, after that incident.

PLAYBOY: You seem pretty sure the Reagan Administration is out to
bludgeon the Latin-American left wing. If a left-wing president were elected in,

say, Colombia, as Salvador Allende was elected in Chile in 1970, do you think the present Administration would cause his overthrow?

GARCÍA MÁRQUEZ: I'm absolutely certain that would happen. Chile all over again, yes. Carter wouldn't have done such a thing, but Reagan wouldn't hesitate. However, that isn't likely to happen. Internal conditions in Colombia are different from those in Chile in the early Seventies.

PLAYBOY: Let's move on to a discussion of your work. Some admirers of *One Hundred Years of Solitude* have said that in telling the saga of the Buendía family, you've managed to tell the complete history of Latin America. Are the critics exaggerating?

GARCÍA MÁRQUEZ: *One Hundred Years of Solitude* is not a history of Latin America, it is a *metaphor* for Latin America.

PLAYBOY: In one of your short stories, *The Incredible and Sad Tale of Innocent Eréndira and Her Heartless Grandmother*, a young prostitute tells her lover, "What I like about you is the serious way you make up nonsense." Is that Gabriel García Márquez talking about himself?

GARCÍA MÁRQUEZ: Yes, that is an absolutely autobiographical statement. It is not only a definition of my work, it is a definition of my *character*. I detest solemnness, and I am capable of saying the most atrocious things, the most fantastic things, with a completely straight face. This is a talent I inherited from my grandmother—my mother's mother—*Doña* Tranquilina. She was a fabulous storyteller who told wild tales of the supernatural with a most solemn expression on her face. As I was growing up. I often wondered whether or not her stories were truthful. Usually, I tended to believe her because of her serious, deadpan facial expression. Now, as a writer. I do the same thing. I say extraordinary things in a serious tone. It's possible to get away with *anything* as long as you make it believable. That is something my grandmother taught me.

PLAYBOY: For our readers who may need a summary, *One Hundred Years of Solitude* traces six generations of the Buendía family in the mythical village of Macondo. It begins with the founding of the village in a time when "the world was so recent that many things lacked names," and ends with the last of the Buendías, an infant born with the tail of a pig, being carried away by ants as the Buendía line is extinguished. Between all that, Macondo experiences the "banana fever," the "insomnia plague," 32 civil wars, revolution, counterrevolution, strikes and a rain that lasts nearly five years. You describe these events in a style called magic realism, in which the fantastical and mythical are blended with the everyday—a priest who levitates when he drinks chocolate, for instance—so let's begin by asking you how much of your fiction has a basis in real life.

GARCÍA MÁRQUEZ: Every single line in *One Hundred Years of Solitude*, in all my books, has a starting point in reality. I provide a magnifying glass so readers can understand reality better. Let me give you an example. In the *Eréndira* story, again, I have the character Ulises make glass change color every time he touches it. Now, that can't be true. But so much has already been said about love that I had to find a new way of saying that this boy is in love. So I have the colors of the glass change, and I have his mother say, "Those things happen only because of love. . . . Who is it?" Mine is just another way of saying the same thing that has always been said about love: how it upsets life, how it upsets everything.

PLAYBOY: Over the past 20 years, we've seen an explosion of magic-realist novels from Latin America. What is it about the Latin world that encourages writers to work in this wild mixture of the real and the surreal?

GARCÍA MÁRQUEZ: Clearly, the Latin-American environment is marvelous. Particularly the Caribbean. I happen to come from the Caribbean part of Colombia, which is a fantastic place—completely different from the Andean part, the highlands. During the colonial period of Colombian history, all the people who considered themselves respectable went to the interior—to Bogotá. On the coast, all that were left were bandits—bandits in the good sense—and dancers, adventurers, people full of gaiety. The coastal people were descendants of pirates and smugglers, with a mixture of black slaves. To grow up in such an environment is to have fantastic resources for poetry. Also, in the Caribbean, we are capable of believing anything, because we have the influences of all those different cultures, mixed in with Catholicism and our own local beliefs. I think that gives us an open-mindedness to look beyond apparent reality. As a child growing up in the Caribbean village of Aracataca, I heard wonderful stories of people who were able to move chairs by simply looking at them. There was a man in Aracataca who had the facility for deworming cows—for healing their infections—by standing in front of the beasts. He would stand in front of the cow and the worms would start coming out of the head of the cow. Now, it's true that I once saw that.

PLAYBOY: How do you explain it?

GARCÍA MÁRQUEZ: Ah, if I could explain it, I wouldn't be trying to tell you about it now. That seemed marvelous to me as a child, and it still does.

PLAYBOY: Let's talk about the real-life prototypes of *One Hundred Years of Solitude*. Was your grandmother the prototype for Úrsula Buendía, the matriarch of the novel?

GARCÍA MÁRQUEZ: Well, she is and she isn't. They are both bakers by trade, and they are both superstitious. But all my characters are composites of people I've known. I take parts of an individual's personality and I paste them together with pieces of other people. As for my grandmother, I lived with her in my grandfather's house from the time I was born until I was eight. My grandfather's house was a house of many women—my grandmother, my grandfather's sister, others. My grandfather and I were the only two males there. The women were incredibly superstitious, crazy—crazy in the sense that they were people with imagination. *Doña* Tranquilina, my grandmother, had the capacity for saying the most extraordinary things without any tact. I'm not sure what her origins were, but she was probably Galician. Galicia is a very strange region of Spain—extremely mystical and tied to the occult. With my grandmother, every natural event had a supernatural interpretation. If a butterfly flew in the window, she'd declare, "A letter is coming today." If milk boiled over on the stove, she'd say, "We must be careful—someone in the family is sick." When I was a child, my grandmother would wake me in the night and tell me horrible stories of people who, for some reason, had a presentiment of their death, of the dead who appeared, of the dead who didn't appear. Often, our house in Aracataca, our huge house, seemed as if it were haunted. All those early experiences have somehow found themselves in my literature.

PLAYBOY: Can you give us an example?

GARCÍA MÁRQUEZ: Certainly. In *One Hundred Years of Solitude*, a group of yellow butterflies always precedes the appearance of Mauricio Babilonia, the lover of Meme Buendía. The realistic base of this story is that there was an electrician who came to our house in Aracataca to fix things. Once, after his visit, my grandmother found a butterfly—which she quickly hit with a dish towel—in the kitchen. "Every time that man comes into this house, we get butterflies," she declared. My grandmother was always saying things like that. She also played the lottery a lot, though she never won. Never.

PLAYBOY: Did you mean it to be ironic that her name was *Doña* Tranquilina?
GARCÍA MÁRQUEZ: For a crazy woman, she was *very* tranquil. Her restlessness was only mental. She was never in any great physical hurry.

Now, my grandfather Nicolás Márquez was the opposite. He was the only person I communicated with in the house. The world of the women—it was so fantastic that it escaped me. But my grandfather brought me back to reality by telling me stories about tangible things—items from the newspapers, war stories from the time he was a colonel on the liberal side in the Colombian civil wars. Whenever my grandmother or my aunts said something particularly wild, he'd say, "Don't listen to that. Those are women's beliefs." My grandfather also had a great practical sense—which I think I inherited from him. Among my friends, it is often said that I'm one of the few writers they know who have a practical sense. It is that practical sense that I use for politics. And also for everyday life. I have a great sense of safety. I am very worried about preventing accidents—I take precautions so that they don't happen. I prefer stairs to elevators. I prefer *anything* to planes. That practical sensibility is not typical of poets. And if, someday, I become a patriarch, a patriarch in the political sense, it will be for that reason—not because I have real power. My friends always consult me on practical matters, and that is something I got from my grandfather.

PLAYBOY: You say your grandfather told you stories of his war experiences. Those stories must have been as disconcerting as your grandmother's tales of the supernatural.
GARCÍA MÁRQUEZ: Actually, no. When he spoke of the civil wars, he spoke of them as almost pleasant experiences—sort of youthful adventures with guns. Nothing like the wars of today. Oh, certainly, the civil wars had many terrible battles and many, many deaths. But during that time, my grandfather also had a great many love affairs and he also fathered a great many children.

PLAYBOY: The central character in *One Hundred Years of Solitude*, Colonel Aureliano Buendía, the son of José Arcadio Buendía, fathers 17 illegitimate children with 17 women during 32 civil wars. Did Nicolás Márquez have 17, too?
GARCÍA MÁRQUEZ: Who knows? The exact number will never be known. As late as 15 years ago, I met people for the first time who turned out to be

aunts. According to my mother, there were 17. She was one of the two children who came from the marriage.

PLAYBOY: So, many of your grandfather's fond memories of the Colombian
civil wars were really fond memories of all these sexual liaisons.
GARCÍA MÁRQUEZ: Well, I think he liked sex—with or without war. To my
memory, he was one of the great fornicators.

PLAYBOY: Oh?
GARCÍA MÁRQUEZ: "Fuckers," as you say in good English.

PLAYBOY: That must have irritated your grandmother.
GARCÍA MÁRQUEZ: It was curious about her. My grandmother was a very,
very jealous woman. But when she'd hear of one of those children's being
born, she reacted like Úrsula Buendía: She took it into her household. My
grandmother said that the family blood couldn't just wander out there, lost.
Anyway, she loved all those children a lot. There was a point in that house
when you couldn't tell which children came from the marriage and which
didn't. My grandmother was also a very strong woman. When my grandfather went off to the war, she didn't have any news of him for a year. She took
care of the house and the security of the family until, one night, there was a
knock on the door. In the dark, in the early hours of the morning, someone
said, "Tranquilina, if you want to see Nicolás, come to the door now." And so
she ran and opened the door and she could see these men on horseback passing, but she didn't see him. All she saw was the horses leaving town. It was a
year later before she received any further news of him.

PLAYBOY: It sounds as if Úrsula is your favorite character.
GARCÍA MÁRQUEZ: Yes. She holds the world together. That is contrary to
what I saw in real life—as a child. The women in my grandfather's household
were often quite *un*worldly. However, I believe that in most cases, women are
the practical sex. It's men who are the romantics and who go off and do all
kinds of crazy things; women know that life is hard. Úrsula is a prototype of
that kind of practical, life-sustaining woman. After Úrsula, I most like her
great-great-granddaughter Amaranta Úrsula. Of all the Buendía offspring,
she's the one who most resembles the original Úrsula—but without the older
woman's complexes and prejudices. Amaranta Úrsula is Úrsula again—but

emancipated now, with the experiences of the world, with modern ideas. However, living in the atmosphere created by Colonel Buendía—the atmosphere of the conservative triumph—she is not permitted to develop her personality. The history of Latin America is a series of such frustrations.

PLAYBOY: While your grandfather was telling you war stories, did he also tell you about the 1928 banana strike? In *One Hundred Years*, Macondo's banana workers, employees of a company that could be United Fruit, go on strike. Three thousand of them are massacred in the Macondo town square, and their bodies are shipped in boxcars to the sea. Thereafter, none of the Macondo townspeople recall the strike; the only one who remembers is a Buendía, and for him, the recollection is the source of his madness.
GARCÍA MÁRQUEZ: That episode didn't come from any storytelling. It is, more or less, based on historical reality. The reasons, the motives and the manner in which the events around the strike occurred were exactly as in the novel—though there were not 3000 dead, of course. There were very few deaths. If 100 people had been killed in 1928, it would have been catastrophic. I made the death toll 3000 because I was using certain proportions in my book. One hundred wouldn't have been noticed. I was also interested in achieving a certain imagery: I wanted the bodies to be taken away in a train, a train such as the ones that were loaded with clusters of bananas. I did research and found that to fill such a train, you'd need at least 3000 bodies. Three thousand in 1928 would have been *all* the residents of the town.

PLAYBOY: So that is how nonfiction gets transformed into art?
GARCÍA MÁRQUEZ: Let me tell you something very curious about that incident. Nobody has studied the events around the real banana strike—and now when they talk about it in the newspapers, even once in the congress, they speak about the *3000* who died! And I wonder if, with time, it will become true that 3000 were killed. That is why, in *The Autumn of the Patriarch*, there is a moment when the patriarch says, "It doesn't matter if it is not true now; it will be with time."

PLAYBOY: *One Hundred Years of Solitude* opens with this line: "Many years later, as he faced the firing squad, Colonel Aureliano Buendía was to remember that distant afternoon when his father took him to discover the ice." Did your grandfather Nicolás Márquez ever take you to discover the ice?

GARCÍA MÁRQUEZ: Well, yes. Something like that. Aracataca was a tropical town—and living there, as I did, in the days before refrigeration, I had never seen ice. One day, my grandfather took me to the company store of the United Fruit Company—Aracataca was a banana center—and he showed me a crate filled with ice-packed fish. Whatever it was that was inside the boxes was so cold that it seemed to me to be boiling. I touched the inside of the box and felt burned. "But this is boiling," I said to my grandfather. And he told me, "No, on the contrary, it is very cold." And then he gave me this substance to touch—and it was ice. From that period of my life, and from my life in general, what remain for me are flashes of memory that I hardly analyze. I prefer only the sensations they leave.

PLAYBOY: Your stories are always full of smells.
GARCÍA MÁRQUEZ: Yes. Odors. I think the evocative power of the sense of smell is the greatest of all the senses, greater than that of taste or hearing.

PLAYBOY: There is an almost erotic sense of smell in all your literature. Is that your way of dealing with sexual passion?
GARCÍA MÁRQUEZ: Yes. It's a matter of my own character.

PLAYBOY: Of all the sensuous pleasures in life, which matters most to you?
GARCÍA MÁRQUEZ: Eating.

PLAYBOY: Eating? Really? Why?
GARCÍA MÁRQUEZ: Well, it is a matter involving feelings—it is impossible to explain. But what I like most is to eat.

PLAYBOY: OK. To return to your own life history, how did you come to live with your grandparents?
GARCÍA MÁRQUEZ: It's a story that's common in the Caribbean. My parents were poor. My father worked as a telegraphist. When my father wanted to marry the daughter of Colonel Nicolás Márquez, her family opposed it; my father had a reputation for going with too many women. So, after the wedding, my father took a job in another town far from Aracataca. When my mother became pregnant with me, in a gesture of reconciliation, my grandparents said, "Come have the baby in our house." Which she gladly did. After a while, my mother returned to the village my father was working in, and so my

grandparents said, "Leave Gabriel with us to raise." The family was poor and, as I said, extended families are common in the Caribbean. Later on, when my parents returned to Aracataca, I went on living with my grandparents—where I was mostly very happy. I did that till I was eight, when my grandfather died.

PLAYBOY: Did you feel abandoned by your mother?
GARCÍA MÁRQUEZ: No, I just thought life was like that. Perhaps, in another kind of society, I might have felt abandoned. But in the Caribbean, it's perfectly natural to live with grandparents and aunts and uncles. It *is* true that for the longest time, my mother was a stranger to me. I remember one morning being told to dress up because my mother was coming for a visit. I have no memory of her before that. I remember going into a room, and there were many women sitting there and I felt disconcerted, because I didn't know which one was my mother. She made some kind of gesture that made me realize that it was she. And she wore a dress from the Twenties, really from the Twenties, with a low waistline and a straw hat. She looked like Louise Brooks. Then she embraced me and I became very frightened, because I felt I didn't love her. I'd heard one was supposed to love one's mother very much, and it seemed evil that I didn't. Later on, when my parents moved to Aracataca, I remember going to their house only when I was sick. I'd have to stay overnight, and I would be given a purgative of resin oil. It's not a pleasant memory.

PLAYBOY: Was it painful for you when your grandfather died?
GARCÍA MÁRQUEZ: No. I practically didn't realize it. Besides, as an eight-year-old, I didn't have any clear notion what death meant. Having a Catholic upbringing, I probably thought he'd gone to heaven and was very content.

PLAYBOY: We ask about his death because you've often told interviewers that nothing interesting has happened to you since you were eight.
GARCÍA MÁRQUEZ: What I mean is that after that I went to live elsewhere with my parents, and I feel that all my writing has been about the experiences of the time I spent with my grandparents.

PLAYBOY: Is your contemporary life less interesting than your childhood?
GARCÍA MÁRQUEZ: It has less mystery. I don't have a grandmother to make up marvelous things for me.

PLAYBOY: The Aracataca of your childhood must have been a marvelous place.

GARCÍA MÁRQUEZ: I think of it as a horrible boom town. It was a banana center for the United Fruit Company—a place where people came to enrich themselves as quickly as possible. But what happens in such a place is that when it suddenly turns into a crossroads for the world, it inevitably fills up with fantastic elements.

PLAYBOY: It's odd that you call Aracataca a horrible boom town. Macondo, the mythic town you created out of Aracataca, is thought to be one of the most charming villages in literature.

GARCÍA MÁRQUEZ: Well, what has happened is that Macondo is a town built with nostalgia. The virtue of nostalgia is that it eliminates all the disagreeable aspects from one's memories and leaves only the pleasant ones.

PLAYBOY: How did the idea come to you to create Macondo out of the memories of Aracataca?

GARCÍA MÁRQUEZ: Well, *One Hundred Years of Solitude* really began when I was a very young man—perhaps 20 years old. I tried to write a novel about the Buendía family titled *La Casa*: the house. The entire drama was to take place in the house—nothing outside. After writing a few chapters, I felt I was not yet ready to write a book as big as that. What I decided to do was start something easier and progressively learn how to write. Mostly, I wrote short stories. Around that time, when I was about 21, my mother asked me to take a trip with her to Aracataca—and that visit had a decisive impact on my career as a writer. You see, at that point, I was living in Barranquilla, a Caribbean city not far from Aracataca. My grandparents had both died, and my mother wanted to sell their house.

At first, I was very happy with the idea of returning to Aracataca. But when we got there, I was staggered. The town had not changed at all. I had the sensation that I had left time, that what had separated me from the town was not distance but *time*. So I walked along the streets with my mother and I realized that she was going through something similar. We walked to the pharmacy, which belonged to people who'd been close friends of the family. Behind the counter sat a lady working on a sewing machine. My mother said, "How are you, my friend?" When the woman finally recognized her, she stood up, and they embraced and cried and said absolutely nothing for more than a half hour. So I had the feeling that the whole town was dead—even those who were alive. I remembered everyone as they had been before, and now they were dead. That day, I realized that all the short stories I had written to that point were simply intellectual elaborations, nothing to do with my reality. When I returned to Barranquilla, I immediately sat down and wrote my first novel [*Leaf Storm*], which takes place in Macondo. Incidentally, on that trip, my mother and I passed a banana plantation that I had often seen as a child. There was a sign on the place; it was called Macondo.

PLAYBOY: When did *One Hundred Years* finally begin taking shape in your mind?

GARCÍA MÁRQUEZ: The trip I described took place around 1950. After that first effort, I made a second try at the novel in Mexico in 1963. I had, by then, a clearer idea of the structure but not of the tone. I didn't know yet how to tell the story so that it would be believed. So, again, I took to writing short stories. But one day, in 1965, I think, I was going to Acapulco by car. And all of a sudden—I don't know why—I had this illumination as to how to write the book. I had the tone, everything!

PLAYBOY: It came to you as a vision?

GARCÍA MÁRQUEZ: Sort of. It was as if I had read everything that was to be in it. So I returned to Mexico City and sat down for the next 18 months to write from nine in the morning till three in the afternoon. I had a family—a wife and two small sons—and I had been supporting them by working in public relations and fixing up movie scripts. All that had to cease so I could write my book. But we had no income, so I pawned our car and gave Mercedes the money. From then on, Mercedes had to be like the women in the Colombian civil wars: She had to run the household and keep life going while I campaigned.

She performed all kinds of wondrous feats. Every day, somehow, she made sure I had my cigarettes, paper, everything I needed to write. She borrowed money. She got credit from stores. When the book was finished, it turned out that we owed the butcher some 5000 pesos—which was an enormous sum. Somehow, the rumor had gotten around the neighborhood that I was writing a very important book, and all the shopkeepers wanted to collaborate. At one point, I realized that Mercedes could not go on anymore alone. I then dropped work on the novel and did a radio script. But the minute I started doing that, it gave me an unbearable migraine headache. Nothing could cure it—the doctors gave me all kinds of things.

Finally, when I went back to my novel, the pain went right away. It took 18 months for the book to be finished. But when it was done, we still had all kinds of problems. Once, toward the end of it all, the typist who had the only copies of many of the chapters of the book was hit by a bus. So the only copies of half the book went flying all over a Mexico City street. Fortunately, the bus didn't kill her, and she was able to get up and reassemble the manuscript. Finally, when it was finished, we needed 160 pesos to send it off to the publisher in Buenos Aires. Mercedes had only 80 pesos left. So I divided the manuscript in half, mailed half off and then pawned Mercedes' Mixmaster and hair drier to pay for the other half. When Mercedes heard that the last of our possessions had gone into postage, she said, "Well, now, all we need is for this novel to be bad!"

PLAYBOY: How did the book's title come to you?
GARCÍA MÁRQUEZ: That came almost when I was writing the last page. Until then, I had no idea what to call the book. I had long abandoned the title *La Casa*. When I made the decision, I made some calculations and discovered that more than 100 years of solitude had passed, but it wouldn't have sounded right to call the book *One Hundred and Forty-three Years of Solitude*. I rounded off the number. It proved to be a good decision. The book was accepted and published in 1967, then became internationally well known when it was translated into English and published in the United States in 1970.

PLAYBOY: Will *One Hundred Years of Solitude* ever be made into a movie, as rumored?
GARCÍA MÁRQUEZ: Never. Producers keep offering me enormous sums for the rights, but I refuse. The last offer, I believe, was $2,000,000. I don't want to see it turned into a movie, because I want readers to go on imagining the characters as they see them. That isn't possible in the cinema. In movies, the image is so definite that the spectator can no longer imagine the character as he wants to, only as the screen imposes it on him.

When I studied the way movies were made, I realized there are limitations in the form that do not exist in literature. I've become convinced that the novelist's work is the freest work that exists. You are totally your own master.

PLAYBOY: Like God?

GARCÍA MÁRQUEZ: Well, somewhat. The problem is that, unlike God, you can't kill characters so easily. You have to kill a character when it really dies. That is what happened to Úrsula Buendía. If you work it out, she must be 200 years old. While I was writing *One Hundred Years*. I realized frequently that she had lived too long, and I tried to have her die. However, she continued. I always needed her for something. She had to be kept until she died naturally.

PLAYBOY: There is also a rumor that there were 1000 pages of *One Hundred Years of Solitude* that you burned. True?

GARCÍA MÁRQUEZ: False. But it's curious how in all legends there are elements of truth. After I finished *One Hundred Years*, I threw out all the notes and documentation so there wouldn't be any trace of them left. That way, the critics would have to take the book on its own merits and not go looking in the original papers. Whenever I write a book, I accumulate a lot of documentation. That background material is the most intimate part of my private life. It's a little embarrassing—like being seen in your underwear.

PLAYBOY: Or having someone learn the secrets to your magic?

GARCÍA MÁRQUEZ: Sure. It's like the way magicians never tell others how they make a dove come out of a hat.

PLAYBOY: Toward the ending of *One Hundred Years of Solitude*, you wrote, "Literature was the best plaything that had ever been invented to make fun of people." Do you think that's true?

GARCÍA MÁRQUEZ: Actually, it was said by a friend of mine and I put it in the book.

PLAYBOY: Do you think it's true?

GARCÍA MÁRQUEZ: I think it's fun when you start to control your book. There isn't anything more wonderful than writing when you truly have the book in your grip. That is what I call inspiration. There is a definite state of mind that exists when one is writing that is called inspiration. But that state of mind is not a divine whisper, as the romantics thought. What it is is the perfect correspondence between you and the subject you're working on. When that happens, everything starts to flow by itself. That is the greatest joy one can have, the best moment. I am never better and my house is never better and my relations with everybody are never better than when a book is turning out well.

PLAYBOY: The last chapter of the novel is filled with lots of jokes and personal asides. You've written Mercedes in as a character and many of your friends, too. Why is that?

GARCÍA MÁRQUEZ: Because I was having fun. It was the end of my 18-month siege, and the book was advancing nicely at that point; I had the feeling nobody could stop it, that I could do anything I wanted with it, that the book was in the bag. In that state, I was so happy, especially after the early agonies, that I started to make those private jokes. There are many more jokes in that section than are apparent to the casual reader. Friends see them and they die laughing, because they know what each one refers to. That was a book that *had* to be finished with great joy—because, in another sense, it is a very sad book. Like life, no?

PLAYBOY: Yes, it is a very sad book. It seemed to say progress is impossible in Latin America: the dreariness of Latin-American political life means that social change can never happen; all things are bound to repeat themselves. It's the common political interpretation.

GARCÍA MÁRQUEZ: I know. I hear that critique a lot. Once, I had a problem with literature professors in Cuba who said, "*One Hundred Years of Solitude* is an extraordinary book, but it has the defect of not giving solutions." To me, that is dogma. My books describe *situations*. They don't have to give solutions. But with *One Hundred Years*, I did want to give the idea that Latin-American history had such an oppressive reality that it had to be changed—at all costs, at any price! In any case, *One Hundred Years of Solitude* doesn't say that progress isn't possible. It says that Latin-American society is so full of frustrations and injustices that it would dishearten anyone. That really indicates a society that *must* be changed.

PLAYBOY: We've talked extensively about *One Hundred Years of Solitude*. Does it offend you when readers act as if it is the only book you've written?

GARCÍA MÁRQUEZ: Deeply. I've often read reviews that said that *One Hundred Years* was the definitive Latin-American novel. That's ridiculous! If it were the definitive book, I wouldn't have gone on writing. Frankly, I think

The Autumn of the Patriarch is, as a literary work, much more important. It's more important as an experimental book. It was a book I couldn't complete until I had the financial security provided by *One Hundred Years of Solitude*, because it was a book that required a lot of time and money to do.

PLAYBOY: Does it bother you when people say they find *The Autumn of the Patriarch* too hard to read?
GARCÍA MÁRQUEZ: It was a difficult book for me to write! Yes, it's true that to read it, a certain literary initiation is needed. Yet I'm hoping that, in time, it will prove as easy to read as my other books. When *Ulysses* came out, it was thought unreadable. Today, children read it. If you ask me, the only shortcoming of *One Hundred Years of Solitude* is that it is too easy to read.

PLAYBOY: *The Autumn of the Patriarch* is a novel about the death of a Latin-American dictator—a popular theme, it seems, in Latin-American literature. Was there anything special in your own life that motivated it?
GARCÍA MÁRQUEZ: Well, again, the roots of this book are in the Aracataca of my childhood. In the town, as I was growing up, lived many Venezuelan exiles—this was during the time of the dictator Juan Vicente Gómez. As often happens with exiles, the dictator became a mythical character. In exile, they magnified him. Their vision of Gomez is part of what motivated the book. But there were other sources, too.

PLAYBOY: When scholars and critics have tried to make elaborate interpretations of your work, you've always put them off. Once, you said something like this: "*One Hundred Years* is not the universal book it is made out to be. It is just the story of the Buendía family, of whom it is prophesied that they shall have a son with a pig's tail; and in doing everything to avoid this, the Buendías *do* end up with a son with a pig's tail." Now, surely, you were doing a little legpulling there?
GARCÍA MÁRQUEZ: Well, that *is* the plot. But it is an exaggeration about as large as that of critics who try to find explanations and symbols where there are none. I maintain that in the entire book, there isn't a single conscious symbol.

PLAYBOY: So you're amused by your many followers who read *One Hundred Years* word for word.

GARCÍA MÁRQUEZ: No. I rather feel a sort of compassion for them. Books are not meant to be read word for word. There is an academic tendency to find not what is in a book but what is beyond the book. In other words, an autopsy.

PLAYBOY: Nonetheless, Alastair Reid, the *New Yorker* writer who is one of the great scholars of your work, claims that the real meaning of *One Hundred Years* is that "no one will ever know us. We all live alone on this earth in our own glass bubbles." Has Reid read your book correctly?

GARCÍA MÁRQUEZ: Absolutely correctly. I'm convinced that everyone has a totally secret and personal part of his personality that is never communicated or revealed. Mercedes and I, for instance, have a very good relationship— we've been together for 25 years. Yet we are both aware that we have obscure areas that neither person can enter. And we've been respectful of that, because we know there's no way to fight it. For instance, I don't know how old Mercedes is. I didn't know her age when we married, and she was very young then. When we travel, I *never* look at her passport or identity card. On airplanes, I'll fill out our landing cards and leave blank the section on hers that requires the birth date. Of course, this is a game. But it's a game that represents very well how there are impenetrable areas that none of us can ever go near. I am absolutely sure that it is impossible to know a person completely.

PLAYBOY: Is the loneliness of *One Hundred Years of Solitude* a reflection of that?

GARCÍA MÁRQUEZ: No. I think that this is something that everyone has felt. Everyone is alone anyway. Compromises and agreements of a social nature are made, but the being is alone. For example, as a writer, I communicate with a lot of people—and quite easily, too. But when I sit down to write, which is the essential moment in my life, I am completely alone. Nobody can help me. Nobody knows exactly what I want to do—and sometimes I don't even know. I can't ask for help. It's total solitude.

PLAYBOY: Is that frightening?

GARCÍA MÁRQUEZ: No. It no longer scares me, because I've shown I can defend myself alone rather well at the typewriter. But I do think that everyone, *everyone* is afraid of that. When you open your eyes in the morning and you are surrounded by reality, the first feeling is always fright.

PLAYBOY: You grew up in a part of the world where the influence of Freud and psychoanalysis was minimal. Could the kinds of phenomena Westerners call the unconscious really be the same kinds of things a magic realist might describe?
GARCÍA MÁRQUEZ: Yes. Maybe. But I never go into those areas. I like to leave the unconscious where it is. To do that has given me good results as a writer.

PLAYBOY: How do you feel when critics make a psychoanalytic interpretation of your work?
GARCÍA MÁRQUEZ: I don't have much admiration for that. Nothing I do is consciously that way. I understand that literary work, especially fiction, exists on the edge of the unconscious, but when somebody tries to explain that unconscious part of my work, I don't read it.

PLAYBOY: How about another approach: Could it be that magic realism is not so much the surreal as the everyday world seen by a more acute eye?
GARCÍA MÁRQUEZ: Well, it is true that I have a great sense of observation. But the other part of it is that I am from the Caribbean and Caribbean people are capable of believing anything. We are very much affected by the influences of so many diverse cultures—African, European, our local beliefs. That gives us an open-mindedness to look beyond apparent realities.

PLAYBOY: Do things happen to you that don't happen to other people? A mutual friend told us he believed you were telepathic.
GARCÍA MÁRQUEZ: Extraordinary things *do* happen often to me. I can imagine they happen to others. The bad thing is that none of this can be systematized. You don't know what a premonition or a telepathic phenomenon is until after it happens. That happens with almost all prophecies—prophecies are always coded. For example, I was on a train recently, traveling to Barcelona. Back home in Mexico, a girl who works in our house was expecting a baby at any moment. So on the train, as I was taking my shoe off, I had the impression that something concerning us was happening in Mexico. I said to Mercedes, "Teresa has just given birth." When we arrived in Barcelona, we telephoned and they told us the exact time when Teresa had given birth. It was more or less when I had said it was in my premonition. Visions are not precise, but they are like magic whispers. I think this happens to practically

everyone, but because of their cultural background, people don't believe it or they don't appreciate it or they don't recognize it. You really need a kind of innocence about the world to see those things.

PLAYBOY: One memorable scene in *One Hundred Years* is of a priest who levitates when he drinks hot chocolate. How did that idea come to you?
GARCÍA MÁRQUEZ: Well, there was a real priest in Aracataca who was thought to be so saintly that people said he rose off the ground whenever he raised the chalice during Mass. When I took that episode and wrote about it, it just didn't sound believable to me. If I don't believe something, neither will the reader. So I decided to see how believable it was with other vessels and liquids. Well, he drank all sorts of things and nothing worked. Finally, I had him drink Coca-Cola and that seemed to be just the thing! However, I didn't want to give Coca-Cola free advertising, so I gave him hot chocolate, which also proved believable. Truly, if he'd gone with Coca-Cola, we would have seen billboards in Latin America that said, GET OFF THE GROUND WITH COCA-COLA.

PLAYBOY: We've heard that you did one draft of *The Autumn of the Patriarch* and threw it away because it read too much like a clone of *One Hundred Years*. True?
GARCÍA MÁRQUEZ: Partly true. I tried the book three times. The first time I wrote it, I based it on a memory I had of Havana in 1959. I had been covering the trial of one of Batista's big generals. He was being tried for war crimes in a large baseball stadium. What interested me, as I watched him, were the literary possibilities in his situation. So when I sat down to write *The Autumn of the Patriarch*, I thought I could use the form of a monolog by the dictator as he sat in the middle of the stadium. However, as I began writing, the idea quickly fell apart. It wasn't real. Latin-American dictators, the great ones, all either died in bed or escaped with huge fortunes. For a second try, I decided to write the novel as if it were a fake biography—that version *did* turn out to be, stylistically, more like *One Hundred Years*. So, sadly, this version was eliminated. Honestly, I don't understand why so many people wanted *The Autumn of the Patriarch* to be like *One Hundred Years*. I suspect that if I wanted commercial success, I could go on writing *One Hundred Years* for the rest of my life. I could cheat, as they do in Hollywood: *The Return of Colonel Aureliano Buendía*. What I finally decided to go with is a structure based on multiple

monologs—which is very much the way life is under a dictatorship. There are different voices who tell the same thing in different ways.

Then, after some time. I reached another block. I personally had never lived under one of the old dictatorships. To make the novel work. I wanted to know what daily life was like in a very old dictatorship. While I was writing, there were two of interest: in Spain and in Portugal. So what Mercedes and I did was move to Franco's Spain, to Barcelona. But even in Spain, after a certain moment, I realized that something was still missing in the atmosphere of the book; things were too cold. So, again, to get the right mood, we moved. This time to the Caribbean—we'd been away a long time. When I arrived in Colombia, the press asked me, "What have you come here to do?" I said. "To try to remember what the guava fruit smells like." Mercedes and I traveled to all the Caribbean islands—not taking notes, simply living. When we returned to Barcelona, the book just streamed forth.

PLAYBOY: Your latest novel, *Chronicle of a Death Foretold*, is being published this year. Didn't we read somewhere that you said you'd never publish another novel while the Pinochet government remained in power in Chile? Pinochet is still running Chile and your book is out. What happened?
GARCÍA MÁRQUEZ: Oh, that was just something I said to the press after *The Autumn of the Patriarch* was published. I was angry. I'd worked seven years on that book, and the first thing they asked me was, "What are you doing next?" When I get asked questions like that, I invent all sorts of answers—anything to make them happy. As it happened, when I finished *The Autumn of the Patriarch*, I didn't have plans for another novel. That answer eliminated that disagreeable question from many an interview.

PLAYBOY: We were told that you often make up stories, little fictions, when you give interviews.
GARCÍA MÁRQUEZ: Who said so?

PLAYBOY: Well, you just did, for one. But that is one of the many legends going around about you—that you "improve" on the stories you tell in your interviews.
GARCÍA MÁRQUEZ: My problem is that I have great affection for journalists, and when I'm fond of a person, I may create something, the way a short story is created, to make sure he or she gets a different kind of interview.

PLAYBOY: Have you invented anything in this interview?
GARCÍA MÁRQUEZ: In which interview? In ours? Now? No! On the contrary, I have tried to refute *all* the fiction there is about me.

PLAYBOY: Good. Can we return for a moment to *Chronicle of a Death Foretold*? In that work—indeed, in almost all your books—you write with great warmth about prostitutes. Is there a particular reason for that?
GARCÍA MÁRQUEZ: Well, I have fond memories of prostitutes and I write about them for sentimental reasons.

PLAYBOY: Is the brothel the place where young Latin-American men learn about sex?
GARCÍA MÁRQUEZ: No, it's more feudal than that. Brothels cost money, and so they are places for older men. Sexual initiation actually starts with servants at home. And with cousins. And with aunts. But the prostitutes were friends to me when I was a young man. Real friends. The environment I grew up in was very repressive. It wasn't easy to have a relationship with a woman who *wasn't* a prostitute. When I went to see prostitutes, it wasn't really to make love but more to be with someone, not to be alone. The prostitutes in my books are always very human and they are very good company. They are solitary women who hate their work. With prostitutes—including some I did not go to bed with—I always had some good friendships. I could sleep with them because it was horrible to sleep alone. Or I could not. I have always said, as a joke, that I married not to eat lunch alone. Of course, Mercedes says that I'm a son of a bitch.

PLAYBOY: The women in your books are very strong. They are the ones who take care of the business of life.
GARCÍA MÁRQUEZ: It's true in my house as well. Mercedes takes care of everything. And my literary agent is also a woman. I am completely supported by women. For me, it's almost a superstition. When I know a woman is involved in something, I know it will turn out well. For me, it is very clear that women hold up the world.

PLAYBOY: The whole world—not half of it?
GARCÍA MÁRQUEZ: Women are concerned with daily reality, while men go around doing all sorts of crazy things. I find that women have a great virtue

in that they lack historical sense. They're interested in the reality of today, the security of today.

PLAYBOY: They don't go off and make 32 civil wars, like Aureliano Buendía, you mean.
GARCÍA MÁRQUEZ: No, they stay at home, run the house, bake animal candies—so that the men can go off and make wars. Another virtue women have is that they are much more loyal than men. The only thing women won't forgive is being betrayed. If, from the beginning, one sets the rules of the game, no matter what they are, women generally accept them. But what they can't stand is if the rules are broken somewhere along the way. If that happens, they can be absolutely unmerciful. On the other hand, men's major virtue is tenderness.

PLAYBOY: Tenderness?
GARCÍA MÁRQUEZ: Right. Tenderness is inherent not to women but to men. Women know that life is very hard.

PLAYBOY: If women have no historical sense, as you said, how do you explain such women as Eva Perón, Indira Gandhi and Golda Meir? Not to mention Joan of Arc?
GARCÍA MÁRQUEZ: Well, I'm speaking in general terms. You bring up fine and great exceptions.

PLAYBOY: Are you glad to see your sons growing up in a world where men and women are more at ease with one another?
GARCÍA MÁRQUEZ: Ah, this is wonderful. I'm dying of envy. Sometimes, when I tell my sons of what it was like for me when I was young, they hardly believe me. For instance, they read *Chronicle of a Death Foretold*, which is the story of an atrocious crime in which two brothers kill a man. A girl is married, and on her wedding night, her husband returns her to her parents because she is not a virgin. So the two brothers kill the man they believe deflowered her. Now, that was a totally common drama in Latin America during my time. But when my sons read it, it seems like science fiction to them.

PLAYBOY: How did you meet Mercedes?

GARCÍA MÁRQUEZ: The whole story is in *Chronicle of a Death Foretold.* We lived in the same town, Sucre, when we were young. We became engaged in 1952, when I was working for the Bogotá newspaper, *El Espectador.* Before the wedding, the paper gave me the opportunity to go to Europe as its foreign correspondent. So I had to choose between doing something I'd always wanted to do and the wedding. When I discussed this with Mercedes, she said, "It's better for you to go to Europe, because if you don't, you'll blame me for the rest of our lives." And so I went. The original plan was for me to stay only a month. However, I wasn't in Europe very long when the dictator Rojas Pinilla shut down *El Espectador,* leaving me stranded in Paris and broke. So I cashed in the return part of my airplane ticket and used the money to continue living in Europe. I stayed three years.

PLAYBOY: How did Mercedes react to that?

GARCÍA MÁRQUEZ: This is one of the mysteries of her personality that will never be clear to me—even now. She was absolutely certain I'd return. Everyone told her she was crazy, that I'd find someone new in Europe. And in Paris, I did lead a totally free life. But I knew when it was over, I'd return to her. It wasn't a matter of honor but more like natural destiny, like something that had already happened. From Paris, I wrote to Mercedes every week. And after we were married, whenever something happened that she was unhappy with, she'd say, "You can't do this, because in your letter from Paris, you said you would never do such a thing." Finally, I told her, "I want to buy back all your letters." [*Mercedes has been quietly listening to this part of the conversation*] How much did I pay for them, Mercé?

MERCEDES BARCHA: One hundred bolívars.

GARCÍA MÁRQUEZ: That was cheap.

MERCEDES BARCHA: It sure was.

PLAYBOY: What did Mercedes do with the money?

GARCÍA MÁRQUEZ: I have no idea. [*Mercedes smiles*] What *I* did was burn the letters. And now I'm truly glad I did that, because if the letters still existed, someone would be after them for publication.

PLAYBOY: A man who has many literary honors thrust on him has to make more than his share of grandiose pronouncements—and you have. Is there anything more you'd like us to know about the quiet man, the private man behind all those pronouncements?

GARCÍA MÁRQUEZ: No. I think we've missed very little. Of course, there are obscure zones in every human being that no one ever touches. But I think that readers of interviews don't want to go into those zones. They prefer to find the person as they want him to be.

PLAYBOY: Then who are you?

GARCÍA MÁRQUEZ: Me? I am the shyest man in the world. I am also the kindest man. On this I accept no argument or debate.

PLAYBOY: Well, since you are the kindest and the shyest human being on the face of the earth, what would you say your greatest weakness is?

GARCÍA MÁRQUEZ: Ah, you've asked me a question I've never been asked before! My greatest weakness? Umm. It's my heart. In the emotional-sentimental sense. If I were a woman. I would always say yes. I need to be loved a great deal. My great problem is to be loved more, and that is why I write.

PLAYBOY: It's fortunate that your writing has brought you so much love. Even people who hate your politics love your books.

GARCÍA MÁRQUEZ: Yes. But I'm insatiable. I *still* need more love.

PLAYBOY: You make it sound like being a nymphomaniac.

GARCÍA MÁRQUEZ: Well, yes—but a nymphomaniac of the heart. And now, what I want is for you to transmit to the readers in the United States this impression of me—with absolute sincerity. I'm very afraid there might be someone in the United States who doesn't love me, and I want that person to love me because of this interview.

PLAYBOY: All right. But we'll give equal time to one last grand question. What do you think the meaning of your life has been so far?

GARCÍA MÁRQUEZ: I can answer you, perhaps, by telling you what I would like to have been in life if I had not become a writer. I'd want to have been a piano player in a bar. That way, I could have made a contribution to making lovers feel even more loving toward each other. If I can achieve that much as a writer—to have people love one another more because of my books—I think that's the meaning I've wanted for my life.

Building a Compass

Gene H. Bell-Villada / 1982

From *South* (London), January 1983, pp. 22–23 and *Boston Review*, v. 12, March–April 1983, pp. 26–27. Reprinted by permission.

The following chat with García Márquez took place in his home on Calle Fuego, in the Pedregal section of Mexico City. It was June 1982. His wife Mercedes—as beautiful and as warmly engaging as rumors say—had opened the front door for me, smiled, and then pointed toward the inside driveway.

"There he is," she said. "There's García Márquez."

As I looked left, I saw *el señor* (as he is sometimes informally referred to) in his BMW, attaching a compass to the dashboard.

"The compass of Melquíades," he joshed.

Doña Mercedes (the original inspiration, incidentally, for Mercedes the mysterious pharmacist, encountered by Aureliano Babilonia during the last days of Macondo) explained that her husband often got hopelessly lost in the Mexican megalopolis, despite his twenty years' residence there. Hence the compass.

Curly-haired and compact (about 5′ 6″ or 1 m. 67 cm.), García Márquez now emerged from the car wearing blue one-piece overalls with a front zipper—his morning writing gear, as it turns out. At this point their son Gonzalo, a very Mexican twenty-year-old, showed up with a shy, taciturn girl friend.

The in-family banter grew lively. In contrast to Gonzalo's Mexican-inflected speech, the novelist's soft voice and dropped s's immediately recalled to me the Caribbean accent of the northern Colombian coast where he had been born and raised.

Even before his receiving the Nobel Prize later that year, the Hispanic press had regularly besieged García Márquez with an attention normally reserved for movie stars and football heroes. My meeting with him, consequently, was obtained only after my first having negotiated countless obstacles. I'd first arrived in Mexico City solely with the intention of chatting with local members of his circle, as part of the preliminary researches for my projected book on him. However, a friend of mine, the writer Jorge Aguilar Mora,

informed me that *el señor* had just returned from serving on the jury of the
Cannes Film Festival, and that it might be worth my while to reach the man
himself.

So my friend telephoned Alva Rojo—the wife of a well-known Mexican
painter—and gave me the receiver, whereupon I explained my business to
her. She in turn gave me the phone number of Luis Vicens, whom I called
directly, and who invited me to drop by for a visit that evening.

Mr. Vicens, an expatriate Catalan bookseller, and an elder buddy of García
Márquez from the 1950s, greeted me with his Colombian wife. We proceeded
to have a spirited conversation about the author's work and national roots,
among other topics. After about two hours, the fellow gave me a scrap of
paper and said, "Well, look, here's Gabo's phone number. Why not give him
a call?"

It would dawn on me only some days later that I was being tested, and that
for some reason I had passed the test.

Later that same evening I called the number. A female voice answered;
I stated my business, and she passed me on to Gonzalo, who listened politely
to my speech and then said, Well, Papá isn't in but could I please call back
Thursday at one o'clock?

Next day I got several busy signals before reaching the first female voice,
who seemed to remember me. She gave the phone to Gonzalo, who then
passed it on to Señora García, who in turn listened to my speech and, after
noting that her husband was out with friends, suggested I call back Saturday
morning at eight A.M.

Seventeen nervous hours later I dialed. For the next thirty minutes there
were non-stop busy signals. At first I feared that the receiver had been
intentionally kept off the hook. Eventually, however, the phone rang and I
spoke to the first female voice, then with Gonzalo, and finally with doña
Mercedes, who said García Márquez was busy writing but could see me at
1 P.M. that day, for exactly ninety minutes since he had a 2:30 date.

After all the delays and uncertainties I was almost taken aback by the
precise nature of her instructions. But indeed the interview would take place
shortly after I arrived at the scheduled hour. The author and Gonzalo soon
led me across the backyard to the novelist's office, a separate bungalow
equipped with special climatization (the author still could not take the
morning chill in Mexico City), thousands of stereo LPs, various encyclopedias and other reference books, paintings by Latin American artists,

and, on the coffee table, a Rubik's Cube. The remaining furnishings included a simple desk and chair, and a matched sofa and armchair set, where our interview was held over beers.

García Márquez asked me not to use a tape recorder, presumably out of concern that I would try to sell the conversation to the media, and so the following is based on notes that I took and then transcribed shortly thereafter. We talked about numerous subjects, including politics, literature, foreign languages, and modern classical music (he loves Stravinsky but dislikes Schoenberg). Throughout our chat, son Gonzalo would drop in to offer a second and third bottle of beer. The following is a distillation of the more pertinent aspects of our interview.

Global fame notwithstanding, García Márquez remains a gentle and unassuming, indeed an admirably balanced and normal sort of man. Throughout our conversation I found it easy to imagine him in a downtown café, sipping drinks with the TV repairman or trading stories with the tacomakers. He loves to chat; were it not for the cautious screening process set up by his friends and family, he could easily spend his entire day talking instead of writing.

Four months after our encounter, the Swedish Academy announced his Nobel Prize. One may speculate as to the additional obstacles that eventually were to become necessary in the wake of such an honor.

GB-V: How many languages has *One Hundred Years of Solitude* been translated into?
GGM: Thirty-seven at my wife's latest count.

GB-V: How did the Japanese version fare? Did readers understand it?
GGM: It caught on fast. Not only did they understand the book, they thought of me as Japanese! But then I've always been a devoted follower of Japanese literature.

GB-V: Outside of Spanish, which language has it sold best in?
GGM: It's hard to track down. The first Russian edition sold a million copies, in their foreign literature magazine. Apparently they're preparing translations into other Soviet languages, too. The Italian version has sold well, I believe. There are also pirated editions in Greek and Farsee—oh, and

in Arabic. Arab readers seem to like the book. I hear those pirated translations aren't very good, though.

GB-V: There's a very famous strike scene in *One Hundred Years of Solitude.* Was it much trouble for you to get it right?
GGM: That sequence sticks closely to the facts of the United Fruit strike of 1928, which dates from my childhood; I was born that year.[1] The only exaggeration is in the number of dead, although it does fit the proportions of the novel. So instead of hundreds dead, I upped it to thousands. But it's strange, a Colombian journalist the other day referred in passing to "the thousands who died in the 1928 strike." As my Patriarch says, it doesn't matter if it's true, because with enough time it *will* be!

GB-V: You maintain a certain lightness of tone in that scene.
GGM: The Yankees are depicted the way the local people saw them, hence the caricature with Virginia hams and blue pills. You see, some of my relatives back then had defended the Americans and blamed the strikers for "sabotaging prosperity" and all that, so this was my reply. Of course, my own view of Americans is a lot more complex, and I attempted to convey those events without any hate. United States may be our enemy, but it's a formidable adversary.

GB-V: Your *One Hundred Years of Solitude* is required reading in many history and political science courses in the U.S. There's a sense that it's the best general introduction to Latin America. How have you felt about that?
GGM: I wasn't aware of that fact in particular, but I've had some interesting experiences along those lines. René Dumont, the French economist, recently published a lengthy academic study of Latin America. Well, right there in his bibliography, listed amid all the scholarly monographs and statistical analysis, was *One Hundred Years of Solitude*! On another occasion a sociologist from Austin, Texas, came to see me because he'd grown dissatisfied with his methods, found them arid, insufficient. So he asked me what my own

---

1. There had long been some controversy as to the exact year of García Márquez's birth. Dasso Saldívar, in his magisterial biography of the author, *El viaje a la semilla*, confirms that the author was actually born a year earlier, in 1927.

method was. I told him I didn't have a method. All I do is read a lot, think a lot, and rewrite constantly. It's not a scientific thing.

GB-V: Some left-wing critics take you to task for not furnishing a more positive vision of Latin America. How do you answer them?
GGM: Yes, that happened to me in Cuba a while ago, where some critics gave *One Hundred Years of Solitude* high praise and then found fault with it for not offering a solution. I told them it's not the job of novels to furnish solutions.

GB-V: So what was your aim in *The Autumn of the Patriarch*?
GGM: I've always been interested in the figure of the Caribbean dictator, who's probably our one and only mythic personage. Where other countries have their saints, martyrs, or conquistadors, we have our dictators. I feel that the dictator is a product of ourselves, of our Caribbean culture, and in that book I tried to achieve a serene vision. I don't condemn him. Of course I portray an earlier sort of dictator, unlike the ones today, who're propped up by a technological apparatus. They're technocrats, whereas those older dictators were often anti-imperialists, like Juan Vicente Gómez, who declared war on England and Germany.

GB-V: What about the technique in that book?
GGM: Since I wanted to create a synthesis, a composite character, I had to resort to a new narrative method. A lot of people thought the book hard going, but more and more readers now find it perfectly normal. Children today can read through much of *The Autumn of the Patriarch*. I'm not equating myself with Picasso, but it's a bit like his Cubist and other techniques, which seemed forbidding at first, yet soon became just another way of putting things together.

GB-V: Did you read *The Emperor Jones*? Or *The Comedians*?
GGM: I had *The Emperor Jones* in mind, together with a lot of other stuff. For ten years I devoured material dealing with Latin American dictators, and also studies of power, such as Suetonius. And afterwards I tried to forget it all! I first read everything by O'Neill when I was in high school, though, whereas Greene taught me to evoke the heat of the tropics. It's interesting, my basic

literary background consists of Golden Age poetry and twentieth-century
U.S. fiction. But then the North American part is obvious. [*He laughs.*]

GB-V: You've said on occasions that Béla Bartók is a prime influence on your
work. Is it the way he combined folklore with classical art?
GGM: That, and his sense of structure. Bartók is one of my favorite
composers. I've learned a great deal from him. My novels are filled with
symmetries of the kind Bartók has in his String Quartets. (People think I'm a
spontaneous writer, but I plan very carefully.) Although I've no technical
knowledge of music, I can appreciate Bartók's sense of form, his architecture.
Bartók also had a profound feeling for his people, and for their music. His
iconography is amazing, too. There's a beautiful photo of Bartók out in the
field, turning the crank on a gramophone for a peasant woman to sing into
it. He worked hard, you can see.

GB-V: Where is your short novel *Innocent Eréndira* set?
GGM: It takes place on the peninsula of La Guajira, which borders with
Venezuela and juts out into the Atlantic, like this. [*He sketches a rough map of
La Guajira on a piece of paper.*]

GB-V: You're a writer with a very intimate knowledge of street life and
plebeian ways. What do you owe it to?
GGM: [*He reflects for a moment.*] It's in my origins; it's my vocation, too. It's
the life I know best and I've deliberately cultivated it.

GB-V: Those smugglers in *Innocent Eréndira*, for instance. How did you get
informed about them?
GGM: Oh, I grew up with smugglers! They were relatives of mine, uncles and
cousins, operating on the Guajira peninsula, the setting for that story. Much
of that contraband is gone today. The stuff they smuggled now gets stocked in
duty-free shops; the rest has become internationalized and Mafia-controlled.

GB-V: With fame, is it hard, keeping up with your popular roots?
GGM: It's tough, but not as much as you'd think. I can go to a local café, and
at most one person will request an autograph. What's nice is that they treat
me like one of their own, especially in hotels up in the States, where they'll
feel good just meeting a Latin American and sharing their gripes about the

U.S. But I never lose sight of the fact that I owe those experiences to the many readers of *One Hundred Years of Solitude*.

Where it does get difficult is at public events—literary cocktails, government functions, the like. The minute I walk through the door, I find myself surrounded by people who want to talk with me. My biggest struggle is leading my private life, so I'm always with old friends, who shield me from the crowds.

GB-V: How has being a journalist influenced your writing?

GGM: Journalism keeps you in contact with reality. I write a weekly syndicated column for ten newspapers and a magazine. And it helps, it's like a pitcher keeping his arm warmed up. You know, literary people have a tendency to get off on all sorts of unreality. Besides, if you stick to writing only books, you're always starting from scratch all over again.

On weekends I head out for my place in Cuernavaca and go through all kinds of magazines, clipping things from *Nouvel Observateur*, *Le Point*, and I used to read *Time* but have since shifted to *Newsweek*. [*He laughs.*]

GB-V: Can you, a Latin American leftist, really stand reading *Time*?

GGM: Well, I admire the techniques of U.S. journalism, the carefulness with facts, for example. Of course, it's all manipulated to fit a point of view, but that's another problem. There are also excellent non-Marxist leftists in the States, like the *Nation* people. I always pay a visit to my friend Victor Navasky when I'm in New York.

GB-V: You're on the U.S. Immigration blacklist. What's the story?

GGM: It's an odd situation. In the early 1960s I was New York correspondent for the Cuban press agency, Prensa Latina. Then, in 1961, I resigned over political disagreements, and left for Mexico. I was denied entry into the U.S. for ten years after that. But in 1971, Columbia University gave me an honorary doctorate, and a one-shot visa came through. Later, the Immigration people decided that if I do something that benefits the U.S., such as deliver a lecture, they'd let me in. So Frank MacShane[2] at Columbia was finding me

---

2. The director of the Creative Writing program at Columbia University in the 1970s and '80s, and author of several literary biographies.

lecture invitations. Eventually a secret pact took shape between the authorities and myself. They don't want the media making an issue over this thing, so if I show them an official document asking me to talk, they'll give me a visa.[3]

At any rate, I've never really understood why they've got me in their black book—or yellow book, to be precise. My political views are clear. They may resemble the views of many a Communist Party man—but I've never belonged to a party. As far as I know, you can't deny people entry just on the basis of their ideas.

[*Gonzalo now stepped in, said quietly "They're here," and stuck around to pick up our beer bottles and glasses. García Márquez and I rounded off a couple of other topics, and he asked if I had any more questions. I quickly searched in my notebook for an appropriate finale.*]

GB-V: And which of your books is your favorite?
GGM: It's always the latest, so right now it's *Chronicle of a Death Foretold*. Of course, there are always differences with readers, and every book is a process. I'm particularly fond of *No One Writes to the Colonel*, but then that book led me to *One Hundred Years of Solitude*.

García Márquez remained his amiable self, and as we strolled through the garden, the three of us made small talk about Mexican taxis, American leftists, life in Paris, and also Harvard College, where the author's older son Rodrigo is a senior majoring in history. At the garden gate we shook hands; Gonzalo cordially offered a ride to the nearest taxi stand, and my conversation with the great novelist ended the way it had begun—with the youngest member of the family.

3. In the 1990s, the administration of President Bill Clinton lifted the long-standing travel ban on García Márquez.

Love and Age: A Talk with García Márquez

Marlise Simons / 1985

From *The New York Times Book Review*, 7 April 1985, pp. 1, 18–19. Reprinted by permission.

Gabriel García Márquez is in the midst of a new novel, and a predictable order is imposed on his life. The 1982 Nobel Prize in Literature is behind him and so is the publication of his most recent novel, *Chronicle of a Death Foretold*. Still, his fans seek out the author of *One Hundred Years of Solitude*—the book that made him a celebrity.

His days now are like his writing—planned meticulously and carried out with carefree style. After six hours at the typewriter, he divides the remainder of the day between reading and listening to music, and friends, writers, politicians—people he calls "my critics, protectors, and co-conspirators."

At times he lives in Cartagena, on Colombia's Caribbean coast, not far from where he was born. The area remains a rich source for him, replenishing his imagination with the myth and anecdote that find their way into his writing. But he and his wife, Mercedes, always return to the highlands and Mexico City, where he writes in the privacy of a studio in his garden. This is where the shy yet gregarious writer and I talked in late February. He has said that his novel in progress has to do with aging. I asked him to discuss his approach to old people in fiction.

MS: You're writing a happy love story, as you've called it, a love affair between two very old persons.
GGM: It's the story of a love that begins when the boy and girl are very young. But it is suspended. It stays in a cocoon. It's renewed when they are in their eighties.

It began with an idea, an image I had. The point of departure for a book for me is always an image, never a concept or a plot. The first image I had for this book is that of an old couple fleeing by boat. An old couple, happy on a

141

boat, dancing on the deck. But I don't want to talk about the book yet. That will bring me bad luck.

MS: You've always said that a writer spends the rest of his life writing about his youth. Now you're inventing a period of your life that you haven't lived yet.

GGM: Yes. I'm anticipating. But in a way I've always done that since I was young. My two first books [both published in the United States as the title stories of collections] were about old people. In *Leaf Storm*, an old man no longer knows what to do and hangs himself. And *No One Writes to the Colonel* is about an old man waiting for a letter that never arrives. If I think about it, about all those characters in *One Hundred Years of Solitude*, I always seem to have observed my elders. I've never written about children.

MS: Perhaps because as a child you lived for some time with your grandparents?

GGM: Yes, that was very important. Basically my grandparents were the models for many of the people in my books because I knew how they talked, how they behaved. To make sure the characters were real, I would always use my grandfather as a reference point. But I was trying to reflect the behavior of my elders without really penetrating what was happening inside them.

I am beginning to become conscious of old age now. This book I'm writing obliges me to think six hours a day about things I had never seriously explored: old age, love and death. It is having an effect on me. You leave a lot of yourself in a book, but a book leaves you with a lot of reflections. I never thought so seriously about death until I began to try and see how it affects people in their old age. I was used to my characters never dying. They were living endlessly.

MS: Except the ones that were hanged, shot or otherwise assassinated.

GGM: Yes, through violence. But they didn't die of old age, there was no aging process. Now that I'm getting older, I'm concerned with how age affects the sentiments, which after all is the most important.

Sex, well I don't know, but I have the impression that sex does not end as long you don't want it to end. While a person does not give up sex, sex does not give up the person. What you cannot do is to stop for a long time because then it is very hard to start up again. So you always have to keep the engine running. It is something I'm dealing with in this book. I don't care what age the characters are, if they had a continuous sex life, they go on. I don't know if this is a fantasy I'm having. But at least I know that my grandfather, who died very old, was still active.

MS: Did you study old age or read how other writers have treated it?
GGM: No, I didn't work that way. I only read Simone de Beauvoir's book, *The Coming of Age.* I try to let the writing, the imagination and invention tell me the secrets of old age. I imagine that afterward, specialists and old people themselves may say that it's not like this. So it may have to be the old age of my book and not that of life.

Curiously, I heard that someone in Colombia just published a study about old age in *One Hundred Years of Solitude.* I haven't read it. I was told that it was done by a gerontologist who said that the treatment of old age was very well done. For me it was another intuition. I wrote the book when I was between thirty-eight and forty.

What I don't do is prepare myself to deal with an overall theme. I may consult on small points. For *One Hundred Years of Solitude* I didn't study the economic or social conditions of Colombia. I could have made a serious investigation about the drama of the foreign banana companies. But I asked a few questions and look what happened. I went to check how many dead there were in the banana workers' strike of 1928. It was a tremendous national scandal. It's not exactly known, but I was told about seventeen. For my book, seventeen would have been a joke. I needed enough bodies to fill a train. I wanted the train instead of being loaded with bananas to be loaded with corpses. History was against me, with seventeen dead. That would not even fill a wagon. So I put three thousand. And so not long ago, during a com-memoration of the event, someone in a speech talked about the massacre of three thousand compatriots.

So what I'm trying to say is that I don't make a study. I am not inclined to theorizing. I do not want to turn any of my experiences into theory and I also read very little literary theory. But of course I may look up some episodes someone has written or check some statistics.

MS: What did you learn from Simone de Beauvoir's book?
GGM: I was very impressed by it. It's a study, a book of reflections on old age, and it includes statistics. Nevertheless, one aspect that is not dealt with much

interests me a great deal. And that is the sex life of the aged. It is mostly dealt with statistically. What interests me is: why is there a tendency to look upon the sexual activities of the aged with aversion? I don't understand why it should be.

It is one of the points I am working out in the book. The couple are not allowed to marry when he is twenty-two and she is eighteen because they are told they are very young. And when they again consider marriage, he is then eighty-two and she is seventy-eight, they're told they can't because they're very old. As far as I'm concerned, this tendency to see the sex life of the aged as repugnant is unjust. There is no doubt that some old people who can have no sex life masturbate until their death.

My parents in some way are the model for the book—maybe not the model, but many of the experiences are theirs. My parents were married for sixty years, they had sixteen children, my mother had a child after she was forty-two. I've always been very curious to know what happened between them after they were seventy. My father died when he was eighty-four. I talked to him about this in very general terms. But you know how it is in Latin America, you don't dare ask such questions, not of one's parents or anyone else.

MS: You've said how much you've always liked being able to drop in at your parents' home every day when you're in Colombia. Now your father has just died [in December]. Do you feel his absence has changed you?
GGM: Since the age of thirteen or fourteen, I haven't lived with my parents. So I've always felt a visitor at home. And this helps me cope better with the emptiness my father left behind. My brothers and sisters who always lived at home are very disconcerted. No one had died in that family—there are the sixteen children, thirty-four grandchildren and fourteen great-grandchildren.

But the death of one's father brings the certainty of death closer. And it creates a certain haste. This haste you get not only from a father's death, you get it anyway as you age. As time is passing, you have to work faster. And above all, to start preparing for a useful old age.

MS: How do you see that?
GGM: Well, for me it's sufficient to be able to write. I can be useful until I'm a hundred years old if I can write. My subject is life and the subject gets larger the longer I live.

MS: Do you think a lot about growing old?

GGM: I'm beginning to. My main fear is the failing of the body. There will be a moment that diets or exercises won't do any good, that the body wastes away. I feel I'm reaching the age of the "never": I never felt this before, I never had this pain, I never breathed this way, I never had to go to the bathroom so many times during the night, I never woke up so early.

But the most interesting thing is what happens in one's heart. That is still a mystery. I'm very curious, as I'm writing this book, to see how the characters go on behaving. It's a true investigation. I could almost say that one writes the novel to see how it will turn out. And to be able to read it.

MS: Do you work very differently now than when you were young?

GGM: The writing process is very different. When you are young, you write almost—well, every writer is different, I'm talking about myself—almost like writing a poem. You write on impulses and inspiration. You have so much inspiration that you are not concerned with technique. You just see what comes out, without worrying much about what you are going to say and how. On the other hand, later, you know exactly what you are going to say and what you want to say. And you have a lot to tell. Even if all of your life you continue to tell about your childhood, later you are better able to interpret it, or at least interpret it in a different way.

When you are older, when the inspiration diminishes, you depend more on technique. If you don't have that, everything collapses. There is no question that you write much more slowly, with much more care, and perhaps with less inspiration. This is the problem of the professional author.

When I was twenty, I wrote a daily story for a newspaper and at times even some editorials on the same day. Then at night, when everyone left the newsroom, I would stay to write a short story or work on a novel.

There is a story called "The Night of the Curlews," one of my first. It was the time when we put out a weekly literary magazine in Barranquilla, called *La Crónica*. At one point the editor suddenly found he was left with two empty pages. So in the evening I sat down and wrote that story.

I couldn't do that today. If I had it completely worked out, I would still need at least two or three weeks to write it. Worse, not many years ago, I wrote a story of fifteen pages and bought a package of five hundred sheets of paper. When I finished the story, I had used up all five hundred to write the fifteen.

Besides, I always used to write at night and write smoking. It's a disadvantage of youth that you almost always write when you are tired. You sit down only after you've done everything you have to do to make a living. Then with time you become more professional and you organize your life.

When the time came that I no longer had to work in a newspaper and could only write, I found it very hard to sit down in the morning and write during the day. Then, as I got older, I had to stop smoking. So I had a choice, wait until I get used to not smoking, or learn to write without it right away. I tried right away and it was extremely difficult. Only then I realized that I used to stop writing not because I was so tired but because I was so intoxicated from the cigarettes. I'm much older now but I wake up feeling fresh.

Another great difference between one age and another to me is memory. I never used to write down all the ideas that occur to me while writing. I believed that if I forgot them they were not important, and the ones that really mattered were those I remembered. Now I write them all down. It makes me very anxious to know that I thought of something but I forgot, something I was going to say, that I read, where I read it, a melody I cannot recall. At a certain age, you begin forgetting names, things. It's a real cause of anguish that one has to learn to overcome. It's not easy. A lot of one's work deals with form and you can get obsessive or desperate about a detail. So now I take notes. I'll scribble a phrase, or a point I may need tomorrow. There are advantages and disadvantages in aging.

I've come to realize, though, there is one thing for which you need to be young. And that is to learn the technique of writing, the tricks of the trade. If you don't learn that when you're young, you won't when you're old.

MS: After the Nobel Prize you said that success, the prize, are a burden that makes it more difficult to write. Do you still feel that way?
GGM: It's a private joke of mine that I have been famous for a long time but nobody knew about it. No, recognition is not a burden for me. I've always had my projects and I haven't changed them. I was working on this book before the prize and I'm still writing it. But it is disturbing for one's private life. It brings many outside interferences, distractions, interruptions. There are many requests to do things, to attend events, they take a lot of time, people don't like to be refused.

Perhaps it's an excess of vanity, but I've always felt all this was going to happen. My commitment to my writing is no different, it's always been very deep. Even in journalism.

Now all my newspaper stories have been dug up in Colombia, whatever I wrote since I was eighteen. Six volumes have already been published and there are two or three to go.

Imagine the shock I got when I heard people wanted to do this. Then I realized it was going to happen anyway, sooner or later. Or they wait till I'm dead and do it then. So I figured the best thing was to have control over it. I read almost all of them and I don't have to regret anything. There are no great gaffes and no important contradictions. But I've always known that whatever you write down, it will pursue you, even after you're dead. There it is. You cannot say, I didn't write that.

MS: But fame has not created greater pressures?
GGM: You could ask me if today I'm more frightened than before when I sit down to write. All my life I've been frightened at the moment I sit down to write.

MS: Every day?
GGM: Every day. Terribly frightened.

MS: When will you finish the book you're writing now?
GGM: Someone asked me the other day how much longer I was going to be in Mexico this time. I said, not how much time, but how many pages. I have about 180 pages to go. It's a matter of three months, I think.

MS: We were talking about how from a very young age you were already writing about old people. How would you feel about doing children's stories, now that you are growing old?
GGM: I already tried writing children's stories. It didn't work. Once I wrote one and I showed it to my two sons who were very small back then. They gave it back to me. They said, "Papá, you think that children are really dumb."

"Soap Operas Are Wonderful. I've Always Wanted to Write One"

Susana Cato / 1987

From the English-language edition of *Granma* (Havana), 17 January 1988.
Reprinted by permission of Susana Cato.

HAVANA—Gabriel García Márquez, Nobel Prize winner for literature, at the age of sixty makes a leap into the world of images.

"The words are within the image. If you think about it, the written word is a very primitive medium. You know what it is to have to put one letter after another and to read it to have to decipher one sound after another without knowing what it means. It's totally primitive, it's almost like cuneiform writing. The image, on the other hand, produces an immediate and much deeper emotion on impact and you don't have to decipher anything, it goes straight to the heart."

As the scriptwriter for a new series called *Amores difíciles* (Difficult Loves), as scenarist for the forthcoming series *Me alquilo para soñar* (I Rent Myself out for Dreaming), the script for which was coordinated by him in a workshop with Eliseo Albergo Diego from Cuba and Doc Comparato from Brazil in the San Antonio de los Baños film school, the writer, now president of the New Latin American Film Foundation, says:

"For me there's no dividing line between cinema and television, they're just images in motion."

At age sixty the Nobel Prize winner does not consider himself a lucky man.

"I believe that luck, just like guardian angels, is something that exists. Nevertheless, they have to be helped along. A prudent man's guardian angel is more effective than the one of a foolhardy man. I think I was given a poor share of luck. Things went badly for me for many years, from birth till I was almost forty.

"Things never went well. I had money problems, work problems. I wasn't able to express myself. It was always apparent that as a writer or as a nobody I had a lot of psychological and emotional problems. I had the feeling that I was the odd man out everywhere and felt very intimidated by it. Then suddenly I don't know what happened. In the last twenty years everything has gone well.

"If my luck had been evenly spread out, I would have had sixty average years."

But today García Márquez feels himself to be "living the best moment, mainly for one reason: from childhood, the idea is implanted in you that sixty is the end of youth. At sixty you are old, you have to dress like an old man, be an old man. Those who believed it became decrepit. I wasn't free of this idea either, because it's a feeling that goes 'in crescendo.' And suddenly you wake up and find you're sixty years old and still feel the same as you ever felt, more even, more settled, more sure of what you're doing, with more capacity to love because now you know how to avoid the pitfalls."

SC: What is love like in the time of AIDS?
GGM: All that AIDS does is add to the risks of love. Love has always been a terribly dangerous emotion, involving great risks. Love itself is a mortal illness. You young people didn't live through the era of syphilis. It was a disease like AIDS. It was venereal, that is to say it came from love. It was deadly and it was incurable for many years. And it produced a fear as great as AIDS! I remember there were posters in Bogotá that said: "If you don't fear God, then fear syphilis." Condoms became fashionable just the way they are now. One has the feeling that things always come full circle. What's more, you shouldn't be afraid of it, you have to die of something. I'm not afraid.

SC: What do you want to die of?
GGM: Love would be good, but not from AIDS. As a subject, love in the time of AIDS would never interest me because AIDS is a plague that is very related to one's behavior. It's like cholera or other plagues that are uncontrollable dangers, they cannot be evaluated, they creep up on you even if you don't move, shut away in your home, like in the story of the "Red Death," when the plague disguises itself in carnival dress and catches the prince unawares in his house. This almost metaphysical dimension of the plague is what interests me.

He talked first about his faith in television.

"I've always wanted to write soap operas. They're wonderful. They reach far more people than books do. Suppose a book sells fantastically well, a million copies in a year. In one night, a soap opera can reach fifty million homes in just one country. So for someone like me, who only wants to be loved for the things he does, a soap opera is far more effective than a novel. The problem is that we're condition to think that a soap opera is necessarily in bad taste, and I don't believe this to be so."

García Márquez believes that if intellectuals were not so contemptuous of television, TV wouldn't be so bad.

"I'm completely convinced that in the end talented people will be responsible for television's progress. I don't have faith in the medium, but in those who create the medium."

To speak badly of television because it's aimed at a mass audience is, according to the author, a form of contempt. "The same was said when I was trying to write novels for a mass audience. *One Hundred Years of Solitude* is a novel that does not omit any of the elements of great literature and it continues to sell and be read by one generation after another. If I'd started with the idea that the public wasn't capable of heeding and responding to this book, then I would never have written it."

After the recent private screening of the pilot for *Difficult Loves*, directed by Ruy Guerra of Mozambique with scenario by García Márquez, he said:

"The only difference between the story *La bella palomera* (*The Beautiful Dove Lady*) and a bad soap opera is that the former is well written. However, the feeling expressed, the drama, the situations, are exactly the same as those of a soap opera: a man goes crazy over a woman he can't have and the husband kills her out of jealousy. That's a soap opera anywhere in the world.

"What's more, if I'm the president of a foundation that has a television school, I can't start by being scornful of TV. I believe in it strongly. At the International Film and Television School we don't think in terms of cinema or television, but in what we're going to say with images."

SC: Cinema has treated you badly.
GMM: No, cinema hasn't treated me badly as far as what has been screened, but for other reasons. Things have gone badly because although I've worked more for cinema than for literature, I don't manage to do all I would like to.

I would like cinema as a form of artistic expression to have the same value in Latin America that literature has at the moment. That's why I'm at the school in the Foundation. That's why I've contributed to the production capital author's fees I should be receiving for the six episodes of *Difficult Loves*, and Latin America is the only part of the world I would do that for.

As to the rejections of the film adaptations of his books he says:

"When people see a film that's based on a book, they want it to be a faithful reproduction. But a cinema adaptation is the transformation the public refuses to accept. That's why I now insist that my books should not be adapted for the screen and I prefer to write specifically for cinema."

SC: But the rhythm, the rush of your words can't be represented in any film adaptation of your texts . . .

GGM: That's the directors' problem, not mine, and it's also their bad luck because people come to see me, not them. So viewers have the habit of judging them through me, of what they've managed to do with my work, the extent to which it's a faithful reproduction or not.

But in Ruy Guerra's production of the fable *The Beautiful Dove Lady* they're going to have a problem, because I do see myself in that film, every bit of it, frame after frame. I can even see the scenes from the script I wrote in Mexico with Ruy, they're exactly the same. It's funny, but the only thing that seemed strange to me is when the protagonist is reading to a sick man, because he's seated on his right and I imagined him on the left. And from now on I'm going to put that he's seated on the left.

As for his Nobel Prize, García Márquez says that the students at his workshops know that a Nobel laureate is capable of saying, "My idea is no good. Yours is better."

"Being a Nobel Prize winner creates more doubts in me than in my students, because a series of historical-biographical factors come into play, like my literary career, which makes me believe that every idea that occurs to me is good. And this creates a conflict in me. It makes me seriously doubt whether every idea that occurs to me really is good. And that's a weight I have to bear, not them."

SC: What's your view of poverty now that you're a rich man?

GGM: For a start, I'm not rich, but rather a poor man with money. It's just that now I don't have a poor man's problems. My view is of the utmost importance because I now know what the real difference is between wealth and poverty. Before I'd imagine it. Now I know how terrible it is, now I know how many things the poor lack, how bad their situation is, how it's necessary to continue thinking the way we do to try to solve the grave problems shared by the majority of mankind, this majority who live without sufficient resources, not to be happy, but not to have the small problems which make daily life a drama. Small problems are big problems for the poor.

To have resolved these problems for myself is what has most inspired me to do everything possible until the day I die to solve the problems of the poor, so that they, like me, can become poor just the same, but with money . . .

SC: What about your friendships with political leaders? How much can a man of the arts influence a political figure?
GGM: It may seem unbelievable but my friendship with political leaders is the least political thing there is. The thing is that I make friends with all kinds of people, architects for instance, and nobody asks me about my friendship with architects. The people I'm least friendly with are intellectuals. I don't know why. Let's say I'm more interested in others. I'm friendly with priests, with singers, with theater people. I love the theater, I'm a great one for theatrics. I don't understand why my friendship with political figures is seen to be so strange. Maybe because they think it has to be a kind of political relationship, whereas we talk about anything and everything.

What I can say is that there's probably an exchange of ideas, but between that and their listening to advice and recommendations, no way. No political leader, no head of state listens to anyone at all. They listen, but ultimately they do what they think should be done. So to influence a head of state is the most difficult thing of all. And in the end they have a lot of influence over you, and get you to do what they want you to do.

Of Fidel Castro he says, "One thing I admire a lot in Fidel is his ability to conceive of an event from its beginnings to its ultimate consequences, his ability to put things in context. I've seen him do it many times. Once some time went by without any presidential candidates being nominated in the United States. Fidel said to me that if they didn't make up their minds, some unknown would slip in and become president. Less than three weeks later, they started to talk about Carter, and Carter eventually became president of the United States."

"It's as if when Fidel sees an iceberg, he were capable of immediately imagining everything there was in the submerged part, which as we all know is seven-eighths of the total volume."

SC: What were your recent talks with Gorbachev like?

GGM: Gorbachev said to me when we were talking about *perestroika*: society has put its brakes on, but not just us. All of humanity has its brakes on. There's no more imagination, creativity has come to a standstill, there's no more faith in man. I don't remember word for word, I'm talking approximately, but Gorbachev said that if a country like his could do something like that and manage to unlock themselves the whole world would be unblocked and it would be a great moment for mankind, and I think he's right.

SC: We know a lot about Simón Bolívar, but we don't know anything about your novel on Simón Bolívar.

GGM: Part of a novel's success is in not talking about it until it's finished.

SC: Why are you so superstitious?

GGM: That's not being superstitious, it's a method of working.

SC: Do you now prefer to be a scriptwriter, or a writer?

GGM: A scriptwriter is a writer. I intend to keep telling my stories, in whatever medium I choose for each. I even thought of a story that wasn't good for the cinema or for a novel, and I wrote it as a play.

This is a reference to his first play, *Diatriba de amor contra un hombre sentado* (Diatribe of Love against a Seated Man), a one-and-a-half monologue to be premiered in Buenos Aires in June 1988. He wrote it especially for Argentine actress Graciela Duffau, "who doesn't go to sleep or sunbathe without the script under her arm." It's a drama that "takes place in Cartagena in a temperature of 120 degrees in the shade and 90 percent relative humidity, when [the character played by] Graciela and her husband return from an informal supper, just before dawn one August 3."

García Márquez on Love, Plagues, and Politics

Marlise Simons / 1988

From *The New York Times Book Review*, 21 February 1988, pp. 1, 23–25. Reprinted by permission.

Gabriel García Márquez is about to publish *Love in the Time of Cholera*, a work he calls a novel of manners: the story of two people whose love, thwarted in their youth, finally flourishes when they are close to eighty.

A Colombian by birth as well as by literary inspiration, he will soon be sixty and seems as busy, vigorous and playful as ever. After mediating in the early 1980s between the Colombian government and leftist guerrillas, he has not returned to Colombia because of widespread violence there. These days, he and his wife, Mercedes, divide their time between Mexico City, their permanent home for the last twenty-five years, and Havana, where he is organizing and directing the Foundation of New Latin American Cinema. Film is an old love of this Nobel laureate, and the dramatic possibilities of television also fascinate him.

Though widely viewed as a political activist of the left, to his friends he is simply unorthodox, a storyteller who objects to theorizing and generalizations and who likes to deal with life in the unexpected anecdotal way it comes. Over several afternoons in Mexico City recently, we talked about his interest in plagues, politics and cinema, as well as his latest book. I asked him to comment on his extraordinary productivity.

MS: You have just finished a play and are writing film scripts and directing a film institute. Are you changing your life?
GGM: No, because I am writing a novel. And I am finishing this one so I can start another. But I have never had so many things going on at the same time. I think I have never felt so fulfilled, so much in the prime of my life.

I'm writing. Six different stories are being filmed. I'm at the cinema foundation. And the play will be opening this year in Argentina and Brazil.

For a long time, of course, things did not work out for me—almost the
first forty years of my life. I had financial problems. I had work problems.
I had not made it as a writer or as anything else. It was a difficult time
emotionally and psychologically. I had the idea that I was like an extra, that
I did not count anywhere. And then, with *One Hundred Years of Solitude*,
things turned. Now all this is going on without my being dependent on
anyone. Still, I have to do all sorts of things. I have to sit on a bicycle in the
morning. I am on an eternal diet. Half my life I couldn't eat what I wanted
because I couldn't afford to, the other half because I have to diet.

MS: And now, in your latest book, *Love in the Time of Cholera*, the theme and
style seem very different. Why did you write a love story?
GGM: I think aging has made me realize that feelings and sentiments, what
happens in the heart, are ultimately the most important. But in some way,
all my books are about love. In *One Hundred Years* there is one love story
after another. *Chronicle of a Death Foretold* is a terrible drama of love. I think
there is love everywhere. This time love is more ardent. Because two loves
join and go on.

I think, though, that I could not have written *Love in the Time of Cholera*
when I was younger. It has practically a lifetime's experiences in it. And it
includes many experiences, my own and other people's. Above all, there are
points of view I didn't have before. I'll be sixty this year. At that age, one
becomes more serene in everything.

MS: Also more generous, perhaps. Because this is a tremendously generous
book.
GGM: A Chilean priest told me it was the most Christian book he'd ever read.

MS: And the style? Do you see this as a departure from your earlier work?
GGM: In every book I try to make a different path and I think I did here.
One doesn't choose the style. You can investigate and try to discover what the
best style would be for a theme. But the style is determined by the subject, by
the mood of the times. If you try to use something that is not suitable, it just
won't work. Then the critics build theories around that and they see things I
hadn't seen. I only respond to our way of life, the life of the Caribbean. You
can take my books and I can tell you line for line what part of reality or what
episode it came from.

MS: There is an insomnia plague in *One Hundred Years of Solitude,* and in one of your stories a plague killed all the birds. Now there is the "Time of Cholera." What is it that intrigues you about plagues?

GGM: Cartagena really had a great plague at the end of the last century. And I've always been interested in plagues, beginning with *Oedipus Rex.* I've read a lot about them. *A Journal of the Plague Year* by Daniel Defoe is one of my favorite books. Plagues are like imponderable dangers that surprise people. They seem to have a quality of destiny. It's the phenomenon of death on a mass scale. What I find curious is that the great plagues have always produced great excesses. They make people want to live more. It's that almost metaphysical dimension that interests me.

I have used other literary references. *The Plague* by Camus. There is a plague in *The Betrothed* of Alessandro Manzoni. I'm always looking up books that deal with a theme I'm dealing with. I do it to make sure that mine is not alike. Not precisely to copy from them but to have the use of them somehow. I think all writers do that. Behind every idea there's a thousand years of literature. I think you have to know as much as possible of that to know where you are and how you are taking it further.

MS: What was the genesis of *Love in the Time of Cholera?*

GGM: It really sprang from two sources that came together. One was the love affair of my parents, which was identical to that of Fermina Daza and Florentino Ariza in their youth. My father was the telegraph operator of Aracataca [Colombia]. He played the violin. She was the pretty girl from a well-to-do family. Her father was opposed because the boy was poor and he [the father] was a liberal. All that part of the story was my parents' . . . When she went to school, the letters, the poems, the violin serenades, her trip to the interior when her father tried to make her forget him, they way they communicated by telegram—all that is authentic. And when she returns, everyone thinks she has forgotten him. That too. It's exactly the way my parents told it. The only difference is they married. And, as soon as they were married, they were no longer interesting as literary figures.

MS: And the other source?

GGM: Many years ago, in Mexico, I read a story in a newspaper about the death of two Americans—a man and a woman—who would meet every year in Acapulco, always going to the same hotel, the same restaurants, following the same routine as they had done for forty years. They were almost eighty-years-old and kept coming. Then one day they went out in a boat and, in order to rob them, the boatman murdered them with his oars. Through their death, the story of their secret romance became known. I was fascinated by them. They were each married to other people.

I always thought I would write my parents' story, but I didn't know how. One day, through one of those absolutely incomprehensible things that happen in literary creation, the two stories came together in my mind. I had all the love of the young people from my parents and from the old couple I took the love of old people.

MS: You have said that your stories often come from a single image that strikes you.

GGM: Yes, in fact, I'm so fascinated by how to detect the birth of a story that I have a workshop at the cinema foundation called "How to Tell a Story." I bring together ten students from different Latin American countries and we all sit at a round table without interruption for four hours a day for six weeks and try to write a story from scratch. We start by going round and round. At first there are only differences . . . The Venezuelan wants one thing, the Argentine another. Then suddenly an idea appears that grabs everyone and the story can be developed. We've done three so far. But, you know, we still don't know how the idea is born. It always catches us by surprise.

In my case, it always begins with an image, not an idea or a concept. With *Love in the Time of Cholera*, the image was of two old people dancing on the deck of a boat, dancing a bolero.

MS: Once you have the image, then what happens?

GGM: The image grows in my head until the whole story takes shape as it might in real life. The problem is that life isn't the same as literature, so then I have to ask myself the big question: How do I adapt this, what is the most appropriate structure for this book? I have always aspired to finding the perfect structure. One perfect structure in literature is that of *Oedipus Rex*. Another is a short story, "The Monkey's Paw," by an English writer, William Jacobs.

When I have the story and the structure completely worked out, I can start—but only on condition that I find the right name for each character. If I don't have the name that exactly suits the character, it doesn't come alive. I don't see it.

Once I sit down to write, usually I no longer have any hesitations. I may take a few notes, a word or a phrase or something to help me the following morning, but I never work with a lot of notes. That's what I learned when I was young. I know writers who have books full of notes and they wind up thinking about their notes and never write their books.

MS: You've always said you still feel as much a journalist as a writer of fiction. Some writers think that in journalism the pleasure of discovery comes in the research, while in fiction the pleasure of discovery comes in the writing. Would you agree?
GGM: Certainly there are pleasures in both. To begin with, I consider journalism to be a literary genre. Intellectuals would not agree, but I believe it is. Without being fiction, it is a form, an instrument, for expressing reality.

The timing may be different but the experience is the same in literature and journalism. In fiction, if you feel you get a scoop, a scoop about life that fits into your writing, it's the same emotion as a journalist when he gets to the heart of a story. Those moments occur when you least expect them and they bring extraordinary happiness. Just as a journalist knows when he's got the story, a writer has a similar revelation. Of course, he still has to illustrate and enrich it, but he knows he's got it. It's almost an instinct. The journalist knows if he has news or not. The writer knows if it's literature or not, if it's poetry or not. After that, the writing is very much the same. Both use many of the same techniques.

MS: But your journalism is not exactly orthodox.
GGM: Well, mine isn't informative, so I can follow my own preferences and look for the same veins I look for in literature. But my misfortune is that people don't believe my journalism. They think I make it all up. But I promise you, I invent nothing either in journalism or fiction. In fiction, you manipulate reality because that's what fiction is for. In journalism, I can pick the subjects that suit my character because I no longer have the demands of a job.

MS: Do you remember any of your journalistic pieces with special affection?
GGM: There was one little one called "The Cemetery of Lost Letters," from the time I was working at *El Espectador*. I was sitting on a train in Bogotá.

And I saw a sign that said, "House of Lost Letters." I rang the bell. They told me that all the letters that could not be delivered—with wrong addresses, whatever—were sent to that house. There was an old man in it who dedicated his life entire to finding their destination. Sometimes it took him days. If it couldn't be found, the letter was burned but never opened. There was one addressed "To the woman who goes to the Church de Las Armas every Wednesday at 5 P.M." So the old man went there and found seven women and questioned each of them. When he had picked the right one, he needed a court order to open the letter to be sure. And he was right. I'll never forget that story. Journalism and literature were almost joined. I have never been able to completely separate them.

MS: What are you trying to achieve at the cinema foundation?
GGM: I'd like to see film-making as an artistic expression in Latin America valued the same way literature is now. We have very fine literature, but it has taken a long time to be recognized. It has been a very hard struggle. And sometimes it is still difficult.

MS: The literature now seems to have a life of its own.
GGM: You know, this really started to happen when we conquered our own readers at home. When they started to read us in Latin America. We had always thought the opposite was important. When we published a book, we didn't care if it was sold here as long as we could get it translated. And yet we knew what would happen. It would be translated and get a few obligatory critical notes from the specialists. The book would stay within the Spanish Studies ghettos of the universities and never get out. When we started to read in Latin America, everything opened up.

The same is beginning to happen with film. There are now good films being made in Latin America. And this is being done not with big productions with a lot of capital. It is done within our own means and with our own methods. And the films are appearing at the international festivals and are being nominated for prizes. But they still have to conquer their own audiences here. The problem lies with the big distributors. They need to spend a lot of money to promote unknown films and then they get no returns. The day our films make money, the whole focus will change. We saw it in literature; we will see it in films in the years ahead.

MS: Politics is important to you. But you don't use your books to promote your political ideas.
GGM: I don't think literature should be used as a firearm. But, even against your own will, your ideological positions are inevitably reflected in your writing and they influence readers. I think my books have had political impact in Latin America because they help create a Latin American identity; they help Latin Americans become more aware of their own culture.

An American asked me the other day what was the real political intention behind the cinema foundation. I said the issue is not what lies behind it but what lies ahead of it. The idea is to stimulate awareness of the Latin American cinema, and that is fundamentally a political objective. Of course, the project is strictly about film-making but the results will be political. People often think that politics are elections, that politics are what governments do. But literature, cinema, painting and music are all essential to forging Latin America's identity. And that's what I mean by politics.

MS: Would you say that is different from placing artistic talent at the service of politics?
GGM: I would never do that. Well, let me be clearer. The arts are always at the service of politics, of some ideology, of the vision the writer or the artist has of the world. But the arts should never be at the service of a government.

MS: What is your vision for Latin America?
GGM: I want to see a Latin America that is united, autonomous and democratic.

MS: In the European sense?
GGM: In the sense that it should have common interests and approaches.

MS: Is that the reason you are now writing about Simón Bolívar?
GGM: Not really. I picked the theme of Bolívar because I was interested in his personality. No one knows what he was really like because Bolívar became enshrined as a hero. I see him as a Caribbean, influenced and formed by Romanticism. Just imagine what an explosive combination . . .

But the ideas of Bolívar are very topical. He imagined Latin America as an autonomous and unified alliance, an alliance that he thought could become the largest and most powerful in the world. He had a very nice phrase for it. He said, "We are like a small mankind of our own." He was an extraordinary man, yet he got badly beaten and was ultimately defeated. And he was defeated by the same forces that are at work today—the feudal interests and traditional local power groups that protect their interests and privileges. They closed ranks against him and finished him off. But his dream remains valid—to have a unified and autonomous Latin America.

You see, I'm looking for different words. I really detest political-speak. Words like "the people," for example, have lost their meaning. We have to fight against fossilized language. Not only in the case of the Marxists, who have petrified the language most, but the liberals too. "Democracy" is another such word. The Soviets say they're democratic; the Americans say they're democratic; El Salvador does, and Mexico too. Everyone who can organize an election says he's democratic. "Independence" is another one. These are words that have come to mean very little. They're disconnected; they don't describe the reality they represent. I'm always looking for words that aren't exhausted.

You know what my biggest failing in life has been? One that can no longer be remedied? It's not being able to speak English perfectly as a second language. If only I had spoken English . . .

MS: Would you have written in English?
GGM: No, no. But after Latin America, my best audience is in the United States, and in the universities there. There's a vast readership that interests me. But I could never become their friend because I don't speak English. I have French and Italian. Of course, it's also their failing for not speaking Spanish. But I think I'm more interested than they are.

MS: What was it like to write the play? Did that give you any trouble?
GGM: Well, it's really a monologue that I wrote for Graciela Duffau, the Argentine actress. It's called *Diatribe of Love against a Seated Man*. An angry woman is telling her husband everything that passes through her head. It goes on for two hours. He is sitting in a chair reading a newspaper and doesn't react at all. But a monologue isn't entirely a play. That is, there are many rules and laws of the theater that don't apply here.

MS: And what is your next writing project?

GGM: I'm going to finish "Bolívar." I need a few more months. And I'm going to write my memoirs. Usually authors write their memoirs when they can no longer remember anything. I'm going to start slowly and write and write. They won't be normal memoirs. Every time I have four hundred pages ready, I'll publish a volume and see. I could go up to six.

The Best Years of His Life:
An Interview with
Gabriel García Márquez

Marlise Simons / 1988

From *The New York Times Book Review*, 10 April 1988, p. 48. Reprinted by permission.

For Gabriel García Márquez, the pleasure and turmoil of writing change from novel to novel. In the case of *One Hundred Years of Solitude*, he thought so long and hard about the story that when he finally sat down to commit it to paper, in came in a great burst. But he had difficulty writing *The Autumn of the Patriarch*, a novel he published seven years before he won the Nobel Prize in 1982. With that book, he recently recalled, "I was doing well when I could finish four lines a day"; the whole project occupied him, off and on, for seven years.

By the contrast, the years when he worked on *Love in the Time of Cholera* were among the happiest of his life. Nostalgically, he wrote about the courtship of his parents and his own journeys by riverboat, both of which were important sources for the book. In Mexico City, his longtime home base, we talked about what writing the novel had been like.

GGM: This book was a pleasure. It could have been much longer, but I had to control it. There is so much to say about the life of two people who love each other. It's infinite.

Also, I had the advantage of knowing the end beforehand. Because in this book, the end was a problem. It would have been in poor taste if one or even both of the characters died. The most wonderful thing would be if they could go on loving forever. So the reader is given the consolation that the boat with the lovers will keep on with its journey, coming and going. Not only for the rest of their lives, but forever.

MS: A kind of Flying Dutchman of love. Have you done a lot of traveling on boats yourself?

GGM: I've known that boat for a long time. I traveled a lot on it when I was twelve. I lived on the coast [in Colombia] but I got a scholarship to study in Bogotá. So I would take the boat from Barranquilla to La Dorada and then the train to Bogotá. That was about the time the river began to deteriorate. Between my first trips and my final ones, I saw the decay in the river that appears in the book.

I had to have two river journeys in the book. The first was that of Florentino Ariza, when he is named telegraphist in the interior. There is no purpose to this one because he arrives, regrets it and turns back. But I had to invent it to be able to describe the river and the landscape. If not, that whole description would have had to come at the end of the book, when the two old people go on their journey. And that would have overshadowed the relationship between the two, which is what mattered there. So that device helped me also to show how the river changed from a fresh and thriving stream and fell into decadence. I must have taken the last trip when I was at the university, when I was about twenty-two. Then the boats stopped running.

All these things for me are part of a nostalgia. Nostalgia is a great source for literary inspiration, for poetic inspiration.

MS: You wrote most of the book in Cartagena?

GGM: Yes, and those two years when I was writing it was a time when I was almost completely happy. Everything went well for me. People spend a lifetime thinking about how they would really like to live. I asked my friends and no one seems to know very clearly. To me it's very clear now. I wish my life could have been like the years when I was writing *Love in the Time of Cholera*.

I would get up at 5:30 or 6 in the morning. I need only six hours of sleep. Then I quickly listened to the news. I would read from 6 to 8, because if I don't read at that time I won't get around to it anymore. I lose my rhythm. Someone would arrive at the house with fresh fish or lobster or shrimp caught nearby. Then I would write from 8 till 1. By midday, Mercedes [his wife] would go to the beach and wait for me with friends. I never quite knew who to expect; there were always people coming and going. After lunch I had a little siesta. And when the sun started going down I would go out on the street to look for places where my characters would go, to talk to people and pick up language and atmosphere. So the next morning I would have fresh material I had brought from the streets.

I also had one of the most curious and enjoyable literary experiences I've ever had. One of the characters was Fermina, an eighteen-year-old girl living in a Caribbean town in the late nineteenth century. She lived with her father, a Spanish immigrant, and with her mother, who I could not figure out. And there was an aunt, her father's sister, who I saw very clearly and who had the same name. I just could not grasp the mother. I would seat them around the table and I could see how they all behaved—except for the mother. At first I thought the aunt was in the way. And I took her out and put her back again. But the mother was the problem. I could not see her, not the face, the name or anything about her. And then one day I woke up and realized what had happened. The mother had died while the girl was still young. And when I saw that the mother was dead, she became alive and real. She grew and had a great presence—in the house, in everyone's memory. It made me so happy to resolve this. I had been stretching the logic of the book. I had been trying to put a dead person among the living, and that was not possible.

MS: And the men? How did you feel about Florentino?
GGM: I don't really like him. I think he is very selfish, like all men are. And as for Fermina, I think she became more bourgeois than she realized. That changed her a lot and made her very pretentious. She only understood that by the time she was very old, when she agreed to go on the boat. To do that, she had to break with her whole life.

But there is another important character, one that has no name—and that is the society of the Caribbean coast, its prejudices and superstitious, its old-fashioned ways. This is what really drives the whole story.

MS: You have said that the thwarted early courtship of your parents served in part as a model for this book. Has your mother read it?
GGM: I don't know if she's read it all the way through. She's eighty-four years old now. I think they have read parts to her. Anyway, she knows what's in it. When I first started writing it in Cartagena, I would go to her house every afternoon and I would question my mother and my father separately. He was still alive then.

MS: Have you read the English translation?

GGM: My English translator is [Gregory] Rabassa. I always trusted him so much; I never had to pay attention. But this time he had other commitments, and another translator was sought. I can read English, but not well enough to judge the way I dare judge a text in French or Italian. But anyhow, there were all sorts of test translations. Of the three sample translations, I read only the first chapter of this one and it was the best, without a doubt. The editors at Knopf agreed. Anyhow, what can I do? I can't worry. There is also the Japanese and the Swedish and the Dutch and so on.

MS: Do the translators contact you and consult you?

GGM: Sometimes it's an editor who sends notes asking little things. Sometimes translators send a list of things they have doubts about. The strange thing is that, regardless of the language, the list of doubts is almost always the same.

MS: I know you get a lot of mail from your readers. What sort of things do they write to you?

GGM: The letters I find most interesting are from people who ask me where I got this theme or that passage or such and such a character. Because they feel it is about something or someone they know. They will say: So and so is just like my aunt. Or: I have an uncle just like him. And that episode happened exactly like that in my village. How did you know about it? People from all over Latin America wrote such things, especially after *One Hundred Years of Solitude*. They felt it was part of their lives.

MS: That's why you still refuse to let the book be filmed? Because that identification will be lost?

GGM: It will be destroyed. Because film does not allow for that. The fact of the actor, of Gregory Peck, becomes the face of the character. It cannot be your uncle, unless your uncle looks like Gregory Peck.

MS: Will *Love in the Time of Cholera* be filmed?

GGM: Maybe. I don't mind as long as it's a Latin American movie. By that I mean one that is directed by a Latin American, that exudes the atmosphere of Latin America, that shows our character, our way of being, our society, because these are the things that define this drama. Anyway it's a problem.

But the answer is for me not to get involved. It has already happened with Francesco Rosi, who made *Chronicle of a Death Foretold*. He showed me the screenplay and I said, "Don't show it to me because if I read it the film will probably never be made. I am thinking of my book and you are thinking of your film. I wrote the book alone, you make the film alone." And that's how it happened and he thanked me.

The General in His Labyrinth Is a "Vengeful" Book
María Elvira Samper / 1989

From *Semana* (Colombia), 14 March 1989. Reprinted by permission of María Elvira Samper. Translated by Gene H. Bell-Villada.

Following several phone calls I'd made to his Mexico City home, he agreed to grant me an interview. On one condition. With one restriction: no talking about politics. "I decided not to talk politics," he said to me, "ever since I realized that you don't know whom to believe, that you don't know who's telling the truth and who's lying." That was exactly what he had said to me previously, the last time I interviewed him, also in Mexico, in May 1985. At that time, President Belisario's so-called peace was a tangle. It was then that García Márquez dropped the first hints of his thesis about disinformation, about the war of information, the manipulation of information. For him it was one of the key factors of that labyrinth in which the peace was all caught up. Now—he says—he doesn't want to get involved in those depths. He doesn't want to talk politics. I accept. It's one of the sacrosanct rights of the interviewee: to say "Yes, but." I accept, because I'm interested in knowing what he thinks now that he's brought his latest novel, *The General in His Labyrinth*, to an end. Already, even before publication, it has sparked controversy. Not exactly historical, but ethical.

García Márquez receives me in his home. He's thinner. "You see, I'm on a diet for models," he says as if to remind me, once more, of his unyielding will power and his quasi-military discipline. And his hair is much grayer. I reflect to myself that, if he formerly thought Mario Latorre fit perfectly his image of the Colonel, now it's the author himself who most resembles him. The obligatory subject, the hors d'oeuvre for lunch, of course, is the situation in Colombia. And although he's warned me that he doesn't want to discuss the subject, he blurts out some notion or other that now, on the fly, I try to remember. "Look, thinks are getting clearer and that makes me feel optimistic. The forces and the sectors of the country are becoming more clearly defined: the guerrillas, the drug trafficking, the military, the paramilitaries, the clergy, the industrialists, the politicians, the civilian government. Colombia is a country where there's a fragmentation of power and each one wields their share according to their interests. The problem is, the civilian government is the one that has the smallest share." I can't resist the temptation to ask him about the way in which he analyzes the problem of the drug traffic, and in some cases the marriage between guerrillas and drug trafficking, and the paramilitary response. And he cuts me off: "I told you I didn't want to discuss those subjects." And I earn my box on the ears: "You journalists are getting killed by the scoop syndrome. The scoop syndrome is going to destroy the country. Look, I've spent three years doing researches. And the mass media want to sniff out and know things just when they take place. Even with a mere telephone call. In their runaround, journalists should take a minute of silence to reflect on the enormous responsibility they face."

I don't venture any more questions. We enter into the material: *The General*, the novel that, after I'd read it with time nibbling at my heels, gives me the feeling that García Márquez has decided to take Bolívar down from his pedestal, so as to show the man—in literal and literary terms—naked.

María Elvira Samper: Although you've always said that after you've published a book it ceases to interest you, how do you feel now that you've brought *The General in His Labyrinth* to its end?
Gabriel García Márquez: This is the only book I'm absolutely satisfied with. First, because I've never worked as hard on any of them. There are three years of research and two years of typing. It's a book that's just as I would have wanted to write it. From a technical, historical, and literary point of view, it's a labor that's exactly how I wanted it to be, with the proportions I wanted to give it. I'm absolutely sure that Bolívar was like that.

MES: Didn't you feel the same serene satisfaction with that unprecedented success, *Love in the Time of Cholera*?
GGM: Nope. With *Love* I felt a lot of fears. For me it was an adventure. There was the risk of schmaltzy melodrama. Bolívar is a literary project I plunged into with all sorts of documentary, technical, and intellectual knowledge, and I think I achieved what I wanted. Besides, though, *The General* has a greater importance than the rest of my work. It shows that all my work corresponds to a geographical and historical reality. It's not Magical Realism and all those things they say. When you read Bolívar you realize that everything else has, in

some way, a documentary, historical, and geographical basis that is verified in *The General*. It's like *No One Writes to the Colonel* again, but now historically based. Ultimately I've only written a single book, the same one that goes round and round, and continues.

MES: The idea of writing about the final journey of Bolívar, where did it come from?
GGM: Well, you see, I'd never thought I would write that book about Bolívar. I wanted to write a book about the Magdalena River. I traveled on the Magdalena River eleven times, round trip. I know that river town by town, tree by tree. It seemed to me that the best pretext to tell about the river was that journey of Bolívar's.

MES: So when did Bolívar start to interest you more than the story of the river?
GGM: There was a moment when I started wondering what that man may have been like, so I could know if he had to speak, if he had to move . . . And I started going deeper and deeper, and then I realized—it's simply amazing!— that that man had absolutely nothing to do with what we'd been taught about him in school. I started reading biographies of Bolívar and began to realize the kind of human being he was. I found him so close, so familiar. He was like many people I know in Venezuela, in Colombia. He was very Caribbean. I started loving him a lot and feeling a great sympathy for him. And above all, I started to feeling angry over what had been done to him.

MES: Which of the biographies that you'd read did you like the most?
GGM: You'll be surprised. The biography by Indalecio Liévano Aguirre is among the best. The problem is that Indalecio was deficient in literature. His prose style is very dry. But as regards his point of view, his knowledge, the organization of the data, the general idea . . . Politically, it's excellent.

MES: What was the image you had of Bolívar when you started to write the novel?
GGM: The image from high school, from the standard history by Henao and Arrubla—"he had a penetrating voice, like the sound of a clarion call, etc, etc." That description comes from O'Leary, but they don't credit him. In reality, I didn't have the slightest idea as to what Bolívar was like. Right now I get to thinking about all those kids who're graduating from school. I don't think they have the slightest idea about Bolívar.

MES: Why, then, did you write his final journey and not *the* biography of Bolívar?

GGM: The problem is that I'm incapable of explaining my book. I wrote in order to explain to myself how all that stuff was. The journey was the least documented part of the life of Bolívar. He, who used to write so many letters, wrote only two or three on that trip. Nobody took notes, nobody kept records. That, then, was what allowed me to write without any major limitations to my imagination. It was marvelous! I could invent everything.

MES: And what about the dilemma of historical novel versus novelized history?

GGM: It's total fiction. The fact that there was no documentation made me feel comfortable. The fact that it was a novel allowed me to get inside Bolívar's head. But I arrived at the conviction that I'd written a biography of Bolívar, in the sense that I believe that that's his personality.

MES: What method did you utilize?

GGM: The method I've utilized is this: if those were the political and historical conditions, if the human situation was that way, if in his letters he said this and that, then in his mind such-and-such was happening. That's why I had to do a novel, because if I set out to write history, I'd limit myself too much. A novel gives you absolute freedom.

MES: And didn't the historical record impose limitations?

GGM: The psychology of the character, his behavior and his personality, are fiction, though based on many documents. It's interesting: there's not a single historical fact that hasn't been super-double-checked. And what does that give me? Well, whatever isn't documented, I've absolute freedom to invent.

MES: So is this were you get Hemingway's "iceberg" theory? The gigantic mass of ice we see floating turns out to be invulnerable, because underneath the water it's sustained by seven-eighths of its volume?

GGM: Yes, what can be noted in *The General* is the enormous amount of information that is submerged.

MES: Did it present a problem for you to confront history, to do historical research?

GGM: Yes. First of all, I was completely lacking in experience and method. Never in my life had I worked on an historical fact, I'd always worked them journalistically. For lack of method I wasted a lot of time, I got discouraged, I got unnecessarily tired. If I were to write another historical book, I'd write it with greater facility because I now have some idea about it.

MES: With all that digging did you find curious things?
GGM: Yes. For example nowhere—and I challenge you to find a fact—does it say that Bolívar wore glasses. Suddenly I found in the inventory of his properties after he died, that there was a pair of lenses [*lentes*] listed. Quickly I went to reconfirm, and found out that *lentes* then was their word for spyglasses.

MES: Why, then, did you decide that Bolívar wore glasses?
GGM: Well, what human being at that age doesn't start suffering from far-sightedness? What human being at that age doesn't use glasses? And especially a man who was an indefatigable reader, who used to read by candlelight. Maybe he could conceal it, but to read documents by candlelight he would've had to wear glasses.

MES: You've said that your books start with an image. When did you hit upon the image of Bolívar naked in the bathtub that opens the book?
GGM: I've said that, but it doesn't necessarily mean that that image has to be the first one in the book, even if that is the case with *One Hundred Years of Solitude*. I started studying Bolívar iconography. I'd see him, but I couldn't conceive that that was the image of the Liberator. I couldn't manage to believe in the existence of that character, couldn't visualize him. But suddenly I found a sentence by Bolívar when young: "I will die poor and naked." And then I saw exactly how he had to be. It wasn't precisely the image of the bathtub, but certainly that of nakedness. Later I found the testimony of an English diplomat who writes about arriving in Bogotá. The diplomat says he went to the presidential palace and that he found some soldiers playing a sort of dice game with stones. Bolívar, naked in a hammock, was tapping his toes to the beat of a republican march he was whistling. Meanwhile O'Leary, sitting on the floor, was writing the phrase that Bolívar had dictated to him. At that moment I saw Bolívar. I dispensed with the chill of Bogotá, with the fact that he was President, with the presidential palace, everything. And I said: that is Bolívar, swinging on a hammock, naked. But it's an anecdote that has been repudiated

by historians. Think of it: everything that the historians deem false was what excited me and what gave me the exact image of Bolívar.

MES: Why did they reject that anecdote?
GGM: Because historians claim that on that date O'Leary was not in Bogotá.

MES: Might there not be instead, deep down inside, a fear of demythologizing the image of Bolívar?
GGM: Of course it's the fear of demythologizing him! My friends, Venezuelan historians who've read the book, after we'd worked on it in depth historically, haven't had any more reproaches for the book. But one of them asked me to put clothes on Bolívar, please.

MES: Like what happened with Michelangelo's frescoes in the Sistine Chapel. Why?
GGM: Because he says that the entire book is very respectful, very reverential. But that business of him being nude . . . Nobody goes around naked. So I said to him: you know it's true. I go around naked at home. And I know lots of people from the coast, especially men, who go around naked.

MES: Nakedness . . . What other trait did you employ to give flesh and blood to the hero?
GGM: Another thing that helped me get an idea of the character was something I found in an account by the painter José María Espinosa, in *Memorias de un abanderado* [Memoirs of a Standard Bearer]. He's painting Bolívar in San Carlos Palace. Manuelita lives across the way. It's a few days before the September attack. Suddenly there's shouting outside. Bolívar stops posing and leans out on the balcony. He sees an officer on horseback crossing the patio at breakneck speed, and tells him, "Well, you're riding at breakneck speed?" And the guy turns around and tells him, "I haven't killed that guy from Cartagena out of respect for I don't know what." That Bolívar who comes out onto the balcony and shouts is the true Bolívar. But no one has considered Espinosa's stories, because he was a painter.

MES: Regarding the paintings and the iconography of Bolívar, which is the portrait that comes closest to your Bolívar?
GGM: I think the closest is the one by an anonymous author, the Bolívar who is in Haiti, which is the one I describe in the lunch with Miranda Lindsay.

MES: Where does Miranda Lindsay come from?
GGM: She's completely fictional. Of all the many women, it was Manuela I kept. There are thirty-five of them, of whom some appear to be historical, others not. So I decided to invent them all, excepting Manuela, who is as she shows up in the book.

MES: If Bolívar loved Manuela so much, then why does he leave her?
GGM: Bolívar always leaves Manuela. The thing is you can see it now, because he has died. It was the last time he saw her and he said he was leaving for Europe. But she still stayed. Now, at the end, she also stays. But she also ends up following him. This time, she arrived at Guaduas. There she was told that the Liberator had died. He left and his end was a terrible end. But a precious one: he was erased from the world.

MES: On some occasion you said that the difficulties that cropped up when you were going to write *One Hundred Years* were those of tone and language. Did you confront any similar difficulties with *The General*?
GGM: Yes, the tone. I've done everything possible so that, without my having to do a pastiche, it'll look like a chronicle of the era.

MES: And yet, the physical and mental condition of Bolívar, who at times was delirious because of illness and fever, could have allowed you more modern literary devices. Stream of consciousness, for example. Weren't you tempted?
GGM: No. I wanted it to resemble a document from the time, so as to protect myself from the limitations.

MES: Is that the reason for the traditional structure of the novel, with an omniscient narrator, and linear time that is scarcely interrupted by evocations and memories . . . ?
GGM: Yes. But there's one thing you perhaps didn't succeed in noticing. At no time does one know exactly what Bolívar is thinking. One knows what the surrounding characters are thinking. But that's not the case for him, because if I as an author know what Bolívar is thinking, I don't have the possibility of speculation or of anything. So I don't enter into the subjectivity of Bolívar. I go into that of the others, even that of the women characters, but not into Bolívar's.

MES: What's that business about the nine versions before the definitive one, which comes out this week? How was the confrontation you set up between the book and the Venezuelan historians?

GGM: When I arrived in Venezuela, in May, I had the book written, pre-cooked. I wrote the book with the bibliographical data and with the ones given me by Eugenio Gutiérrez Celis and Fabio Puyo. Then I asked about a historian who best knew Bolívar's human side. They told me it was Vinicio Romero. He knew all of his slightest writings. I called him and he indeed gave me an abundance of details. I'd send him entire questionnaires, which he'd then answer. What most interested me was that Bolívar be seen as a man, as a human being.

MES: Was it your chief intention to demythologize him, show him, as you yourself say in the novel, when glory has exited his body?

GGM: Yeah. Look. Fidel Castro was asked a few days ago, in Caracas, if it's an irreverent image of the Liberator. And he said, "The image is pagan." That was what I wanted, and I believe I achieved it. So much do I respect Bolívar that I didn't want the book to be launched at the Quinta de Bolívar, with those women disguised as Manuelita Sáenz selling the book. *The General* was written, among other reasons, so that the memory of Bolívar won't keep being subjected to that sort of thing.

MES: Aren't you afraid of unleashing a polemic with the publication of your book?

GGM: That is a polemic between Bolivarians and Anti-Bolivarians. What I had to say, I said already. They're not going to get one more word out of me on that. Such is my opinion and since my business is a novel, I say that's how it was. The rest are interpretations, which don't concern me. I leave them to their devices!

MES: Do you despise Santander?

GGM: No, but he made the country that we have today.

MES: How is it?

GGM: A great country, but one that's all screwed up by one thing that comes from the mentality of Santander, which is that the institutions don't correspond to the reality.

MES: If Santander hadn't interposed himself in Bolívar's way, would Colombia be a different country?
GGM: The differences between Venezuela and Colombia are very great, and they are the result of nothing more than the differences in institutions. In Venezuela, the federal wars were won. They've long had civil marriage, divorce, separation of Church and State, secular education. That's the difference between the two countries: their institutions. Santander was a great governmental leader, but to make a country, I believe, you need to reanalyze it completely.

MES: How so?
GGM: I think we're acting, thinking, conceiving, and trying to follow a country that is not real, but one that is on paper. The Constitution, the laws . . . everything in Colombia is magnificent, everything on paper. It doesn't correspond at all to reality. In that sense, Venezuela is closer to Bolívar's ideas than Colombia. Colombia as a country is *Santanderista*. The institutions, the legal and administrative structure is *Santanderista*, but the country is Bolivarian. That's a whole other matter. There's a democratic tradition that's been repressed for many, many years, which is the only hope remaining to us and to Colombia.

MES: It seems odd that you talk about hope. In your works there appears to be at heart a certain tragic conception of history and of the human condition. Solitude appears to be the only reality, the last thing that remains. Why such fatalism?
GGM: That is a hasty interpretation. Not everything ends in solitude. I would say that I try to lay out on the table all the negative factors that there are, so that we can realize what needs to be done.

MES: Also there is in *The General* the enduring juxtaposition and counterpoint of solitude vs. love.
GGM: You're defining *One Hundred Years*.

MES: Perhaps, but I find that in Bolívar, too. In the face of abandonment, deterioration, and loneliness, the only thing that Bolívar seems to salvage as positive is love.
GGM: Well, that's what there is in all of my books, not, as you say, the final solitude. They're the opposites, solitude and love. Perhaps love is the only option, the only salvation that remains to us.

MES: After having read so much about Bolívar, having documented so much, is there anything that has ended up definitely clear to you about the Liberator?
GGM: After sitting down to read calmly the book that I wrote, what I believe is that Bolívar wouldn't stop at any halfway measures so long as to arrive at what he wanted. He wanted the continent to be a single country. And free. He truly wanted an infinite *patria*: Latin America. It was the only thing in which he had no contradictions.

MES: If the end justified the means, then there did exist in Bolívar what we might call the "totalitarian temptation"? And it wasn't just a slander from the Santanderista opposition?
GGM: It did exist. It was clear that Bolívar was ready to appeal to any means for the unity and independence of Latin America. If what was necessary was totalitarianism, he was willing to be totalitarian; if it was democracy, then he'd be democratic.

MES: What about the need for monarchical power?
GGM: That is very clear. When Bolívar requested lifelong presidency and lifelong senate, he was masking what he felt: the need for monarchy. He feels that the life of one man is not enough for so grand a labor as he conceives it.

MES: So Santander had his reasons for nipping him in the bud?
GGM: There are new tendencies right in Venezuela, Santanderistas who believe that today one knows what Bolívar was, and that he owes his grandeur to Santander, who served as a brake and prevented him from overflowing into absolutism.

MES: Bolívar was a man of great contradictions.
GGM: Bolívar was himself and his opposite. All of the contradictions are true. The problem of doing Bolívar's biography is that you'll find a sentence that, for example, proves that he was pro-monarchy, and soon you'll find another that proves the contrary. All of the doubts shown by Bolívar in my book can come up when you study Bolívar.

MES: You have always said that in each one of your fictional characters there is something of yourself. Is there that something in Bolívar?
GGM: I feel identified with Bolívar in many aspects. For example, in that business of not fixating much on death because it distracts you from the

fundamentals, which are what you're doing in life. And that interpretation I have of Bolívar is perfectly verifiable from his letters and his conduct. He didn't want to know anything about doctors or about his illness. He must have known he was on the verge of death; he felt there was nothing he could do about it. If he started investigating it . . . An illness is like a job: you've got to dedicate yourself completely to it. I too have that same notion. I don't let the idea of death distract me from what I'm doing, because what'll turn out is that one pretends one is alive.

MES: What else did you lend to Bolívar?
GGM: What you'd least imagine of myself: his bad temper, which he used to control as well as I do. The fact is that a novelist creates characters with bits and pieces of oneself.

   Another thing that caught my attention, and that I explored a lot, was his relationship to women. I think I say everything there. There is a point at which I stop and say what I think about him. I don't believe he loved anyone. Maybe his wife, and what happened was that he became fearful of love.

MES: Is that why he says, "I'll never fall in love again. It's like having two souls at the same time"?
GGM: Yes, but that's not by Bolívar. It's by me.

MES: By you, who have nothing but high praise for love?
GGM: Well, just a minute. Bolívar says that. What's mine is the idea that being in love is like having two souls. And that is marvelous.

MES: Let me venture a hypothesis: The colonel (in *No One Writes to the Colonel*) and the general have many traits in common. But it's curious, in both of them, though it may seem absurd, what's as important as their grandeur is the problem of constipation.
GGM: You won't find in any biographer of Bolívar the problem of constipation. I found it in Reverend, the doctor, but only in passing. He says they gave him a spoonful of I don't know what stuff and some pills for chronic constipation. When you say "chronic constipation," you already know the character of the guy. Because I've said that the world is divided into those who shit well and those who shit bad.

MES: Or between Santanderistas and Bolivarians?
GGM: For the record: that statement is yours.

MES: Did you become a Bolivarian?
GGM: Yes. And the only thing I know is that we do not know the history of Colombia. So a task I've taken on, now that the book is finished, is to create a foundation—the Foundation to write the true history of Colombia. I'm going to earmark the results of the Bolívar book for this foundation. I'm going to organize a group of young historians, who aren't tainted, to try to write the true history of Colombia, not the official story, so that they'll tell it in a single volume—readable, like a novel—what that country is like. Because I insist to you, not just Colombia but Latin America has to be analyzed all over again. Both *The General* and the Foundation are efforts at seeking the roots of everything that is happening today in Colombia.

MES: Is there anything that can be salvaged?
GGM: The creative imagination. In Colombia, in spite of all the horrors, creativity continues. It's incredible. Even the creativity of Colombian delinquents is superior to that of the outlaws in any other country. And that of the artists, well, just look. In Colombia there's theater, painting, literature . . . There's everything. But the State doesn't give scarcely a cent for culture, for creativity. The State doesn't spend on education or on public health, either. And Colombian capitalism, the Colombian oligarchs, they don't sacrifice anything, and so everyone has to fight for survival in any way possible. That's why they say that the economy is doing just fine while the country is doing badly. But then we have a stingy government, one that is completely Santanderista!

MES: So, more digs against Santander?
GGM: That was the notion that Santander had about the State.

MES: Do you think of *The General* as a book that has no cracks or fissures?
GGM: The only weakness I've noted is that the book is vengeful against those who did to Bolívar what they did.

MES: I insist there is anti-Santanderismo behind all that.
GGM: I say that there is no anti-Santanderismo, because actually the discord between Santander and Bolívar was reciprocal. The thing is, since in this case

I speak with the voice of Bolívar, then it looks as if there are more arguments from Bolívar than from Santander. Nevertheless I've tried to have Santander be seen as he was. I think he was an admirable man. But the true liberal was Bolívar. Santander stood precisely for the conservative thinking of Spain. He was the creator of some perfect institutions on paper, but with a very limited vision. Bolívar, by contrast, was a liberal unleashed, who was trying to create the largest and most powerful alliance in the world.

MES: A utopia.
GGM: There are those who claim that Bolívar had the vision of an eighteenth-century man and thus had no concept of the Nation. That the idea of the great Latin American alliance bordered on dystopia. On the other hand, they say Santander's mind is that of the nineteenth century, and that he well understood the problem of national borders. So we have in Colombia a curiosity, which is that the creator, the founder of the Liberal Party, was a conservative: Santander. The party that remained being the conservative one, it was attributed to Bolívar. I don't know how the Liberals and the Conservatives manage right now. Well . . . they're all conservatives now, they're all Santanderistas.

MES: In your view, what are the fundamental personality differences between Bolívar and Santander?
GGM: Santander was devious and viper-like. Bolívar was a foul-mouthed Caribbean. The greatest difference was in style.

MES: How do you explain the cult of Bolívar, which undoubtedly is greater than that of Santander?
GGM: That disproportionate and pious cult of Bolívar is nothing more than an atavistic feeling of guilt on the part of those who treated him like a dog. But I continue to believe that that Bolívar, so beat down and fucked over, is far greater than the image they've tried to sell us.

On the Lot with García Márquez

Andrew Paxman / 1996

MEXICO CITY—Winner of the Nobel Prize in Literature in 1982, Colombia's Gabriel García Márquez is best known for novels that explore the social history of Latin America through the lives of individual Colombians—novels like *One Hundred Years of Solitude* and *Love in the Time of Cholera*.

Less well-known is García Márquez's involvement in film. Having studied at Rome's Cinecittá, he began to write screenplays for Mexican directors in the early 1960s. Directors who have since worked for him include Arturo Ripstein and Tomás Gutiérrez Alea. However, only one of his novels has been adapted to film: *Chronicle of a Death Foretold* by Francesco Rosi (1987).

García Márquez is also president of the Foundation for New Latin American Cinema in Cuba, which he set up in 1985. He teaches an occasional course in screenwriting at the Foundation's International Film & TV School.

The author's latest foray into cinema is the Jorge Alí Triana-directed *Edipo Alcalde* (Oedipus the Mayor), which relocates Sophocles's tragedy to a Colombian town. *Variety* correspondent Andrew Paxman met García Márquez over coffee at Mexico's historic Churubusco Studios, where "Oedipus" is in post-production.

Q: What interested you about *Oedipus Rex*?
A: It's a perfect structure, where the investigator finds that he himself is the murderer. A long time ago I knew I wanted to make a film of it, but only recently realized I could adopt it to the reality of Colombia.

181

Now that I'm seeing the first cut, I realize that it could be a plot that was originally conceived for Colombia. There's a mix of all kinds of culturally ingrained violence, and everyone's to blame. It's a matter of collective responsibility.

Q: How do you like writing for the screen?
A: Personally, it bores me. It's a technical task, which I haven't studied well, and it makes me feel like I'm in a straitjacket. I take a lot of time revising, as if it was literature. So I definitely shouldn't be writing screenplays!

Q: In *Oedipus* we see a world governed by destiny. If the same is true of Colombia, isn't it true that one can't do anything about its problems?
A: You can't conclude that. What we have to do now is struggle for an identity and for the reaffirmation of independence. Every time there's a presidential election in the U.S., they take the world to the edge of war. I'm impatient for the elections to finish, so that the problems in Colombia, Mexico, Venezuela, and Cuba can all be resolved a little.

Q: Do you feel that the U.S. is the cultural enemy of Latin America?
A: In Latin America, the U.S. invests enormous quantities of money in cultural centers and so on, and they haven't achieved what we've done in the U.S. without spending a cent. We're changing their language, the music, the food, the way of loving, the way of thinking, we're beginning to make our films there. Our level of penetration in the U.S. is now what they'd like here. And that's fine by me. What I fear is political penetration.

Q: What about the overwhelming domination of U.S. films?
A: We don't have the right to let it bother us, because we don't have a competitive film industry. Thirty years ago our books didn't sell in English or French; our books began to sell abroad once we had conquered our own markets. We need to make films that our own audiences like—and those we make now try to win at Cannes.

The great revelation of cinema was Italian neo-realism, especially the screen-writer Zavattini. He created a cinema that was cheap, sentimental, very simple—but very good cinema. That formula, it's always seemed to me, is the great formula for Latin America.

Q: Why have you resisted film adaptations of most of your novels?
A: I think that a book leaves a margin of creation for the reader. He may imagine that a colonel is just like his uncle, or another character is like his grandmother. The margin is a type of gift that the book brings to the reader.

  This entire something disappears in film, because the cinematic image is so convincing that it doesn't leave any margin of creation.

Q: So why did you let Rosi make *Chronicle of a Death Foretold*?
A: First, he's a very good friend of mine. When the book came out I was in Paris, and he called me and said he wanted to have lunch with me. I was delighted—we hadn't seen each other for years. We went to lunch, a very long lunch. And then he left.

  The next day, his screen-writer Tonino Guerra called me and said, "You're a couple of idiots! Francesco Rosi came all the way to ask you to let him film *Chronicle of a Death Foretold*, and he didn't even dare to ask you!" So I called him up and said, "Hey, Francesco. Do it!"

Q: Would you do that again?
A: With no one. It was a moment of weakness.

Q: How often are you asked?
A: (*Laughs and throws up his hands in mock despair.*)

Q: Have you seen any U.S. films that you like?
A: *Apollo 13*. Why? Because they made it an adventure about the people who stayed behind. The only theme that exists in the world is the suffering and the joys of people. The most powerful image is when the two parachutes on the returning capsules open up, and you think of the wives and other people watching.

Gabo Changes Jobs

Susana Cato / 1996

From *Cambio 16 Colombia*, 6 May 1996. Reprinted by permission of Susana Cato. Translated by Gene H. Bell-Villada.

Thirty-five years ago, Gabriel García Márquez left journalism. After a long absence he has returned to the trade with *News of a Kidnapping*, a 336-page reportage to be presented this week at the Bogotá Book Fair. The work is the fruit of three years' researches, during which the Nobel laureate interviewed more than fifty individuals around the world. The result is a book in which there's not an iota of fiction. All of the facts where painstakingly checked. And yet, says Gabo, "It looks more like a novel than any novel does."

On 21 May 1948, *El Universal* in Cartagena ran the column "Punto y aparte" (Period, New Paragraph), the first journalistic piece by a law student called Gabriel García Márquez. Today, almost half a century later, at a far remove from that world "so recent that many things lacked names, and in order to indicate them it was necessary to point," the unknown journalist has become not only one of the most famous writers of the twentieth century, but a news item himself. Just two weeks ago he captured the world's chief headlines when the kidnappers of Juan Carlos Gaviria asked the author to be President of Colombia. "Nobody with an ounce of common sense will make any decision under the pressure of a kidnapping," the Nobel laureate replied.

The subject is one he knows about. His never-forgotten trade led him to investigate for three years the kidnappings of ten Colombians—five women and five men—at the hands of the "Extraditables." *News of a Kidnapping*, to be published this week, is not only the culmination of the author's journalistic *cum* literary technique—its odd-numbered chapters deal with the world outside, the even-numbered ones with captivity, the world inside. It's also an example of news reporting that is humanized, with flesh-and-blood protagonists, whereby García Márquez opens up—as he did in *The Story of a Shipwrecked Sailor*—that fascinating space often denied victims by journalistic cool-headedness: that of memories.

Susana Cato: In *News of a Kidnapping*, the protagonists live, they have recognizable first and last names, and they talk on the telephone with their author. How hard was it for you to write it?

Gabriel García Márquez: Every book is hard. *One Hundred Years of Solitude* was because of the enormous mythic weight it carried inside. *The Autumn of the Patriarch* also was because of its enormous weight of historical fiction. *News of a Kidnapping* is difficult because of its enormous weight of journalistic reality.

SC: Nobody believes at this point that it might be hard for you to get hold of reports as it is for ordinary mortals. The happy and undocumented reporter[1] from forty years ago isn't the same as the Nobel prizewinner who'll never be denied an interview.

GGM: I didn't secure that privilege through connections or through money, but by climbing step by step through the profession of journalist. When I was your age I had to struggle against the same difficulties that you've now encountered for me to grant you this interview. And don't forget that to do a job like this, a Nobel prizewinner needs more humility than a cub reporter does.

SC: It seems to me that the biggest difficulty lies not in who writes it, but in its being a subject that the protagonists would like to talk about comfortably.

GGM: It was very difficult indeed, but for more interesting reasons. First I spoke to "Maruja" Pachón and her husband, Alberto Villamizar. They both had the idea for the book, and they are the core and the guiding thread of the story, and actually we went on working together over three years. But at first it was disheartening. Maruja had perhaps made the unconscious decision to forget those terrible six months; she had to make a great effort in order to recount them. It was necessary to start twice and to go back several times—at least twenty hours of recording—so that she could finally recall the more human details, which were the ones we wanted.

---

1. A reference to a collection of journalistic reports by García Márrquez, entitled *Cuando era feliz e indocumentado.*

SC: And you, sir, who have invented a cup of chocolate that makes someone levitate, couldn't you have invented details on whim?
GGM: If I'd wanted, I could have. But the challenge was to play fair. What I wanted was to write a report with all its rules and in which there's no room for invention. Today I'm glad: the book hasn't a single imagined line or a single fact that wasn't checked within the limits of what's humanly possible. Still, I'm sure that reading it will take work, because it resembles a novel more than any of my novels do. That, I believe, is its chief merit.

SC: I'm nevertheless surprised at the openness of the characters. People don't like seeing their emotions exposed.
GGM: No one resisted telling about their experiences since, among other reasons, most were victims. They had nothing to hide, quite the opposite. And if something amazed me, it was the extent to which most of them had managed to overcome their pain. However, I was grateful to them all for keeping the secret of what we were doing, for almost two years. It was incredible how they did it in the most whisper-mongering country in the world. I interviewed no less than fifty people and there wasn't a single leak. Since I had the problem that, if I showed up at some official or private organization to gather facts, it would become news, I secured the aid of the journalist Luz Ángela Arteaga, who obtained the most difficult data by pretending it was for some project of her own. And Margarita Márquez Caballero, my first cousin and private secretary, handled all the material and transcribed over four dozen cassettes in absolute silence. I forgot about a fact myself, because she had the discretion not to tell it to me.

SC: Were the victimizers equally disposed? Why don't you speak with Pablo Escobar?
GGM: With the victimizers it would have been different, because they probably would've wanted to take advantage of the report to justify themselves. Pablo Escobar was still alive in prison when I started doing the investigation, and I know that he got wind of the book I was writing. I'd resolved to discuss it with him in person only when I'd completed the first draft, but he died before that. I'm sure I would have put myself in his place so as to be fair to him. In good reporting there can be neither good guys nor bad guys, but concrete facts, so that readers can draw their conclusions.

SC: And yet, the conclusion drawn by *Newsweek* in its latest issue is that the book shows that, deep down inside, you admire Pablo Escobar.

GGM: I too felt surprised at that conclusion. It's strange that such clear-headed, seasoned journalists could confuse objectivity with admiration. Pablo Escobar interested me as a human instance: a man who began as a car thief and succeeded in building an illicit multinational firm that broke down all the defense barriers of the United States, a country whose monitors took pride in their ability to detect a missile from the moment it might leave the Soviet Union.

As a serious reporter you cannot disregard such a feat, and in the book it's seen that way. In any case, Escobar fled and died before I could interview him. So in the book he remained what he'd been in Colombia during those years: an invisible force that nobody could see and that nobody knew where he was. But nobody doubted that he was an immense power, with an immense capacity for destruction.

SC: How did you get hold of so much secret information without interviewing him directly?

GGM: I had at my disposal all of the letters that Escobar addressed to the authorities, to the families of the hostages, and to his own lawyers. They were an invaluable fount of information, not only about the facts themselves, but about Escobar's own personality. There's no doubting their authenticity, especially their epistolary style, which is of an astounding precision and expressiveness for a man of his educational level. Whenever it came to accusing someone, especially the authorities, he'd use his real handwriting, affix his signature, and add his thumbprint.

SC: You have a moon in Virgo, which compels you to a love of detail. That has been a trademark of your books. Could you tell us about some unbelievable detail that you gave shape to in *News of a Kidnapping*?

GGM: Precisely because I try to write for all beliefs, I asked the astrologer Mauricio Puerta to do Pablo Escobar's chart. He had, at birth, the worst possible conjunction. When he turned himself in he seemed to have just three destinies: prison, hospital, or death. There was a fourth destiny, which in his case was unimaginable: a convent. But when he escaped he no longer had any return route, according to his astrological chart, because by then his predominant tendency was a sudden death.

SC: So why did you interview the Ochoa brothers, who were victimizers as much as Escobar and his people were?

GGM: With the Ochoa brothers it was different. The three are in jail and are about to complete their sentence. But what is not known and will be revealed in the book is that within prison they set up a communications channel with Pablo Escobar and Alberto Villamizar. Thanks to that, the two last kidnapping victims—Maruja Pachón and Pachito Santos—got out alive, and Escobar turned himself in. The Ochoas—who were convicted for drug trafficking and illicit profits, but not for homicide or terrorism—did work that should have been taken into account to reduce their sentence, in keeping with the law. Not only was it not done, though, but they didn't lay claim to it, either.

SC: What did you do to talk with them? What was the encounter like?

GGM: Getting to see the Ochoas was no problem. They receive visitors, they have food brought to them from home. But if I'd shown up there, the news would've been a scandal, and would have obliged me to divulge the secret of the book I was writing. So I needed to wait for a good opportunity. I got it from a group of high-level U.S. journalists whom President Samper had invited last year, so that they could study the drug trafficking situation in Colombia. While they were conversing with the Ochoas I'd avail myself of the opportunity to speak to each of them separately about some of my remaining doubts. I sent my queries in my first draft when it was ready, and not only did they provide some truly relevant notes but they corrected some errors of fact and furnished some new data.

SC: Even with Escobar dead, the impression is that circumstances in Colombia are still the same ones you have in your book. More so, for those of us who live outside of Colombia, it would seem as if the news stories of kidnapping, drug trafficking, and terrorism are the same as ever. Isn't it strange that, in your country, nothing changes at all?

GGM: It's worse. For me, what's odd is that I feel myself living inside my book. César Gaviria, who was President at the time, now finds himself in the same circumstances where the families of the kidnapping victims in my book ended up. Alberto Villamizar, the husband of Maruja Pachón, who is the central protagonist, is the kidnapping czar today, and is doing the same things he did to free his wife and Francisco Santos.

On the other hand, Escobar kept the hostages to make the Constituent Assembly prohibit the extradition of Colombian citizens. Today, as it turns out, the kidnappers of Juan Carlos Gaviria are asking that extradition not be reinstated and that Vice-President De La Calle not replace Samper, because they've been led to believe that De La Calle favors extradition. Which is not true. I think that, when they singled me out as a candidate, it's because they knew that I always opposed and still oppose the extradition of Colombian citizens, out of a basic principle of national dignity: no mother sends her children to the house next door to be punished. It is she who punishes them, and only she has the right to do so. A difference between kidnappings today and those in my book is that the ones happening right now are pointless, because there doesn't seem to be any possibility that extradition will be reestablished. However weak institutions in Colombia might be, we need to strengthen them instead of discard them as feeble.

SC: You have said that you see no difference between novel and news reporting. Why did you choose reportage instead of fiction, where everything is in your imagination and you therefore run fewer risks?

GGM: A piece of journalism is a complete news item, but with an important factor: the humanizing details. That is to say, the true subject of this book is the suffering of the protagonists, not only that of the victims and their families, but even, also, that of the kidnappers. Let me be responsible and clear: there is no crime more barbarous than a kidnapping. No kidnapping victim ever gets over it completely. In my book, every time a door opened, at any time, day or night, the victims didn't know whether they were being brought food or a death sentence. They were all informed by radio and TV, and on so many occasions they could see their families. Yet their relatives couldn't see them, nor did the relatives know they were being seen. It was like seeing life from the standpoint of death.

Even the actual kidnappers, some of whom were quite humane, would try to calm them down. But the victims believed that the perpetrators were going to kill them and that their kindly executioners wanted them to suffer less. Besides, you had to be a bit suicidal to take on the job of keeping watch over the kidnapping victims, because some of the guards were convinced that, once they got out of there, they'd be killed so as to be kept from blabbing. And certainly, many were killed. The human drama of a kidnapping is so heart wrenching and complex that it can't be invented in a novel. In sum: I always wanted to write a book in which we Colombians could see our own horror as in a mirror. And I hope this is the one.

SC: What do Colombians plan to do so that they won't enter the twenty-first century in the same situation they're in now?

GGM: And how do you believe we can think about the twenty-first century when we're still trying to enter the twentieth? Remember, I've spent three years making sure that there not be a single false item in a book, for a country in which no one any longer knows where is truth and where is falsehood. What is the future of fiction writing when a presidential candidate doesn't realize that his holy advisors are receiving millions of dollars in dirty funds for his campaign? Where the accusers aren't taken into account because, in the midst of the many truths they told, they also inserted so many lies? Where the President in turn reconstitutes himself as the accuser of his accusers with the argument that they did receive the cash but didn't invest it in the campaign because they went off with it? Where—according to all this—three of his ministers are at the prison gates for having handled money that didn't exist and having covered up a crime that didn't happen? Where several of the fifteen judges who judge the President are being accused of the same crime they're supposed to judge? Where there are six Congress people in jail, and more than twenty under investigation, and the Attorney General is imprisoned, and the General Comptroller is accused of larceny? Where the Government has no time to govern and the State is falling to pieces, and society is divided between those who believe everything and those who believe nothing, without much grounds for one or the other? And where ultimately the drug lords who're in jail and accused of having given dirty money leave the President, his advisers, the country and everybody groundless, because they maintain that they didn't give so much as a cent? What the hell! In a country like this, we novelists have no choice but to change jobs.

Days of Magic Realism: Gabriel García Márquez Is a Fantastic Figure Himself, As a Rare Visit Proves

David Streitfeld / 1997

From *The Washington Post*, 12 September 1997, pp. C1–2. © 1997 by The Washington Post. Reprinted by permission.

Showers of flowers, levitating priests, rainstorms that last five years—the books of Gabriel García Márquez are filled with unlikely events.

But if you want to hear something really bizarre, try this: To celebrate seventy years of life, a half-century as a professional writer, three decades of overnight fame, and fifteen years as a Nobel laureate, the master has come to Washington and let, ever so slightly, the spotlight fall upon him.

He spent a half-day with students at Georgetown, and appeared last night at the American Film Institute to launch a small festival of his works. It doesn't sound like much, but the fact that a fan could actually buy a ticket and see García Márquez in person is just about unprecedented in this country. Everybody wants him, so he says no to all. Except this week. Maybe he's just glorying in his survival. Five years ago he had a malignant tumor in his thorax and morbid thoughts in his soul, but there's been no recurrence of either. He's positively chipper. "Young people always think the old are going to die at any minute," he says, accusingly. "They don't know the youth mortality is much higher."

As he says this, he is entering Kramerbooks on Dupont Circle. The few patrons in the store's café are too deep into their own lives to notice who has arrived. He orders a Coke with lots of ice.

Does he want to talk about what he calls in his latest book "the biblical holocaust that has been consuming Colombia for more than twenty years"?

"I never talk about Colombian politics when I'm outside Colombia."

American politics, then. In a couple of hours, he was going to meet with No. 1 fan Bill Clinton. What was on the agenda?

"I never talk about American politics when I am in America."

Then he adds mysteriously, "I have flattered Clinton so much," before shutting up again. Finally, he explains that last spring he had sent the president an early copy about the recent turmoil in Colombia, *News of a Kidnapping*.

"Clinton got it on the 16th of the month," the writer says. "Five or six days later, I got a letter. It was dated the 17th. He said he read it all in one sitting, from beginning to end. He also said, 'Thank you for being the prophet of my presidency.'"

Clearly, the president had seen a comment by García Márquez last year about how he was sure that, if reelected, Clinton would eventually be ranked as one of this country's great leaders.

Really, maestro?

He looks up sharply. "I said he's going to *be* a great president, and I still think he has the potential."

As always, García Márquez is wary about how he is quoted. With good reason. For at least a decade, nearly every utterance by the writer has been widely circulated by the attentive media. Usually, he says, inaccurately.

Take the secondhand statement, reported in March by Reuters and others, that he was "disgusted" with his homeland. Supposedly, García Márquez was going into exile until President Ernesto Samper, whose term has been dogged by accusations his election was financed by drug money, left office in August 1998.

It seemed a protest in keeping with a novelist who makes grand gestures against the current of history, most famously when he said in the early '70s that he wouldn't write again as long as the dictator Pinochet was in power in Chile. That turned out to be seventeen years.

"I never thought he'd last so long," García Márquez admits now. "Even though you may think it's not true, I really am a realist. Time convinced me I was wrong. What I was doing was allowing Pinochet to stop me from writing, which means I had submitted to voluntary censorship." In 1975 he wrote *The Autumn of the Patriarch*, generally considered to be the best modern portrait of a tyrant in any language.

As for leaving Colombia, what García Márquez really hoped for was to stay in his beloved Cartagena. "Then I realized the political and social reality right now is so intense I couldn't write in peace. So I went to Mexico, which the press interpreted to mean I wouldn't come as long as Samper was president."

García Márquez has a playful style when talking, but on this point he grows practically stern: "For me to say I'm not going to come back to a country while a president is in power is to do him an honor, an homage that I will not give to anyone."

If nearly any other writer said this, it would sound grandiose. From García Márquez, it is simply blunt.

This is what it is like to be a famous person in a country with the highest kidnapping rate in the world, where one city had more than 1,200 murders in two months, that is the leading producer of cocaine and heroin, where four presidential candidates were assassinated before the 1990 campaign, where the editor of a leading newspaper was not only killed but a bust in his memory blown up and then his newspaper dynamited.

For three years, you work on a book about a series of kidnappings that transfixed Colombia in the early '90s, during the presidency of César Gaviria. If your book has a hero, it is Gaviria, who is shown remaining cool and steadfast against Pablo Escobar, the drug lord who masterminded the kidnappings to pressure the government to give him asylum.

You dedicate the book to all Colombians "with the hope that the story it tells will never befall us again." But just as it is coming off press in May 1996, Gaviria's younger brother is kidnapped by an obscure group called "Dignity for Colombia." Among their demands: that you become the new president.

"Pull this country out of the mess it's in," they order, adding that it would show "disrespect" to deny Colombians your "lucidity and honesty at this time of darkness and corruption."

This sort of thing never happens to Norman Mailer.

"I would have been a horrible president," says García Márquez, who rejected the kidnappers' demand. (Gaviria was released after seventy-two days in hellish captivity.) "It would be like asking me to pilot a jumbo jet. I wouldn't know how to do it . . . When a country needs leaders, they look among the people who appear in the newspaper. Tennis champions, maybe. Pablo Escobar thought he had the right to be president. At heart, he wanted to be."

News from a Kidnapping is written in a deliberately dry style as far away from García Márquez's traditional magic realism as possible. Nevertheless, the portrait of the drug lord bears a passing resemblance to the fantastical dictator in *Autumn of the Patriarch*, whose influence is felt everywhere but who is hardly ever seen in the flesh.

Escobar, García Márquez writes, "had employees who spent the day engaging in lunatic conversations on his telephones so that the people monitoring his lines would become entangled in mangrove forests of non sequiturs and not be able to distinguish them from the real messages . . . [Sometimes he] traveled in a public minibus that had false plates and markings and drove along established routes but made no stops because it always carried a full complement of passengers, who were his bodyguards. One of Escobar's diversions, in fact, was to act as driver from time to time."

Life, once again, is imitating fiction. Or perhaps it is merely making García Márquez's old point: that his fiction, populated by men with wings, resurrections, ghost ships and deaths foretold, is much less fantastic than it seems.

"Whether I'm working in journalism or literature, I'm always describing the same reality. There are some things about reality that I don't use in my fiction because people wouldn't believe them."

This is what it is like to be the most famous writer in the world: Everyone wants to celebrate you, all the time. That's especially true this year, with all these anniversaries. He turned everything down, but says he came these few days to Washington, because it was done under the auspices of the Organization of American States, "which represents all of Latin America."

There's a personal element, too: César Gaviria is now head of the OAS, and he and his wife, Ana Milena, have acted as the writer's hosts here, picking him up at the airport, throwing a small dinner party for him, and so on. García Márquez has a hard time refusing a friend.

Still, he made certain conditions. No speeches. No interviews. (Well, one.) Instead, he wanted to meet students, which he did for four hours with sixty undergraduate and graduate students at Georgetown, on Wednesday. No press was allowed, and only one professor.

He doled out advice—"Never put a fact in a novel unless you're very sure of it, because if it's wrong some reader somewhere will discover it." He read from his novel in progress, and asked the students' advice. They were properly impressed. "He didn't need to do this," said Brenden Varma. "He was completely unpretentious, and gave the impression he actually cared about our intellectual capacity."

While this program was ending, friends of the writer were paying tribute in another Georgetown auditorium. They had come from far-flung corners—Chile, Colombia, New Jersey—to discuss their first experience with *One Hundred Years of Solitude*.

The Argentine novelist Tomás Eloy Martínez told how in 1967 an editor he knew called him and insisted he come over right now and read something. It was raining very heavily that day, and by the time Martínez got to the editor's house he was drenched. He wiped his feet on some papers that had thoughtfully been placed on the floor. On closer inspection, these turned out to belong to the manuscript of *One Hundred Years of Solitude*. They had been dropped, one by one, as the editor read in excitement. The damage wasn't irreparable, but it was a close thing: García Márquez had been too poor to make a photocopy.

Antonio Skármeta aimed to top that with his account of living in New York during the same era. But nothing he wrote was of interest to editors; he said he often felt like the screenwriter of *King Kong*, who was told by the producer, "This is really good, but leave the gorilla out of it."

One day Skármeta went to the post office to pick up a package. When he returned to his miserable home, someone was lying on his bed. "This is my bed!" Skármeta said. "Can you prove it?" the intruder asked. The writer pointed to his name next to the doorbell. They argued, they tussled, and suddenly there was a knife in the interloper's hand. But instead of slicing Skármeta, he merely slit the name off the door and left. This was not an atmosphere conducive to reading, but when the writer opened his package and found a new novel called *One Hundred Years of Solitude*, he plunged in.

"Many years later, as he faced the firing squad, Colonel Aureliano Buendía was to remember that distant afternoon when his father took him to discover ice. At that time Macondo was a village of twenty adobe houses, built on the bank of a river of clear water that ran along a bed of polished stones, which were white and enormous, like prehistoric eggs. The world was so recent that many things lacked names, and in order to indicate them it was necessary to point."

The reader's rhapsody is impossible to describe. Skármeta had come to New York because he felt the impossibility of being both Chilean and a novelist, because the prevailing style in his native country scorned the anecdotal and the earthy and believe that the implications in the text were many times more important than the text itself.

By focusing on a small Caribbean town yet incorporating the universe, by describing the misery of reality and the energy of life, García Márquez showed Skármeta the way out. He went back to Chile and wrote, among other things, the novel that became the very popular movie, *The Postman*.

Multiply Skármeta's experience by thousands and you get some idea of the effect of the novel on the hemisphere's artists. Multiply it by millions and you will have some idea of its popularity. Have thirty million copies been sold in all languages and editions, or is it forty million? Both figures have been given by reputable sources, although in truth the exact number is lost in the mist of time.

The Georgetown panelists were García Márquez's friends, but that didn't mean there wasn't the occasional bit of criticism. Belisario Betancur, Colombian president from 1982 to '86, said his feelings about the writer were filled with contradictions. "First of all he didn't vote for me . . . He's a great writer, but a very bad politician."

After the Nobel Prize in 1982, a Colombian stamp was issued in García Márquez's honor. "I hope," the writer commented, "it's only used for love letters." Some of his recent books are also love letters, on a grander scale. *Love in the Time of Cholera*, the 1985 novel that is generally accounted one of his best books, is a sustained investigation into a romance that takes decades to reach fruition. And he's working on a novel whose three parts share a common thread among older people.

Part of this work was inspired by another Nobel laureate's work, Yasunari Kawabata's *House of the Sleeping Beauties*. "This is the only book I've ever read that has made me envious. I read it and said, 'Why didn't I think of this?' "

He explains the plot. "In Kyoto there is a house where aristocratic older men can go see beautiful young women. They are naked but drugged. If the men touch them, they wake up and it breaks the rules. So they can only watch—and the men discover the immense pleasure of looking without touching. It's a beautiful book."

The male character in his own book, he adds, says "he doesn't worry about sex anymore, because it doesn't depend on him, it depends on her. There's a French proverb: there are no impotent men, only women who don't know what to do."

That's going to go over big at the National Organization for Women.

"It's flattery, no?" he protests. "Once, in Caracas, I said that all men were impotent. Women were thrilled. They said I was their hero."

Index